# STUDY GUIDE

*for use with*

First Canadian Edition

# MANAGERIAL ACCOUNTING

PREPARED BY WENDY SCHULTZ, UNIVERSITY OF MANITOBA

THOMSON

NELSON

# TABLE OF CONTENTS

# CHAPTER 1
# THE STRATEGIC CONTEXT

## CHAPTER OVERVIEW

This chapter discusses planning and operating in a global business environment. Companies should establish mission statements on which to base their strategic planning. Plans should include goals and objectives. Several kinds of constraints may affect a company's goals and objectives.

Organizational structure shows the distribution of responsibility and authority within an organization. Core competencies indicate the organization's internal strengths and capabilities and, therefore, help select appropriate business functions to do internally or to outsource.

Strategic management involves the deployment of resources in achieving the company's strategic objectives. The main focus of strategic management is the value chain, which is the series of activities that convert inputs into products and services. The accounting system provides financial and nonfinancial information that managers need for strategic management.

This chapter also explains the differences between financial accounting, management accounting, and cost accounting.

## CHAPTER STUDY GUIDE

For a business to operate effectively in the global economy, it must meet two requirements. First, managers must understand the factors that affect international markets to identify the locations in which the company has the strengths and desire to compete. Second, managers must devise a business strategy to achieve the company's goals and objectives within the company's operating markets.

This chapter introduces management accounting for use in both traditional and the new global organizations, and shows how, as an organizational control, management accounting assists with the implementation of an organization's strategy.

Management accounting is defined as the gathering and application of information used to plan, make decisions, evaluate performance, and control an organization. Management accounting has two-way interactions with other organizational units. The management accounting unit both gathers information from and provides information to other units. Management accounting gathers two time-based types of information: "expected" and "what happened." "Expected" information includes what might or should be. "What happened" information reports what has already taken place.

The focus of financial accounting is providing information to external uses such as creditors and investors. Financial accounting information must follow generally accepted accounting principles. Financial accounting emphasizes the organization as a whole.

In contrast to financial accounting, management accounting can be applied in all types of organizations to provide information for internal users. Managers may need management accounting information expressed in financial or nonfinancial terms. Management accounting emphasizes providing relevant information to managers. Management accounting is more flexible than financial accounting because management accounting does not have to follow generally accepted accounting principles. Management accounting information may be quantitative, qualitative, actual, or estimated. The key criterion of management accounting is that it should meet management's needs. Exhibit 1-1 lists some differences between financial accounting and management accounting.

Cost accounting is a part of management accounting that deals with calculating the cost of making products or providing services.  Cost accounting overlaps financial accounting and management accounting.  The financial accounting system uses cost accounting information to compute the cost of inventories and cost of goods sold.  Management accounting uses cost accounting information to assess product profitability, to prepare budgets, to evaluate performance, to make pricing decisions, and to make investment decisions.  Exhibit 1-2 illustrates the relationship of cost accounting to financial accounting and management accounting.

Management accounting is one of many controls that ensure, with varying degrees of success, that employees and managers do what is required.  Controls are necessary because individuals are sometimes unable or unwilling to act in the company's best interest.  There are two reasons why employees might not do what the organization requires:  (1) employees may lack the necessary ability, training, or information and, therefore, may not understand what is expected or how best to perform jobs, and (2) employees may lack goal congruence with the company.  Controls are needed to compensate for personal limitations and to ensure that only appropriate activities are being performed.

Three approaches to control or influence the behaviour of employees are (1) specify appropriate activities, (2) specify appropriate results, and (3) recruit or develop appropriate personnel.

Specific action controls attempt to ensure that employees perform certain activities and/or do not perform others.  Action control specifies the appropriate activities to be undertaken, via work rules, policies and procedures, and codes of conduct.  The managerial accounting information reporting on the activities would be nonfinancial.

A result control specifies what must be accomplished, leaving the selection of activities to the employees and managers.  Results accountability can be accomplished through setting expectations for performance with standards, budgets, and management by objectives, which will be discussed in subsequent chapters.  Management accounting information reporting on the results could be financial or nonfinancial.

To control via personnel, the capabilities of employees can be upgraded through selective hiring of only those who are likely to do what the organization desires.  Personnel control can be accomplished by creating an organizational culture that compels employees to do what is organizationally correct.  Personnel control does not require management accounting information.

In addition to management accounting, there are other controls that need to be considered when developing management accounting practices.  These other controls include financial accounting, management information systems, employee and manager performance evaluation systems, and organizational culture.

A company should start its strategy development with a mission statement that states what the company wants to achieve and how the company will meet its customers' needs with its products and services.  The mission statement may change over time as a company adapts to the changing business environment.

A company's strategy links its mission statement to actual activities.  Managers should fit the company's internal skills with opportunities in the marketplace to achieve the company's strategic goals and objectives.  Larger companies will have a general strategy and a strategy for each business unit.  Managers should coordinate the strategies of the business units with the company's general strategy.

Management accounting serves managers in designing, implementing, and evaluating the organization's strategy by providing information about expectations of what a strategy will accomplish and cost, and the strategy's actual past performance.

All activities within a company should support its strategy.  Exhibit 1-3 provides an example of strategic purchasing.

An organization establishes goals and objectives.  Goals are the results, expressed in qualitative terms, that the organization wants to attain.   The organization expresses objectives in quantitative terms and a specified time frame.  Management accounting provides information for setting the goals and objectives.  Subsequently, management accounting provides information on the organization's success with accomplishing those goals and objectives.

Organizational structure shows how an organization distributes authority and responsibility within the organization.  Authority is the right to use the organization's assets to accomplish a task or reach an objective.  Responsibility is the obligation to accomplish a task or reach an objective.  When top management retains all authority for making decisions, the management structure is centralized.  Alternatively, if the organization distributes authority to many people throughout the organization, decentralization exists.  For decentralization to work well, there must be employee empowerment.  Employee empowerment means that the organization gives its employees the authority and responsibility to make their own decisions about their work.  Most organizations have an organizational structure that falls between centralization and decentralization.

A core competency is any critical function or activity in which the company has higher proficiency than does its competitors.  Core competencies are important because they form the foundation of obtaining and retaining a competitive advantage.  Examples of core competencies include technological innovation, engineering, product development, and customer service.

For companies that operate in a competitive market structure, management may decide to avoid or reduce competition through compression of competitive scope, differentiation, or cost leadership.  A company that chooses compression of competitive scope concentrates on a specific market niche to the exclusion of all others.  A company that chooses differentiation seeks to distinguish its products or services from those of competitors by adding value to the product so that customers will be willing to pay a higher price.  Companies practicing cost leadership focus on becoming the low-cost producer and passing the cost savings on to customers in lower prices.

An environmental constraint is any restriction on strategy caused by external cultural, fiscal, legal/regulatory, and political situations and by competitive market structures.  Because management cannot directly control environmental constraints, they are usually long-term rather than short-term constraints.

Management accounting provides both financial and nonfinancial information important for designing, implementing, and evaluating strategies.  A focus of management accounting is on costs involved with strategies, including unit costs and total costs, as well as the costs for organizational units.

Strategic management includes the organizational planning for deployment of resources to produce value for customers and shareholders.  The strategic management of resources is concerned with the following issues: (1) how to deploy resources to support strategies, (2) how resources are used in, or recovered from, change processes; (3) how customer value and shareholder value will serve as guides to the effective use of resources, and (4) how resources are to be deployed and redeployed over time.

The foundation of the strategic management of resources is the value creation chain.  The value creation chain is the group of processes and activities that change inputs into products and services that have value for the company's customers.  The value creation chain includes internal and supplier processes.  Management can use the value creation chain to classify activities as value-adding activities or non-value-adding activities.  Management can seek to reduce or eliminate non-value-adding activities so that the company can become more efficient and effective.

Exhibit 1-4 presents a simple model of the value creation chain.  The value creation chain is based on the belief that value is created for customers in goods and services by activities.  These activities are divided into five major categories:  (1) sourcing, (2) enhancing, (3) aggregating, (4) disseminating, and (5) interacting.

Sourcing involves obtaining raw or crudely produced materials in order to add value at later stages.  Enhancing involves making basic products from raw materials.  Aggregating consists of putting together various enhanced products to produce a complex product.  Disseminating involves distributing products or services to customers or consumers.  Interacting consists of the activities undertaken by the customer in obtaining the good or service being produced by the value creation chain.

Regardless of their value creation chain stage, companies require management accounting information in order to manage relationships required with their activities.  Managers require information in order to plan, control, evaluate performance, and make value creation chain decisions.

The value creation chain is the set of all activities that convert materials into products and services for the final consumer.  Vertical integration is a measure of the extent to which the value creation chain resides within a single organization.  Companies that are highly vertically integrated have more in-house links to the value creation chain than links to other companies.  Companies with low vertical integration depend on their suppliers or customers to create more links to the value creation chain.

Outsourcing is contracting with outside manufacturers or vendors to provide necessary goods or services instead of producing or providing them internally.  A company can outsource almost any process or activity required to make a product or provide a service.  Companies have outsourced many processes including marketing and sales, accounting, engineering, manufacturing, customer service, and product distribution.  In the accounting area, companies are increasingly outsourcing the payroll function, financial accounting, and all aspects of information technology.  By outsourcing processes and activities that are not within a company's core competencies, a company can concentrate its resources on strategically important functions.  The outsourcing decision should be made only after proper analysis.  Exhibit 1-5 lists some relevant quantitative and qualitative considerations for an outsourcing decision.

Although management often views outsourcing decisions as short-run decisions, these additional considerations reveal that outsourcing decisions have potential long-run effects.  Managers should view outsourcing decisions with a long-range perspective.  A company must recognize that it gives up a degree of control when it outsources an activity.  Therefore, management should carefully weigh the viability of activities that it may outsource.  Because of nonmonetary factors, management may decide not to outsource an activity though a supplier's costs are lower.  Reasons not to outsource an activity under these circumstances include the following: (1) the activity or function could be essential to the company's long-term viability; (2) the company may be pursuing a core competency concerning the function; and (3) the company cannot resolve issues such as product/service quality, time of delivery, flexibility of use, or reliability of supply.  In these cases, the company may reevaluate its activities for the function to discover how to perform the function at a lower cost.

If a company chooses to outsource an activity, it should prepare a thorough list of criteria to use for contract manufacturer or vendor selection and communicate these criteria to potential suppliers.  The nonmonetary criteria are more important than cost considerations.

Once a company has chosen a vendor, it should monitor and evaluate the vendor's performance regularly.  Such performance evaluations should include correct pricing on invoices, the quality of the parts, and on-time delivery.

In making outsourcing decisions, a company should first define its primary reasons for outsourcing.  Exhibit 1-6 lists the top ten reasons to outsource.

Management accounting evolves over time based on the needs and demands of its users. Its evolution is also influenced by the practitioners of management accounting.

With globalization, organizations are either expanding globally or being affected by global competitors. The global economy includes the international trade of goods and services, movement of labour, and flows of capital and information. Improved transportation, communication, and trade agreements have led to increased international trade. Global considerations result in more complexity. Management accounting must now provide additional information for managers to plan, make decisions, evaluate performance, and control organizations within a complex business environment.

Organizations are also influenced by information technology in terms of computerized transaction processing and electronic telecommunication. In order to fit within this new context, management accounting has made the following changes: (1) a change from manual and then mainframe accounting systems to enterprise resource planning (ERP) systems, and (2) a shift to manage at the activity level rather than at the level of financial transactions. ERP systems provide management accounting with accounting information as well as a wide range of processing activities and operational information. The greater level of detail with activities has resulted in increased complexity. ERP systems allow management accounting to deal with the complexity of global competition with management at the detailed activity level.

In spite of the great demand for management accounting information, the lack of credibility that stigmatizes public accountants in the post-Enron environment could easily be transferred to management accounting. More than ever, adherence to ethical standards is required. Ethical standards represent beliefs about moral and immoral behaviours. Beliefs about morality vary between different individuals. The moral perspective, however, will be more similar within a given society than across societies. In a business context, ethical standards are norms for individual conduct in making decisions and engaging in business transactions. Because laws and ethical standards differ across countries, companies should develop their own ethical standards and strive to follow them consistently in all of their operating areas.

Appendix A to the textbook provides a primer for assessing behaviour for ethicalness.


## SELF TEST

### TRUE/FALSE

1. T F Management accounting reports must follow generally accepted accounting principles.

2. T F Financial accounting focuses on reporting to external users.

3. T F Cost accounting serves the needs of the financial accounting system by determining the cost of inventories and the cost of goods sold.

4. T F A company's strategy is its long-term, dynamic plan that will fulfill its organizational goals and objectives by satisfying its customers.

5. T F A company should begin its strategy formulation with an analysis of its core competencies.

6. T F A company may change its strategy, but a company should never change its mission statement.

7. T F Objectives differ from goals in that a company expresses its objectives in quantitative terms and places a time limit on achieving the objectives.

8.  T (F) Authority is the obligation to accomplish a task or achieve an objective.

9.  (T) F For decentralization to work effectively, an organization must provide employee empowerment.

10. (T) F A core competency is any critical function in which an organization has higher proficiency than do its competitors.

11. (T) F Exerting managerial influence on operations so that they will conform to plans is controlling.

12. T (F) Across many industries, companies generally outsource their core competencies to reduce costs.

13. (T) F Besides costs, control over product quality and on-time delivery are two important factors in outsourcing decisions.

14. (T) F The global economy includes the international trade of goods and services, movement of labour, and flows of capital and information.

15. T (F) Ethical standards represent codified societal rules and change as the society changes.


## MULTIPLE CHOICE

1.  The global economy includes the international:

    A. trade of goods and services.
    B. movement of labour.
    C. flows of capital and information.
    (D.) all of the above.

2.  Management accounting information:

    A. must be factual only.
    B. must be quantitative in nature.
    C. must comply with generally accepted accounting principles.
    (D.) can be quantitative, qualitative, factual, or estimated.

3.  Which area of accounting focuses on determining the cost of making products or performing services?

    (A.) cost accounting
    B. financial accounting
    C. management accounting
    D. tax accounting

4.  Management accounting:

    A. must follow generally accepted accounting principles.
    B. is primarily concerned with the needs of investors.
    C. emphasizes verifiability over relevance.
    (D.) emphasizes the reporting of timely, relevant information.

5. Cost accounting primarily overlaps:

    A. financial accounting and tax accounting.
    B. management accounting and auditing.
    C. financial accounting and management accounting.
    D. financial accounting and auditing.

6. Which of the following is not a Canadian accounting designation?

    A. CA
    B. CGA
    C. CMA
    D. CPA

7. Controls are needed:

    A. to compensate for personal limitations.
    B. to ensure that only appropriate activities are being performed.
    C. both a and b
    D. neither a nor b

8. _____ attempt to ensure that employees perform certain activities and/or do not perform others.

    A. Specific action controls
    B. Result controls
    C. Personnel controls
    D. Activity controls

9. Which of the following approaches to control does not require management accounting information?

    A. specific action control
    B. result control
    C. personnel control
    D. all of the above approaches to control require management accounting information

10. Which of the following is another control that needs to be carefully considered when developing management accounting practices?

    A. financial accounting
    B. management information systems
    C. organizational culture
    D. all of the above

11. What is the basic set of assumptions about the organization and its goals and business practices?

    A. organizational culture
    B. organizational structure
    C. organizational behaviour
    D. organizational constraints

12.  A long-term dynamic plan that fulfills organization goals and objectives through satisfaction of customers' needs and wants within the company's operating markets defines:

  A.  mission statement.
  B.  core competencies.
  C.  strategy.
  D.  organizational culture

13.  An organization should begin its strategy formulation with a(n):

  A.  mission statement.
  B.  evaluation of its core competencies.
  C.  evaluation of its organizational culture.
  D.  evaluation of employee empowerment.

14.  In a business, strategies by management should promote a primary goal of:

  A.  employee satisfaction.
  B.  employee safety.
  C.  profit generation.
  D.  customer satisfaction.

15.  What are desired results expressed in qualitative terms?

  A.  goals
  B.  objectives – Quan & time constraints
  C.  core competencies
  D.  constraints

16.  What reflects the way in which an organization distributes authority and responsibility?

  A.  organizational culture
  B.  organizational structure
  C.  organizational behaviour
  D.  organizational constraints

17.  What is the obligation to accomplish a task or achieve an objective?

  A.  employee empowerment
  B.  organizational constraint
  C.  authority
  D.  responsibility

18.  What exists when top management retains all authority for making decisions?

  A.  employee empowerment
  B.  core competencies
  C.  centralization
  D.  decentralization

19.  For decentralization to work effectively, a company must provide for:

    A.  outsourcing.
    B.  employee empowerment.
    C.  responsibility.
    D.  authority.

20.  Which of the following is an example of a core competency?

    A.  technological innovation
    B.  engineering
    C.  after-sale service
    D.  all of the above

21.  Which of the following is an environmental constraint?

    A.  taxation structures
    B.  legal/regulatory situations
    C.  competitive market structures
    D.  all of the above

22.  The foundation of strategic management is the:

    A.  value creation chain.  *(VCC)*
    B.  accounting system.
    C.  product life cycle.
    D.  organizational culture.

23.  What set of processes and activities converts inputs into products and services that have value to the company's customers?

    A.  product life cycle
    B.  value creation chain
    C.  strategic management
    D.  accounting system

24.  What involves the organizational planning for deployment of resources to create value for customers and shareholders?

    A.  strategic management
    B.  product life cycle
    C.  organizational structure
    D.  organizational culture

25.  The value creation chain includes:

    A.  internal processes only.
    B.  supplier processes only.
    C.  both internal and supplier processes.
    D.  neither internal nor supplier processes.

26.  To become more efficient and effective, companies must reduce or eliminate:

    A.  all cost drivers.
    B.  all activities.
    C.  employees.
    D.  activities that add no value within the value creation chain.

27.  Contracting with external vendors to provide necessary parts or services rather than producing them internally is:

    A.  outsourcing.
    B.  insourcing.
    C.  horizontally intregrating.
    D.  value creation chain analysis.

28.  Which qualitative factor should management consider in outsourcing decisions?

    A.  product quality
    B.  on-time delivery
    C.  stability of the supplier
    D.  all of the above

29.  Companies should never outsource:

    A.  payroll.
    B.  core competencies
    C.  financial accounting.
    D.  information technology.

*reveals your competitive advantage.*

30.  _____ represent beliefs about moral and immoral behaviours.

    A.  Ethical standards
    B.  Moral standards
    C.  Legal standards
    D.  Cultural standards

## ESSAY QUESTIONS AND PROBLEMS

1.  Explain the differences between financial accounting and management accounting.

2.  What is cost accounting?

3.  Why are individuals sometimes unable or unwilling to act in the organization's best interest?  Why are controls needed?

4.  What are the three approaches to control or influence the behaviour of employees?

5.  What should a company include in its mission statement?

6. What is a core competency?  Why are a company's core competencies important in developing strategy?

7. Explain the differentiation and cost leadership strategies.

8. What are environmental constraints on a company's strategy?

9. What is strategic management?  What issues are important for strategic management?

10.  What is the value creation chain?  How can companies use the value creation chain to become more efficient and effective?

11.  What are the five categories of activities that make up the value creation chain?  Briefly define each stage of the value creation chain.

12.  What is outsourcing?  What are some advantages of outsourcing?

13. What activities are good candidates for outsourcing?  What activities should a company not outsource?

14. What is the global economy?  What is the impact of the global economy on management accounting?

15. Define and explain ethical standards.

## SELF TEST ANSWERS

### TRUE/FALSE

| | | | | | | | | | | |
|---|---|---|---|---|---|---|---|---|---|---|
| 1. | F | 4. | T | 7. | T | 10. | T | 13. | T |
| 2. | T | 5. | F | 8. | F | 11. | T | 14. | T |
| 3. | T | 6. | F | 9. | T | 12. | F | 15. | F |

### MULTIPLE CHOICE

| | | | | | | | | | | |
|---|---|---|---|---|---|---|---|---|---|---|
| 1. | D | 7. | C | 13. | A | 19. | B | 25. | C |
| 2. | D | 8. | A | 14. | C | 20. | D | 26. | D |
| 3. | A | 9. | C | 15. | A | 21. | D | 27. | A |
| 4. | D | 10. | D | 16. | B | 22. | A | 28. | D |
| 5. | C | 11. | A | 17. | D | 23. | B | 29. | B |
| 6. | D | 12. | C | 18. | C | 24. | A | 30. | A |

ESSAY QUESTIONS AND PROBLEMS

1.      Financial accounting is historical in nature and provides information for investors, creditors, and other external users.  Financial accounting statements must comply with generally accepted accounting principles. Financial accounting emphasizes the organization as a whole.  Financial accounting emphasizes reliability and verifiability over relevance.

        Management accounting provides information for internal use by managers.  Management accounting does not have to comply with generally accepted accounting principles.  Management accounting often deals with segments of an organization rather than the organization as a whole.  Management accounting emphasizes relevance over reliability.  There is more flexibility in producing management accounting information.  Forecasts and estimates often form the basis for management accounting information.  Management accounting information can produce reports with nonfinancial and financial terms.

2.      Cost accounting bridges the financial accounting and management accounting functions.  As part of financial accounting, cost accounting provides product cost measurements for inventories and cost of goods sold on the financial statements.  As part of management accounting, cost accounting provides some of the quantitative, cost-based information managers need to assess product profitability, prepare budgets, and make investment decisions.

3.      There are two reasons why employees and even managers might not do what would be deemed appropriate by the organization:  (1) employees may not always understand what is expected or how best to perform jobs, as they may lack the necessary ability, training, or information, and (2) employees may lack goal congruence with the organization.  Thus, controls are needed to compensate for personal limitations and to ensure that only appropriate activities are being performed.

4.      The three approaches to control or influence the behaviour of employees are:  (1) specify appropriate activities, (2) specify appropriate results, and (3) recruit or develop appropriate personnel.  Specific action controls attempt to ensure that employees perform certain activities and/or do not perform others.  Action control specifies the appropriate activities to be undertaken, via work rules, policies and procedures, and codes of conduct.  A result control specifies what must be accomplished, leaving the selection of activities to the employees and managers.  Results accountability can be accomplished through setting expectations for performance with standards, budgets, and management by objectives.  To control via personnel, the capabilities of employees can be upgraded through selective hiring of only those who are likely to do what the organization desires.  Personnel control can be accomplished by creating an organizational culture that compels employees to do what is organizationally correct.

5.      A company's mission statement should state clearly what the company wants to achieve and communicate how the company will meet its intended customers' needs with the products and services it provides. A company's mission statement may change over time.

6.      A core competency is any important task or activity in which one company has a higher proficiency than do its competitors. Technological innovation, engineering, product development, and customer service are some examples of core competencies. Core competencies are important in developing strategy because they are the foundation of competitiveness and competitive advantage.

7. A company choosing a differentiation strategy distinguishes its product or service from that of competitors by adding enough value that customers are willing to pay a higher price. Differentiation can be based on the product itself, the delivery system by which it is sold, the marketing approach, or other factors. A company choosing a cost leadership strategy avoids competition by becoming the low-cost producer/provider and, therefore, charging low prices that emphasize cost efficiencies. In this strategy, competitors cannot compete on price and must differentiate their products/services from the cost leader.

8. Environmental constraints are limitations on strategy as a result of external cultural, fiscal, legal/regulatory, political, and competitive market structures. Because a company's management cannot directly affect environmental constraints, they tend to be long-term constraints.

9. Strategic management is the company's planning for use of its resources to create value for customers and shareholders. The following issues are important in strategic management of resources: (1) how to deploy resources to support strategies, (2) how resources are consumed by or recovered from change processes, (3) how customer value and shareholder value will guide the use of resources, and (4) how resources are to be deployed and redeployed over time.

10. The value creation chain is the set of processes that converts inputs into products and services for the company's customers. The value creation chain includes internal and supplier processes. Companies use the value creation chain to identify activities that add value and activities that do not add value. Companies seek ways to reduce or eliminate activities that do not add value to become more efficient and effective.

11. The value creation chain is based on the belief that value is created for customers in goods and services by activities. These activities are divided into five major categories: (1) sourcing, (2) enhancing, (3) aggregating, (4) disseminating, and (5) interacting.

Sourcing involves obtaining raw or crudely produced materials in order to add value at later stages. Enhancing involves making basic products from raw materials. Aggregating consists of putting together various enhanced products to produce a complex product. Disseminating involves distributing products or services to customers or consumers. Interacting consists of the activities undertaken by the customer in obtaining the good or service being produced by the value creation chain.

12. Outsourcing is contracting with outside manufacturers or vendors to provide necessary goods or services instead of producing or providing them internally. By analyzing their value creation chain and core competencies, managers can discover their company's relative strengths. They can consider outsourcing the value creation chain processes that suppliers can do more efficiently and effectively. By outsourcing processes that are not within a company's core competencies, a company can concentrate its resources on core functions.

13. Activities that are good candidates for outsourcing include marketing and sales, accounting, engineering, manufacturing, customer service, and product distribution. In the accounting area, the payroll function is increasingly being outsourced, as is financial accounting and all aspects of information technology. A company should not outsource core competencies or activities needed for competitive advantage.

14. The global economy includes the international trade of goods and services, movement of labour, and flows of capital and information. The overall result is increased complexity of transactions due to global considerations. Management accounting must provide additional information to managers to plan, make decisions, evaluate performance, and control organizations within a complex business environment.

15. Ethical standards represent beliefs about moral and immoral behaviours. Such beliefs are personal, and thus ethical standards will vary with individuals. Ethical standards are more common within a particular society than they are across societies. In particular, legal and ethical standards differ from one country to another.

# CHAPTER 2
# COST TERMINOLOGY AND COST FLOWS

## CHAPTER OVERVIEW

Managers must understand information about costs in fulfilling their managerial functions. An adjective usually precedes the word *cost*. Managers view costs in different ways depending on how they will use the cost information. This chapter explains cost terms and why understanding them is important. This chapter also describes how product costs flow through a manufacturing company's accounts. Product costs include direct materials, direct labour, and manufacturing overhead. Costs not associated with the acquisition or manufacture of inventory are period costs.

Companies classify costs as variable, mixed, or fixed depending upon how they behave with a change in the activity level. This chapter illustrates how to use the high–low method to separate mixed costs into their fixed and variable components. The appendix illustrates how management can use least-squares regression analysis to separate mixed costs into their fixed and variable elements.

This chapter also explains how to calculate the cost of goods manufactured and the cost of goods sold for a manufacturing company.

## CHAPTER STUDY GUIDE

Managers must be able to understand and communicate information about costs using common management accounting terms. Cost is the monetary measure of the resources given up to acquire a good or service. Costs can be described in many ways. Thus, the word *cost* usually has an adjective before it that identifies the type of cost.

A cost object is anything to which costs attach or are directly related. Costs that the company can easily trace to a cost object are direct costs. Costs that the company cannot easily trace to a cost object are indirect costs. The company assigns or allocates indirect costs to cost objects using cost predictors, cost drivers, or arbitrary allocation bases. Companies also classify costs as period costs or product costs. Period costs are incurred in the nonproduction area. Product costs are all the costs incurred to produce a product or provide a service. Product costs are also called inventoriable costs and include the costs of direct material, direct labour, and manufacturing overhead.

Direct materials are those materials that the company can conveniently trace to a product. Direct materials include purchased raw materials and manufactured components. Because direct costs are so expensive to record, management may decide that the additional clerical cost of treating an insignificant cost as direct is greater than the benefit. If the company can trace materials directly to a product but the cost of such materials is insignificant, the company will usually consider such cost as indirect materials costs. Indirect materials costs are a part of manufacturing overhead.

Direct labour cost is the cost of labourers who work directly on making a product or providing a service. Direct labour cost is traceable to a cost object. For a company to consider a cost to be direct rather than a part of overhead, the company must be able to trace the cost conveniently and economically to the product or service. Management treats some direct labour costs as indirect costs for two reasons: (1) tracing direct labour cost to products may be cost inefficient, and (2) erroneous information about product or service costs might result from treating direct labour as a direct cost.

A good example of the second reason is the treatment of the overtime premium paid when employees work more than 40 hours a week. If the company treats the overtime premium as a direct cost, the products made during a week that includes overtime would cost more than products made in other weeks. Because scheduling is often random, products made during weeks in which employees work overtime should not have to bear the cost of the overtime premium. Management should more appropriately consider the overtime premium a part of manufacturing overhead. Thus, all products made during the year would bear a small part of the overtime premium cost. An exception would be if a customer demands a product so quickly that employees must work overtime to satisfy that customer. Such an order should bear all of the overtime premium.

Manufacturing overhead includes all production costs that are not directly or conveniently traceable to manufacturing a product or providing a service. Direct labour cost has become a progressively smaller proportion of product cost in recent years and overhead has become a much larger portion. This trend is due to the increased use of robots and other forms of automation.

The processing of raw materials into finished products occurs in three stages:
(1) work not started (raw materials), (2) work in process, and (3) finished work (finished goods). Exhibit 2-1 illustrates the stages of production and their corresponding costs. In the first stage, the cost incurred shows the prices paid for raw materials and supplies. Accrual accounting requires the accumulation and attachment to the goods of all costs connected with the conversion of the raw materials or supplies. The total costs incurred in the first two stages are equal to the total production cost of finished goods in stage three.

The cost accounting system accumulates costs in each of the three stages. The primary accounts used are (1) raw materials, (2) work in process, and (3) finished goods. These accounts serve as a database for cost, management, and financial accounting.

Service firms do not have the same level of cost complexity as manufacturing companies. The work-not-started stage consists only of supplies. When the service firm begins work, it adds the cost of supplies used to the direct labour cost and overhead cost incurred for the job. Calculating the cost of services provided is becoming increasingly important for service firms.

The sum of direct materials, direct labour, and overhead costs is total product cost. Prime cost is the sum of direct materials cost and direct labour cost. Conversion cost is the sum of direct labour cost and manufacturing overhead cost. Exhibit 2-2 shows the typical components of prime cost and conversion cost for a manufacturing company.

Cost behaviour reflects the way a cost responds to a change in activity level. Every cost will change given enough time or a large enough change in the activity level. Thus, for managers to analyze cost behaviour properly, they must specify a time frame and an activity level. The time frame is usually the longer of the operating cycle or one year. The activity level encompassing the company's normal operating range is the relevant range.

Managers often use cost drivers and cost predictors to estimate how changes in the activity level will affect costs. A cost driver is an activity or occurrence that has a direct cause-effect relationship to a cost. A change in the cost driver will cause a change in the cost. For example, production volume will drive total production cost. A cost predictor is a variable that has a consistent relationship with a cost. The change in the variable may not have a direct cause-effect relationship with the change in the cost. A third variable might be affecting the predictor and the cost in the same way. To be used as a predictor, the activity measure must change with the cost in a foreseeable manner.

Variable costs are costs that change in total in direct proportion to a change in the activity level.  Variable costs per unit remain constant when the activity level changes.  Fixed costs remain constant in total within a specified range of activity.  Fixed costs per unit decrease when the activity level increases because there are more units to absorb a constant amount of fixed costs.  When the activity level decreases, fixed costs per unit increase because there are fewer units to absorb a constant amount of fixed costs.  The activity level is usually units produced for production costs and units sold for selling expenses.  The classification of fixed and variable costs is valid only within the relevant range of activity.  In the long run, all costs are variable.  Exhibit 2-3 summarizes how variable costs and fixed costs each react in total and on a per-unit basis with a change in the activity level.

Some product costs are variable while others are fixed.  Direct materials cost is a variable cost.  Companies in Western cultures have usually treated direct labour cost as a variable cost.  In other cultures, notably Japan where employees often have lifetime employment contracts, management views direct labour cost as fixed.  Some companies in Japan are trying to change these lifetime employment contracts so that direct labour cost will become a variable cost.  Manufacturing overhead costs may be variable, fixed, or mixed.

Mixed or semivariable costs have a fixed component and a variable component.  Managers usually separate mixed costs into their fixed and variable components.  If the activity level increases, mixed costs will increase in total because of the variable cost component and decrease on a per-unit basis because of the fixed cost component.

The cost of electricity is a common example of a mixed cost.  There is normally a fixed cost per month and a variable cost based on the number of kilowatt hours consumed.  Exhibit 2-4 illustrates electricity cost graphically.

A step cost is a variable or fixed cost that shifts upward or downward when activity changes by a certain interval or step.  Step variable costs have small steps, and step fixed costs have large steps.   When step costs exist, a specific relevant range of activity must be considered when estimating costs at various levels of activity.  Within this relevant range, step variable costs are treated as completely variable and step fixed costs are treated as completely fixed.  Exhibits 2-5 and 2-6 illustrate graphically a step variable and a step fixed cost.

Accountants consider all costs to be linear rather than curvilinear.  Thus, accountants use a straight line to describe any type of cost behaviour within a relevant range of activity.  The formula for a straight line is $y = a + bx$ where $y$ = total cost,  $a$ = fixed cost,  $b$ = per-unit variable cost, and $x$ = activity base or cost driver in units of the activity base or cost driver.  Exhibit 2-7 illustrates uses of the straight-line cost formula.

Management accountants must separate mixed costs into their fixed and variable components.  The high–low method is the simplest method of doing so.  The high–low method uses activity and cost information from an actual set of cost observations to calculate the variable and fixed cost estimates.

The first step in using the high–low method is to identify the high level of activity and the low level of activity.  They must be within the relevant range.  The next step is to compute the differences in total costs and activity levels.  The change in the total costs divided by the change in the activity level provides the per-unit variable cost.  This result is true because fixed costs do not change when the activity level changes.  Thus, the only costs that change are the variable costs.  The per-unit variable cost times the number of units (either at the high or the low) equals total variable costs.  Total costs less total variable costs equals fixed costs.  Management accountants can use the formula $y = a + bx$ to predict total mixed costs and the fixed and variable elements of such mixed costs at any activity level within the relevant range.  Exhibit 2-8 provides a step-by-step illustration of the high–low method.

Regression analysis is a more complex method that management accountants can use to separate mixed costs. Regression analysis often results in a more reliable estimate of the cost formula than does the high-low method. The appendix illustrates regression analysis.

Whether management accountants use the high–low method or regression analysis to analyze mixed costs, they should remember three important points. First, costs determined are only estimates. Second, the degree of accuracy of the cost estimate depends on the validity of the activity measure used to predict the variable cost. Third, if significant changes are occurring in a company, historical information may not be reliable in predicting future costs.

Total overhead costs incurred for the year are not known until the end of the year, when all invoices have been received. In order to charge overhead to products during the year, a company must use a predetermined overhead rate.

Variable overhead changes in total in direct proportion to a change in an activity level. The company should calculate a predetermined overhead rate for each variable overhead cost pool. Variable manufacturing overhead is then charged to production by multiplying the variable overhead rate by the actual volume of the related activity base.

The activity level used to assign overhead costs to production should have a logical relationship to the incurrence of the overhead cost. Production volume would be a logical choice if the company made only one product. For companies that make multiple products, production volume is not an appropriate activity level. The activity measure chosen should be common to all costs in the cost pool being allocated. Frequently used measures include direct labour hours, direct labour cost, machine hours, production orders, and physical quantities of raw materials used. Some companies use only one or perhaps two (fixed and variable) overhead cost pools. Other companies compute a separate overhead rate for each department.

Traditionally, most companies have used volume-based measures such as direct labour hours or direct labour cost as the activity level. In the new manufacturing environment, direct labour costs make up a much smaller percentage of product cost. Direct labour does not drive or cause many components of overhead cost. Managers could falsely assume that by reducing direct labour hours, overhead costs would decrease. Companies must recognize the need to change their cost information systems as companies automate, increase the number and variety of products, and incur greater overhead costs.

Many companies are using multiple cost pools and new activity measures to assign overhead costs. Exhibit 2-10 illustrates detailed predetermined overhead rate calculations for various activities. Having predetermined overhead rates allows management to compare budgeted and actual results. Management can investigate causes of significant variances.

Fixed overhead is constant in total but varies on a per-unit basis inversely with changes in the activity level. Therefore, management must choose a specific activity level to compute the predetermined fixed overhead on a per-unit basis.

Management usually selects expected capacity. Expected capacity is the anticipated activity level for the upcoming year. Other possible capacity measures include theoretical capacity, practical capacity, and normal capacity. Theoretical capacity is the activity level the company could achieve if all production factors operate perfectly. Practical capacity is activity level that is equal to theoretical capacity less allowances for unused resources and regular operating interruptions such as holidays. Normal capacity is the long-run average activity level that the company could reasonably achieve.

Once the company has calculated its predetermined overhead rates, the company uses them throughout the next year to apply (assign) overhead costs to work in process. The company transfers overhead costs along with the other production costs to finished goods at the completion of production.

The company debits the actual overhead costs to the manufacturing overhead account(s). Applied overhead is the amount of overhead assigned to work in process. To apply overhead to work in process, the company debits work in process and credits the manufacturing overhead account(s). The company applies overhead to work in process by multiplying the predetermined overhead rates by the level of activities.

Actual overhead will almost never equal applied overhead resulting in a balance in the manufacturing overhead account(s) at the end of the year. If actual overhead is greater than the applied overhead, the company has underapplied overhead resulting in a debit balance. If actual overhead is less than the applied overhead, the company has overapplied overhead resulting in a credit balance. The manufacturing overhead accounts used for recording actual and applied overhead amounts are temporary accounts. The company must close the balance in the overhead account(s) at year-end. If the balance is not material, the company closes it to cost of goods sold in a manufacturing company or to cost of services rendered in a service firm. If the balance is material, the company must allocate it pro rata among work in process, finished goods, and cost of goods sold or cost of services rendered. Exhibit 2-12 gives an example of the disposition of overapplied variable overhead.

Traditionally, business used a combined overhead rate for three reasons: (1) clerical ease, (2) clerical cost savings, and (3) the lack of any formal requirement to separate costs by behaviour. The disadvantage of using a combined overhead rate is that it reduces a manager's ability to detect the causes of underapplied or overapplied overhead. Exhibit 2-13 illustrates a case in which underapplied overhead is related to fixed costs, but management could not detect this fact from the combined rate.

Companies can use the combined overhead rate for a specific cost pool or for all overhead costs. Combining overhead cost pools obscures the underlying cause-effect relationships between activities and overhead costs, which makes reducing costs, improving productivity, and discovering the causes of underapplied or overapplied overhead more difficult. Thus, the lack of detailed information impairs management's ability to carry out its functions of planning, controlling, and decision making.

Separate departmental overhead rates are better than a combined overhead rate. Machine hours may be an appropriate activity base to use in assigning overhead costs in a highly automated department. In a labour-intensive department, direct labour hours may be more appropriate.

Product costs are accumulated for inventory purposes and expensed to cost of goods sold. All product costs flow through the work in process account, to finished goods, and then to cost of goods sold. In a perpetual inventory system, a company continually updates its inventory and cost of goods sold accounts. In the past a drawback to a perpetual system was the higher cost of maintaining it. Technological advances such as computers and bar coding have caused the cost of maintaining a perpetual inventory system to drop significantly. Therefore, the textbook will assume that all companies use a perpetual inventory system. Exhibit 2-14 provides a good example of the journal entries used to record the flow of costs through the accounting system. Exhibit 2-15 shows T-accounts that reflect the posting of the journal entries in Exhibit 2-14.

A manufacturing company computes its cost of goods sold differently from a merchandising company. The cost of goods sold for a merchandising company equals the beginning inventory plus purchases less the ending inventory. A manufacturing company must compute its cost of goods manufactured before it can compute cost of goods sold. The cost of goods manufactured corresponds to the purchases account for a merchandising company. The cost of goods manufactured also represents the total production cost of the completed goods transferred to finished goods inventory during the period. The cost of goods manufactured does not include the cost of work in process at the end of the period. Exhibit 2-16 presents a schedule of cost of goods manufactured.

A manufacturing company computes its cost of goods sold by adding the cost of goods manufactured to the beginning finished goods inventory to arrive at the cost of goods available for sale. Then the company subtracts ending finished goods inventory from the cost of goods available for sale to compute the cost of goods sold. Exhibit 2-17 presents a schedule of cost of goods sold.

## APPENDIX--LEAST-SQUARES REGRESSION ANALYSIS

Least-squares regression analysis is a statistical method for separating mixed costs into their fixed and variable elements. Least-squares regression analysis is superior to the high–low method in that least-squares regression analysis considers all representative data points and figures out the line that best fits the data points. This line of best fit is the one that minimizes the sum of the squares of the deviations between the data points and the line. Exhibit 2-18 illustrates least-squares regression analysis graphically.

In contrast, the high–low method just considers the high and low points. Also, the high and low points could be outliers or points that are not representative of the usual cost relationships. The company should exclude outliers from the data points used in least-squares regression analysis also.

When dealing with multiple independent variables, companies can use least-squares regression analysis to learn the independent variable (activity correlated with variable costs) with the strongest correlation to the dependent variable (total costs). If the company uses only one independent variable to predict the dependent variable, the process is called simple regression. If the company uses more than one independent variable, the process is known as multiple regression. Simple regression uses the linear formula $y = a + bx$ in which $y$ = total costs,
$a$ = fixed costs, $b$ = per-unit variable costs, and $x$ = the activity level. Least-squares regression analysis computes the fixed costs ($a$) and the per-unit variable cost ($b$). The company then uses this formula to predict total mixed costs for any activity level within the relevant range.

## SELF TEST

### TRUE/FALSE

1.  T  F  A cost reflects a monetary measure of the resources given up to acquire a good or service.

2.  T  F  Costs that remain constant on a per-unit basis as the activity level changes are fixed costs.

3.  T  F  The sum of prime cost and conversion cost equals product cost.

4.  T  F  Predetermined overhead rates are always calculated in advance of the year of application.

5.  T  F  Per-unit fixed costs decrease with an increase in the activity level.

6.  T  F  A mixed cost has a variable element and a fixed element.

7.  T  F  Cost drivers have a cause-effect relationship to a cost.

8.  T  F  Costs incurred in the manufacture of inventory are product costs.

9.  T  F  Step costs are always variable.

10. T  F  A cost object can be a product, a customer, a department, a division, or a territory.

11. T F Costs that are directly traceable to a cost object are known as overhead costs.

12. T F Actual overhead will usually equal applied overhead.

13. T F If the amount of underapplied or overapplied overhead is not significant, the company should close it to

## APPENDIX--LEAST SQUARES REGRESSION ANALYSIS

14. T F Regression analysis generally yields more reliable results than the high–low method in separating mixed costs into their fixed and variable elements.

15. T F One weakness of regression analysis is that it cannot help management select the independent variable that is the best predictor of total costs.

## MULTIPLE CHOICE

1. The sum of direct materials cost and direct labour cost is:

    A. period cost.
    B. prime cost.
    C. conversion cost.
    D. standard cost.

2. The sum of direct labour cost and manufacturing overhead cost is:

    A. period cost.
    B. prime cost.
    C. conversion cost.
    D. standard cost.

3. On a per-unit basis variable costs are:

    A. fixed.
    B. variable.
    C. mixed.
    D. zero.

4. What are the three categories of product costs?

    A. direct materials, manufacturing overhead, and work in process
    B. direct materials, direct labour, and work in process
    C. direct materials, direct labour, and manufacturing overhead
    D. direct materials, manufacturing overhead, and standard costs

5. What are the inventories of a manufacturing company?

    A. raw materials, work in process, and manufacturing overhead
    B. manufacturing overhead, work in process, and finished goods
    C. raw materials, direct labour, and manufacturing overhead
    D. raw materials, work in process, and finished goods

6. Which of the following would be considered a period cost?

    A. salaries of the advertising department
    B. overtime paid to production employees
    C. plant maintenance supplies
    D. direct materials

7. On a per-unit basis, fixed costs _____ as the activity level increases.

    A. decrease
    B. increase
    C. remain constant
    D. may increase or decrease

8. An activity measure whose changes are accompanied by consistent, observable changes in a cost item is a:

    A. relevant range.
    B. mixed cost.
    C. cost predictor.
    D. cost driver.

9. A measure of activity believed to have a direct cause-effect relationship to a cost is a:

    A. cost predictor.
    B. cost object.
    C. relevant range.
    D. cost driver.

10. Anything to which costs attach or are related is a(n):

    A. cost predictor.
    B. cost driver.
    C. cost object.
    D. allocated cost.

11. As the activity level increases, total mixed costs:

    A. decrease.
    B. increase.
    C. may increase or decrease.
    D. remain constant.

12. On a per-unit basis, mixed costs _____ as the activity level increases.

    A. increase
    B. decrease
    C. remain constant
    D. may increase or decrease

13. Beginning work in process plus total current period manufacturing costs less ending work in process equals:

    A. cost of goods sold.
    B. cost of goods manufactured.
    C. total overhead costs.
    D. cost of goods available for sale.

14. If one plots mixed costs on a graph, the point where the total cost line intercepts the $y$ axis represents:

    A. total fixed costs.
    B. total variable costs.
    C. per-unit variable cost.
    D. per-unit fixed cost.

15. In describing the straight-line formula $y = a + bx$, which of the following statements is correct?

    A. "$a$" is the fixed portion of total cost.
    B. In the high-low method, "$b$" equals change in activity divided by change in cost.
    C. As "$x$" increases, "$y$" decreases.
    D. "$y$" is the activity base (or cost driver).

16. Manufacturing companies usually charge a small amount of underapplied overhead to:

    A. Work in Process.
    B. Finished Goods.
    C. Cost of Goods Sold.
    D. Miscellaneous Expense.

17. If the amount of underapplied or overapplied overhead is significant at the end of the accounting period, a manufacturing company should close the balance by allocating it pro rata among:

    A. direct materials, work in process, and manufacturing overhead.
    B. direct materials, work in process, and finished goods.
    C. direct materials, work in process, and cost of goods sold.
    D. work in process, finished goods, and cost of goods sold.

18. If the cost of goods sold is less than the cost of goods manufactured, then:

    A. work in process inventory has increased during the period.
    B. finished goods inventory has increased during the period.
    C. total costs to account for must be less than cost of goods manufactured.
    D. finished goods inventory has decreased during the period.

USE THE FOLLOWING INFORMATION TO ANSWER QUESTIONS 19, 20, AND 21

Harris Company had total maintenance costs of $30,000 in March when the company used 60,000 machine hours. In April the total maintenance costs were $34,000 and the total machine hours were 80,000.

19.  What is Harris Company's estimated variable maintenance cost per machine hour?

    A.  $0.20
    B.  $0.425
    C.  $0.50
    D.  $5.00

20.  What is Harris Company's estimated monthly fixed cost for maintenance?

    A.  $18,000
    B.  $30,000
    C.  $32,000
    D.  none of the above

21.  Harris Company's estimated total maintenance costs in a month that 65,000 machine hours were used is:

    A.  $13,000.
    B.  $27,625.
    C.  $31,000.
    D.  none of the above.

22.  Martin Company applies overhead on the basis of machine hours.  Martin Company estimated that its total overhead costs would be $600,000 and its total machine hours would be 200,000.  At the end of the year, actual overhead was $595,000 and actual machine hours were 199,000.  For the year overhead was:

    A.  underapplied by $2,000.
    B.  overapplied by $2,000.
    C.  underapplied by $3,000.
    D.  underapplied by $5,000.

23.  Fritz Company had a $6,000 credit balance in its overhead account at the end of the year just before closing. Actual overhead was $300,000.  Fritz applies overhead at the rate of $10 per machine hour.  How many machine hours did Fritz Company use during the year?

    A.  28,800
    B.  29,400
    C.  30,000
    D.  30,600

24. Bonner Company applies overhead on the basis of machine hours. The company had fixed overhead of $50,000 and variable overhead of $250,000 at an activity level of 50,000 machine hours. The relevant range is 40,000 to 100,000 machine hours. What would you expect the total overhead costs to be at an activity level of 75,000 machine hours?

    A. $ 65,000
    B. $375,000
    C. $425,000
    D. $450,000

25. Beckler Company had a beginning balance in its Work in Process account of $36,000. During the year, the company added $500,000 of direct materials and $100,000 of direct labour to work in process. The cost of work completed was $950,000. The ending balance in Work in Process was $268,000. How much overhead did Beckler Company apply to Work in Process during the year?

    A. $314,000
    B. $368,000
    C. $582,000
    D. $904,000

26. The balance in Pittman Company's overhead account at the end of the year was $90,000 debit (underapplied). Pittman Company considers this to be a material amount. At the end of the year Work in Process, Finished Goods, and Cost of Goods Sold had the following balances:

| | |
|---|---|
| Work in Process | $ 50,000 |
| Finished Goods | $150,000 |
| Cost of Goods Sold | $300,000 |

After Pittman Company closes its Overhead account, what will be the ending balance in the Cost of Goods Sold account?

    A. $210,000
    B. $246,000
    C. $354,000
    D. $390,000

27. Assume the same facts as in question 26 except that the balance in the Overhead account at the end of the year was $3,000 credit (overapplied). Pittman Company considers this amount not to be significant. After Pittman Company closes its Overhead account, what will be the ending balance in the Cost of Goods Sold account?

    A. $297,000
    B. $298,200
    C. $301,800
    D. $303,000

USE THE FOLLOWING INFORMATION TAKEN FROM DOW MANUFACTURING COMPANY'S
ACCOUNTING RECORDS TO ANSWER QUESTIONS 28 AND 29

| | |
|---|---:|
| Total current period manufacturing costs | $750,000 |
| Ending work in process | 35,000 |
| Cost of goods manufactured | 741,000 |
| Cost of goods available for sale | 911,000 |
| Cost of goods sold | 875,000 |

28. What was Dow's beginning balance in Work in Process?

    A. $ 9,000
    B. $26,000
    C. $36,000
    D. $44,000

29. What was Dow's ending balance in Finished Goods Inventory?

    A. $ 9,000
    B. $ 36,000
    C. $134,000
    D. $170,000

## APPENDIX--LEAST SQUARES REGRESSION ANALYSIS

30. A company should eliminate outliers in analyzing mixed costs using:

    A. the high–low method only.
    B. regression analysis only.
    C. neither the high–low method nor regression analysis.
    D. the high–low method and regression analysis.

## ESSAY  QUESTIONS AND PROBLEMS

1. Explain how fixed, variable, and mixed costs behave both in total and on a per-unit basis with a change in the
activity level.

2.  What is the difference between a cost predictor and a cost driver?

3.  Define each of the following:  (A) expected activity, (B) theoretical capacity, (C) practical capacity, and (D) normal capacity.  Which of these do companies usually use as the measure of activity in computing their predetermined overhead rates?  Why?

4.  Why would management treat some direct labour costs as indirect costs?

5.  What are the advantages and disadvantages of using a single overhead rate for the entire plant?

6. The following information is from the accounting records of Horton Company for calendar year 20XX:

| | Beginning of Year | End of Year |
|---|---|---|
| Raw Materials | $ 50,000 | $ 75,000 |
| Work in Process | $ 93,000 | $ 84,000 |

Other Information:

| | |
|---|---|
| Raw materials purchases | $280,000 |
| Direct labour cost | $220,000 |
| Variable manufacturing overhead cost | $440,000 |
| Fixed manufacturing overhead cost | $210,000 |

Prepare a Schedule of Cost of Goods Manufactured for Horton Company.

7. Watson Company is a small manufacturing company. During the week, employees who work directly on making products worked a total of 900 hours. Of these 900 hours, 100 hours were overtime hours for which the employees receive time-and-a-half pay. The regular pay rate is $14 an hour. Watson Company considers the overtime premium to be manufacturing overhead. Calculate Watson Company's direct labour cost, manufacturing overhead cost, and total payroll for the week.

8. Miller Manufacturing makes one product only. For the month of July the company made 2,000 units and incurred the following product costs:

| | |
|---|---|
| Raw materials | $ 80,000 |
| Direct labour | 30,000 |
| Variable overhead | 40,000 |
| Fixed overhead | 52,000 |
| Total product costs | $202,000 |

(A) Determine the variable cost per unit, the fixed cost per unit, and the total cost per unit for the month of July.

(B) Assume that Miller plans to make 2,600 units in August. Estimate the total product costs that Miller would incur. Estimate the variable cost per unit, the fixed cost per unit, and the total cost per unit.

(C) Assume that the company plans to make 1,300 units in September. Estimate the total product costs that Miller would incur. Estimate the variable cost per unit, the fixed cost per unit, and the total cost per unit.

9. Prepare journal entries in general journal form to record the following transactions:

(A) Purchased $40,000 of raw materials on account.

Dr. Raw materials      40,000
    Cr.     A/P            40,000

(B) Issued $8,000 of direct materials and $2,000 of indirect materials into production.

WIP      8000
OH      2000
    RM         10,000

(C) Incurred $40,000 in direct labour cost and $50,000 of indirect labour cost.

Dr. WIP     40,000
Dr. OH     50,000
    Cr. Wages Pay.    90,000

(D) Transferred $65,000 in variable overhead costs and $20,000 in fixed overhead costs to work in process.

WIP     85,000
    FOH       20,000
    VOH       65,00

(E) Production completed during the period was $44,000.

Finished Goods    44,000
    WIP        44,000

10. Prepare journal entries in general journal form to record the following:

(A)  Sold goods on account for $650,000.

A/R          650,000

    S\s                    650,000

(B)  Recorded the cost of goods sold in the amount of $370,000.

Cost of goods sold   370,000

    FG                      370,000

11.  Keller Company's beginning and ending inventory accounts for June were as follows:

|  | Beginning | Ending |
|---|---|---|
| Raw Materials | $ 59,000 | $ 29,000 |
| Work in Process | 120,000 | 90,000 |
| Finished Goods | 200,000 | 240,000 |

During June, Keller Company purchased $40,000 of raw materials.  All raw materials are direct materials. During June, Keller Company also incurred $80,000 of direct labour cost and $500,000 of manufacturing overhead cost. Determine the following:

(A) prime cost added to production during June

DL + DM used

= 80,000 + 70,000

= 150,000    ✓

RM

59,000

40,000 | 70,00

27,00

(B) conversion cost added to production in June

DL + MOH

= 80,000 + 500,000

= $580,000    ✓

(C) the cost of goods manufactured in June

$COGM = Bg. WIP + DL + DM + MOH - End WIP$

$= 59,000 + 80,000 + 10,000 + 500,000 - 29,000$

$= \$680,000$ ✓

(D) the cost of goods sold in June

$CGS = Bg. FG + COGM - End FG$

$= 200,000 + 680,000 - 240,000$

$= \$640,000$ ✓

12.  Young Company expects the following overhead costs at each of the following activity levels.  All activity levels are within the relevant range.

|  | Direct Labour Hours | | |
| --- | --- | --- | --- |
|  | 10,000 | 15,000 | 20,000 |
| Total variable costs | $80,000 | $120,000 | $ 160,000 |
| Total fixed costs | 90,000 | 90,000 | 90,000 |
| Total overhead costs | $170,000 | $210,000 | $ 250,000 |

Compute (A) the predetermined variable overhead rate, (B) the predetermined fixed overhead rate at the expected activity level of 15,000 direct labour hours, and (C) the predetermined combined overhead rate at the expected activity level of 15,000 direct labour hours.

a) $PVOHR = \dfrac{120,000}{15000} = \$8$

b) $PFOHR = \dfrac{90,000}{15000} = \$6$

c) $POOR = \dfrac{210,000}{15000} = \$14$

13.  The following are the maintenance costs and machine hours of Rios Company for the first six months of the year:

| Month | Maintenance Costs | Machine Hours |
|-------|-------------------|---------------|
| January | $5,976 | 9,000 |
| February | $5,700 | 8,300 |
| March | $7,465 | 11,100 |
| April | $6,100 | 9,700 |
| May | $7,900 | 12,300 |
| June | $7,434 | 11,900 |

Use the high–low method to estimate the following:

(A)  variable maintenance costs per machine hour

$$b = \frac{7900 - 5700}{12300 - 8300} = \frac{2200}{4000} = \$0.55$$

$$(0.55)(12,300) = \$6765$$
$$(0.55)(8,300) = \$4565$$

(B)  fixed maintenance costs per month

$$7900 - 6765 = 1135$$
$$5700 - 4565 = 1135$$

$$1135 + 0.55x$$

14.  Deitz Company applies overhead on the basis of machine hours.  For the current year, Deitz estimated that the total overhead costs would be $600,000 and that the total machine hours would be 120,000.  At the end of the year Deitz had incurred $598,000 in actual overhead costs and had used 119,000 machine hours.

(A) Compute the predetermined overhead rate.

estimate                    actual

$$total \ OH = 600,000$$

$$MH = 120,000$$

$$\frac{\$600,000}{120,000} = \$5 \qquad \frac{\$598,000}{\$119,000} = \$5.02$$

(B) Compute the ending balance in the overhead account. Was overhead underapplied or overapplied?

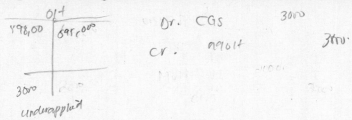

(C) Prepare the journal entry to close the overhead account. Assume that the underapplied or overapplied overhead was not material.

Dr. CGS          3000

Cr.    mult          3000.

## APPENDIX--LEAST-SQUARES REGRESSION ANALYSIS

15. Steuart Company is attempting to predict its maintenance costs more accurately. Maintenance costs are a mixed cost. Maintenance costs and machine hours for the first four months of the year are as follows:

|  | Maintenance Costs | Machine Hours |
|---|---|---|
| January | $5,860 | 1,000 |
| February | 5,290 | 900 |
| March | 6,120 | 1,080 |
| April | 5,270 | 860 |

Determine the *a* value (fixed costs per month) and the *b* value (variable cost per machine hour) using least-squares regression analysis.

## SELF TEST ANSWERS

### TRUE/FALSE

| | | | | | | | | | |
|---|---|---|---|---|---|---|---|---|---|
| 1. | T | 4. | T | 7. | T | 10. | T | 13. | T |
| 2. | F | 5. | T | 8. | T | 11. | F | 14. | T |
| 3. | F | 6. | T | 9. | F | 12. | F | 15. | F |

### MULTIPLE CHOICE

| | | | | | | | | | |
|---|---|---|---|---|---|---|---|---|---|
| 1. | B | 7. | A | 13. | B | 19. | A | 25. | C |
| 2. | C | 8. | C | 14. | A | 20. | A | 26. | C |
| 3. | A | 9. | D | 15. | A | 21. | C | 27. | A |
| 4. | C | 10. | C | 16. | C | 22. | B | 28. | B |
| 5. | D | 11. | B | 17. | D | 23. | D | 29. | B |
| 6. | A | 12. | B | 18. | B | 24. | C | 30. | D |

### ESSAY QUESTIONS AND PROBLEMS

1.      Fixed costs remain constant in total. On a per-unit basis, fixed costs decrease with an increase in the activity level and increase with a decrease in the activity level. Total variable costs increase proportionally with an increase in the activity level and decrease proportionally with a decrease in the activity level. On a per-unit basis, variable costs remain constant when the activity level increases or decreases. Mixed costs have a fixed cost component and a variable cost component. Total mixed costs increase with an increase in the activity level and decrease with a decrease in the activity level. The increase or decrease in total mixed costs is due to the variable cost element. Because of the fixed cost component, the increase or decrease is not proportional to the change in the activity level. On a per-unit basis, mixed costs decrease when the activity level increases and increase when the activity level decreases. These changes are due to the fixed cost element.

2.      A cost predictor is an activity measure that when changed results in a consistent, observable change in a cost. The change in the variable may not have a direct cause-effect relationship with the change in the cost. A third variable might be affecting the predictor and the cost in the same way. A cost driver has a direct cause-effect relationship to a cost. A change in the cost driver will cause a change in the cost.

3.      Expected activity is the level of activity that the company anticipates for the upcoming year. Theoretical capacity is the maximum potential activity that could occur during the year. Practical capacity is the theoretical capacity less expected interruptions such as start-up time and holidays. Normal capacity is a measure of the average level of activity over a long period of time such as five to ten years. Companies usually choose expected activity in setting predetermined overhead rates. They choose expected activity because it results in product costs that closely approximate actual costs.

4.      Management treats some direct labour costs as indirect costs for two reasons:
(1) tracing direct labour cost to products may be cost inefficient, and (2) erroneous information about product or service costs could result from treating direct labour as a direct cost. A good example of the second reason is the treatment of the overtime premium paid when employees work more than 40 hours a week. Because scheduling is often random, products made during weeks in which employees work overtime should not have to bear the cost of the overtime premium. An exception would be when a customer demands a product so quickly that employees must work overtime to satisfy that customer.

5.      Several advantages come with using a single overhead rate for the entire plant.  One advantage is reduced clerical expense.  Another is less complexity because the company does not have to separate fixed and variable costs.  Neither are there separate cost pools for various overhead drivers.

Several disadvantages can also occur, however, when using a single overhead rate for the entire plant. Product costs may be distorted.  The distortion in product costs happens because the company uses a single activity measure to assign all overhead costs.  The company ignores the activities that drive overhead costs. Managers could attempt to reduce overhead costs by reducing the level of activity used to apply overhead.  If this activity does not drive overhead costs, the results will be disappointing.  Distorted cost information could also cause managers to make poor strategic decisions.  Managers could set a price too high or too low.

6.      Horton Company

Schedule of Cost of Goods Manufactured
For the Year Ended December 31, 20XX

| | | |
|---|---|---:|
| Beginning work in process | | $  93,000 |
| | | |
| Beginning raw materials | $  50,000 | |
| Add:  Raw materials purchases | 280,000 | |
| Raw materials available | $330,000 | |
| Less:  Ending raw materials | 75,000 | |
| Raw materials used | $255,000 | |
| Direct labour | 220,000 | |
| Variable overhead | 440,000 | |
| Fixed overhead | 210,000 | |
| | | |
| Total current period manufacturing costs | | 1,125,000 |
| Total costs to account for | | $1,218,000 |
| Less:  Ending work in process | | 84,000 |
| Cost of goods manufactured | | $1,134,000 |

7.  

| | | | |
|---|---|---|---|
| Total hours for week | 900 | Overtime hours for week | 100 |
| Regular pay rate | x  $14 | Overtime premium rate per hour | x  $7 |
| Direct labour cost | $12,600 | Manufacturing overhead | $700 |

Total payroll = $12,600 + $700 = $13,300

8.     Raw materials, direct labour, and variable overhead are the variable product costs. Fixed overhead is a fixed product cost. Variable costs are fixed per unit and change in total proportionally with a change in the activity level. One computes the variable cost per unit of $75 by dividing the $150,000 total variable costs for July by the 2,000 units produced. Fixed costs remain constant in total when the activity level changes. Thus, on a per-unit basis fixed costs increase with a decrease in the activity level and decrease with an increase in the activity level. The total cost per unit changes because of the change in the per-unit fixed cost.

|                      | (A)       | (B)       | (C)        |
|----------------------|-----------|-----------|------------|
|                      | July      | August    | September  |
| Raw materials        | $  80,000 | $104,000  | $  52,000  |
| Direct labour        | 30,000    | 39,000    | 19,500     |
| Variable overhead    | 40,000    | 52,000    | 26,000     |
| Total variable costs | $150,000  | $195,000  | $  97,500  |
| Fixed overhead       | 52,000    | 52,000    | 52,000     |
| Total product costs  | $202,000  | $247,000  | $149,500   |
| Number of units      | 2,000     | 2,600     | 1,300      |
| Per unit:            |           |           |            |
| Variable cost        | $ 75      | $ 75      | $ 75       |
| Fixed cost           | 26        | 20        | 40         |
| Total cost           | $101      | $ 95      | $115       |

9.     (A)  Raw Materials Inventory .................... 40,000

              Accounts Payable ......................................... 40,000

       (B)  Work in Process Inventory ................ 8,000

            Variable Manufacturing Overhead ...... 2,000

                   Raw Materials .......................................... 10,000

       (C)  Work in Process Inventory ................ 40,000

            Variable Manufacturing Overhead ...... 50,000

                   Salaries and Wages Payable ...................... 90,000

       (D)  Work in Process Inventory ................ 85,000

                   Variable Overhead ..................................... 65,000

                   Fixed Overhead ......................................... 20,000

       (E)  Finished Goods Inventory ................. 44,000

                   Work in Process Inventory ....................... 44,000

10.    (A)  Accounts Receivable .......................... 650,000

                   Sales ............................................................ 650,000

       (B)  Cost of Goods Sold ........................... 370,000

                   Finished Goods Inventory ........................ 370,000

11.     (A) Prime costs are the direct materials cost and the direct labour cost.  The direct materials cost added to production is computed as follows:

| | |
|---|---:|
| Beginning inventory of raw materials | $ 59,000 |
| Add:  Raw materials purchased | 40,000 |
| Raw materials available for use | $ 99,000 |
| Less:  Ending inventory of raw materials | 29,000 |
| Direct materials added to production | $ 70,000 |
| | |
| Direct labour cost | 80,000 |
| Prime cost added to production | $150,000 |

(B) Conversion costs are the direct labour cost and the manufacturing overhead cost.

| | |
|---|---:|
| Direct labour cost | $ 80,000 |
| Manufacturing overhead cost | 500,000 |
| Conversion cost | $580,000 |

(C)

| | | |
|---|---:|---:|
| Beginning work in process | | $120,000 |
| | | |
| Beginning inventory of raw materials | $59,000 | |
| Add:  Raw materials purchased | 40,000 | |
| Raw materials available for use | $99,000 | |
| Less:  Ending inventory of raw material | 29,000 | |
| Direct materials added to production | $70,000 | |
| Direct labour cost | 80,000 | |
| Manufacturing overhead cost | 500,000 | |
| Total manufacturing costs for June | | 650,000 |
| Total costs to account for | | $770,000 |
| Less:  Ending work in process | | 90,000 |
| Cost of goods manufactured in June | | $680,000 |

(D)

| | |
|---|---:|
| Beginning finished goods inventory | $200,000 |
| Add:  Cost of goods manufactured | 680,000 |
| Cost of goods available for sale | $880,000 |
| Less:  Ending finished goods inventory | 240,000 |
| Cost of goods sold in June | $640,000 |

12.     (A) To compute the variable overhead rate, divide the total variable costs by the activity level (e.g., direct labour hours):

$120,000 ÷ 15,000 DLH = $8 per DLH

        (B) To compute the predetermined fixed overhead rate at the expected level of activity, divide the total fixed costs by the expected activity level:

$90,000 ÷ 15,000 DLH = $6 per DLH

(C) To compute the combined overhead rate for the expected level of activity, divide the total costs by the activity level:

$210,000 ÷ 15,000 DLH = $14 per DLH

The combined overhead rate is also equal to the sum of the variable overhead rate and the fixed overhead rate: $8 + $6 = $14 per DLH

13.     The first step is to identify the high month and the low month.  Calculate the change in costs and the change in machine hours.

|  |  | Maintenance Costs | Machine Hours |
|---|---|---|---|
| High | May | $7,900 | 12,300 |
| Low | February | 5,700 | 8,300 |
|  | Changes | $2,200 | 4,000 |

(A) The variable maintenance cost per machine hour is the change in costs divided by the change in machine hours.

$2,200 ÷ 4,000 machine hours = $0.55 per machine hour

(B) Compute the fixed costs per month by subtracting the total variable costs from the total costs.  You can do this for the high month or the low month.

|  | May | February |
|---|---|---|
| Total maintenance costs | $7,900 | $5,700 |
| Total variable costs: |  |  |
| $0.55 per MH x 12,300 MH | 6,765 |  |
| $0.55 per MH x  8,300 MH |  | 4,565 |
| Fixed costs | $1,135 | $1,135 |

14.     (A) The predetermined overhead rate equals estimated overhead divided by the estimated machine hours: $600,000 ÷ 120,000 = $5 per machine hour

(B) Actual overhead                       $598,000
    Less:  Applied overhead:
    $5 per MH x  119,000 MH =             595,000
    Underapplied overhead                $   3,000

The ending balance in the overhead account would be a $3,000 debit balance.

(C) Cost of Goods Sold                    3,000
        Manufacturing Overhead                    3,000

15.

| x | y | xy | $x^2$ |
|---|---|---|---|
| 1,000 | 5,860 | 5,860,000 | 1,000,000 |
| 900 | 5,290 | 4,761,000 | 810,000 |
| 1,080 | 6,120 | 6,609,600 | 1,166,400 |
| 860 | 5,270 | 4,532,200 | 739,600 |
| 3,840 | 22,540 | 21,762,800 | 3,716,000 |

Mean of $x$ = 3,840 ÷ 4 = 960   Mean of $y$ = 22,540 ÷ 4 = 5,635

$b = \dfrac{21,762,800 - 4(960)(5,635)}{3,716,000 - 4(960)(960)} = \dfrac{124,400}{29,600} = 4.203$

$a = 5,635 - 4.203(960) = 1,600.12$

# CHAPTER 3
## COST-VOLUME-PROFIT ANALYSIS

## CHAPTER OVERVIEW

Managers use accounting information to plan and control the operations of the business and to make decisions.  For many of these decisions, managers must classify costs according to how they behave with a change in volume.  Using cost-volume-profit analysis (CVP), managers can calculate the effects on profit for changes in volume, price, and costs.  Manufacturers, wholesale and retail trade firms, and service businesses all use CVP.  CVP analysis is valid for the short run only.

The breakeven point is that quantity of sales volume at which the company will experience zero profit or loss.  Since most companies want to operate above breakeven, CVP analysis extends the breakeven point computation by adding a desired profit factor.  The margin of safety of a firm indicates how far a company is operating from its breakeven point.  A company's degree of operating leverage shows what percentage change in profit would occur given a specified percentage change in sales from the current level.

The appendix provides an overview of absorption and variable costing.

## CHAPTER STUDY GUIDE

A useful starting point in understanding cost-volume-profit (CVP) analysis is understanding the breakeven point.  At the breakeven point, total revenues equal total costs resulting in a zero profit.  The breakeven point in units is the number of units that a company must sell to have a zero profit.  The breakeven point in sales revenue is the sales revenue in dollars that a company must generate to have a zero profit.  Because managers seldom want to operate at a level that simply breaks even, CVP adds a profit element to breakeven calculations so that managers can plan for volume levels that result in profits.

To use CVP analysis, managers must classify costs by how they behave with a change in volume.  Some costs are fixed, some costs are variable, and some costs are mixed.  Fixed costs remain constant in total when volume increases or decreases.  However, per-unit fixed costs decrease when volume increases and increase when volume decreases.  Total variable costs increase proportionately to an increase in volume.  Also, total variable costs decrease proportionately with a decrease in volume.  Per-unit variable costs remain constant when volume increases or decreases.  Managers usually assume that revenue is constant on a per-unit basis.  These cost and revenue behaviours hold true only within the relevant range.

Mixed costs have a fixed cost element and a variable cost element.  Managers must separate mixed costs into their fixed and variable elements before using CVP analysis.  Mixed costs increase in total when volume increases because of their variable cost element.  Mixed costs per unit decrease when volume increases because of their fixed cost element.  Managers can use techniques such as the high–low method or regression analysis to separate mixed costs.

Contribution margin is revenue less variable costs.  The breakeven point in units is equal to the fixed costs divided by the contribution margin per unit.  On a per-unit basis, contribution margin is constant because revenue and variable costs are constant on a per-unit basis.  The breakeven point in revenue equals the breakeven point in units times the sales price per unit.  The result may not be feasible because the company cannot sell partial units or because lot size restrictions may apply.  In such cases, managers can round the result to a feasible solution.  The data presented in Exhibit 3-1 are used to illustrate the computation of the breakeven point.

The contribution margin ratio is contribution margin divided by revenue. Another way to compute the breakeven point in revenue is to divide the fixed costs by the contribution margin ratio. To find the breakeven point in units, divide the breakeven point in revenue by the sales price per unit. The variable cost ratio is 100% minus the contribution margin ratio.

Cost-volume-profit (CVP) analysis is the process of examining the relationships among revenues, costs, and profits within a relevant range of activity and for a specified time. All kinds of companies can use CVP analysis.

To compute how many units the company must sell to achieve a target profit before tax, add the target profit before tax to the fixed costs and divide this sum by the contribution margin per unit. To calculate the revenue that the company must realize to achieve a target profit before tax, add the target profit before tax to the fixed costs and divide this sum by the contribution margin ratio. Exhibit 3-2 illustrates CVP analysis with a target profit before tax.

Managers can also compute the number of units that the company must sell or the sales revenue that the company must realize to achieve a target profit after tax. To convert the target profit after tax to a target profit before tax, divide the target profit after tax by 1 minus the tax rate. Then one can use the formulas for target profit before tax. Exhibit 3-3 illustrates CVP analysis with a target profit after tax.

Managers may want profit before tax to be a specified per-unit profit. Managers treat the desired per-unit profit before tax as an additional variable cost in the CVP formula. The number of units that the company must sell to earn a desired per-unit profit before tax is equal to the fixed costs divided by the difference between the per-unit contribution margin and the desired per-unit profit before tax.

If the manager wants profit before tax to be a specified percentage of sales, the specified percentage times the sales price will equal the desired per-unit profit before tax. Managers can calculate the amount of revenue the company must realize to earn a profit before tax equal to a specified percentage of revenue. To do so, managers divide the fixed costs by the difference between the contribution margin ratio and the desired profit before tax percentage. The desired profit before tax percentage must be less than the contribution margin ratio. Exhibit 3-4 illustrates the calculation of the number of units and the amount of sales revenue that a company must realize to earn a desired per-unit profit before tax.

To calculate the number of units that the company must sell to earn a desired per-unit profit after tax, managers must convert the per-unit profit after tax to a per-unit profit before tax. Managers do this by dividing the per-unit profit after tax by the difference between one and the tax rate. Managers can compute the revenue that the company must realize to earn a profit after tax equal to a specified percentage of revenue. Managers must first convert the specified percentage of profit after tax to a specified percentage of profit before tax. Again, managers do this by dividing the desired percentage of profit after tax by the difference between one and the tax rate. Exhibit 3-5 illustrates the calculation of the number of units and the amount of sales revenue that a company must realize to earn a variable profit after tax.

Income statements can be used to prove the accuracy of computations made using the formula approach to CVP analysis. Exhibit 3-6 proves each of the computations made in Exhibits 3-2 through 3-5.

The solutions provided by breakeven analysis and CVP analysis are valid only with the specified selling price and cost relationships. A change in the sales price, variable costs, or fixed costs, will cause a change in the breakeven point and the sales required to earn a desired profit.

Other things being equal, the breakeven point will increase if the total fixed cost or per unit variable cost increases, or the per unit sales price decreases. Exhibit 3-7 illustrates the effect of these changes on the breakeven point. The breakeven point will decrease if the total fixed cost decreases or the contribution margin increases. Incremental analysis can be used to determine how revenue and cost changes will affect a company's breakeven point or sales volume required to realize desired profits.

A breakeven graph can be prepared to show the relationships between costs, volume, and profit. The x-axis represents volume in units and the y-axis represents dollars. The variable cost line and the total revenue line intersect at the origin. The area between the total revenue line and the variable cost line represents contribution margin. Exhibit 3-8 illustrates this relationship. The total cost line intersects the y-axis at the amount corresponding to fixed costs. The area between total cost and variable cost represents fixed cost. The breakeven point is the point at which the total revenue line crosses the total cost line. Volume above that point results in a profit, and volume below that point results in a loss. Exhibit 3-9 illustrates a breakeven graph.

Another type of graph is a profit-volume graph. A profit-volume graph depicts the amount of profit or loss at each sales level. The vertical axis represents profit or loss in dollars and the horizontal axis reflects sales in units. Amounts above the horizontal axis reflect profits, and amounts below the horizontal axis represent losses. The total fixed costs are shown on the vertical axis as a negative amount. The breakeven point in units is shown on the horizontal axis. A line is drawn that passes between the plotted points and extends upward beyond the breakeven point. This line can be used to determine the amount of profit or loss for any sales volume. Exhibit 3-10 illustrates a profit-volume graph.

Although graphs provide a visual display of cost-volume-profit analysis, they do not give precise answers to questions for which managers need answers. The company must compute these answers by using algebraic formulas.

Although CVP analysis usually assumes that the company sells one product only, companies that sell multiple products can use CVP analysis also. Companies with multiple products must compute a weighted average contribution margin ratio assuming a constant sales mix. Then the company can compute the total revenue that it must realize to break even or earn a desired profit. The total sales times the sales mix percentage equals the sales of a particular product. Exhibit 3-11 illustrates CVP analysis with multiple products.

Nine underlying assumptions limit CVP analysis: (1) all variable cost and revenue behaviour patterns are constant per unit and linear within the relevant range; (2) total contribution margin is linear within the relevant range and increases proportionally with volume; (3) total fixed costs are constant within the relevant range; (4) managers can separate mixed costs accurately into their fixed and variable elements; (5) sales and production are equal; (6) no capacity is added during the period under analysis; (7) the sales mix remains constant for a multiproduct company; (8) either no inflation exists or it affects all cost factors equally; and (9) labour productivity, production technology, and market conditions do not change during the period.

Thus, CVP analysis is only as good as the validity of the underlying assumptions. In today's business world, many companies are discovering that many costs they previously classified as fixed actually vary with activities other than volume. The company may not incur certain variable costs after the first year of providing a product or service. Also, CVP analysis is primarily a tool for making short-term decisions.

The margin of safety is the excess of a company's estimated or actual sales over its breakeven point. It is the amount by which sales can drop before losses begin to be incurred. The margin of safety can be expressed as units, dollars, or a percentage. Exhibit 3-12 illustrates the calculation of the margin of safety.

The relationship of a company's variable and fixed costs is reflected in its operating leverage. Companies that have high variable costs and low fixed costs have a low operating leverage and a relatively low breakeven point. Companies with a low operating leverage can show a profit even when they experience wide swings in volume levels. Conversely, companies that have a cost structure that includes high fixed costs and lower variable costs have a high operating leverage and a relatively high breakeven point. Companies with a high operating leverage must establish higher sales volumes initially in order to cover fixed costs. However, each unit sold after breakeven produces large profits. The degree of operating leverage indicates how sensitive a company is to sales increases and decreases by measuring how a percentage change in sales affects company profits. Exhibit 3 –13 illustrates the calculation of the degree of operating leverage. The degree of operating leverage is highest at the breakeven point. As the company moves away from breakeven sales, margin of safety increases, but the degree of operating leverage declines.

## APPENDIX 3A--ABSORPTION AND VARIABLE COSTING

The most common product costing approach is absorption costing. Absorption costing treats direct materials, direct labour, variable manufacturing overhead, and fixed manufacturing overhead as product or inventoriable costs. Thus, absorption costing treats all manufacturing costs as product costs. Exhibit 3-14 illustrates the absorption costing model.

An absorption costing income statement presents costs according to their functional classifications. A functional classification is a group of costs that a company incurs for the same basic purpose. Examples include cost of goods sold, selling expenses, and administrative expenses. An absorption costing income statement shows the difference between sales and adjusted cost of goods sold as gross margin. Gross margin less the operating expenses is income before income taxes.

Variable costing treats only direct materials, direct labour, and variable overhead as product costs. Variable costing considers only the variable manufacturing costs as product costs and treats fixed overhead as a period cost. Another name for variable costing is direct costing. Exhibit 3-15 illustrates the variable costing model.

A variable costing income statement presents cost according to their behaviour as variable or fixed and then perhaps according to functions within the behavioural classifications. A variable costing income statement shows the variable cost of goods sold. Product contribution margin is the difference between sales and variable cost of goods sold. Product contribution margin less variable selling and administrative expenses equals total contribution margin. Total contribution margin less the sum of fixed overhead and fixed selling and administrative expenses is income before income taxes. A variable costing income statement is also known as a contribution income statement.

Companies must use absorption costing for external financial reporting. Managers, however, may prefer variable costing to help them fulfill their managerial duties. Variable costing allows managers to see more easily the effect on costs of a change in the activity level. Some companies may keep their accounting records on a variable costing basis and make worksheet adjustments to convert them to an absorption costing basis.

Two basic differences exist between absorption and variable costing: (1) under absorption costing, fixed manufacturing overhead is considered a product cost; under variable costing, it is considered a period cost; and (2) absorption costing classifies expenses by function, whereas variable costing categorizes expenses by behaviour.

Although different in some aspects, absorption costing and variable costing have four underlying similarities:  (1) both methods use the same basic cost information; (2) both methods treat direct materials, direct labour, and variable manufacturing overhead as product costs; (3) both methods treat selling and administrative expenses as period costs; and (4) both methods use similar accounts.

Exhibits 3-16, 3-17, and 3-18 are presented to compare absorption and variable costing procedures and presentations.

Absorption and variable costing provide different income figures when sales are not equal to production. The differences are caused by including fixed manufacturing overhead as a product cost under absorption costing but considering it a period cost under variable costing.  When production is greater than sales, net income under absorption costing will be higher than net income under variable costing.  When sales exceed production, net income under variable costing will be higher than net income under absorption costing.  When sales equal production, no difference will occur in net income under each of the two methods.

Exhibit 3-19 summarizes the differences between absorption and variable costing.

## FORMULAS:

CM = Sales - Variable costs
CM Ratio = CM ÷ Sales
Change in CM = Change in sales x CM ratio
BEP (units) = FC ÷ CM per unit
BEP (revenue) = FC ÷ CM ratio
Units for PBT = (FC + PBT) ÷ CM per unit
Revenue for PBT = (FC + PBT) ÷ CM ratio
Units for PAT = {FC + [PAT ÷ (1 - TR)]} ÷ CM per unit
Revenue for PAT = {FC + [PAT ÷ (1 - TR)]} ÷ CM Ratio
Units for $P_uBT$ = FC ÷ (CM per unit - $P_uBT$)
Revenue for $P_uBT$ = FC ÷ (CM ratio - Desired PBT as a percentage of sales)
Units for $P_uAT$ = FC ÷ {CM per unit - [$P_uAT$/(1 - TR)]}
Revenue for $P_uAT$ = FC ÷ {CM ratio - [Desired PAT as a percentage of sales ÷ (1 - TR)]}
$P_uBT$ = $P_uAT$ ÷ (1 - TR)
Margin of Safety (units) = Estimated units – Breakeven units
Margin of Safety (dollars) = Estimated (actual) sales dollars – Breakeven sales dollars
Margin of Safety (percentage) = Margin of safety (units or dollars) ÷ Estimated (actual) sales (units or dollars)
DOL = CM ÷ PBT

**SELF TEST**

TRUE/FALSE

1.  T  F  At the breakeven point, contribution margin equals fixed costs.

2.  T  F  Within the relevant range, per-unit variable costs are fixed.

3.  T  F  Contribution margin is equal to selling price minus variable production costs.

4.  T  F  The contribution margin ratio is equal to contribution margin divided by fixed costs.

5.  T  F  Profit before taxes plus fixed costs equals the contribution margin.

6.  T  F  Incremental analysis is a process focusing only on factors that change from one course of action or decision to another.

7.  T  F  On a breakeven graph, the breakeven point is the point at which the total cost line intersects the total revenue line.

8.  T  F  On a profit-volume graph, amounts shown above the horizontal axis represent losses.

9.  T  F  A company refers to the relative combination of the quantities sold of its products as its contribution mix.

10.  T  F  The margin of safety helps management to determine how close to breakeven the company is operating and provides an indication of risk.

11.  T  F  A cost structure that includes very high fixed costs reflects low operating leverage.

12.  T  F  The degree of operating leverage is equal to contribution margin divided by profit before tax.

## APPENDIX 3A-- ABSORPTION AND VARIABLE COSTING

13.  T  F  Variable costing treats fixed manufacturing overhead as a product cost.

14.  T  F  Companies must use absorption costing for external financial reporting purposes.

15.  T  F  Variable costing income statements are more useful internally for planning, controlling, and decision making than absorption costing statements are.

## MULTIPLE CHOICE

1. Variable costs:

   A. are fixed per unit.
   B. vary per unit.
   C. decrease per unit as the activity level increases.
   D. remain constant in total as the activity level increases.

2. Fixed costs:

   A. remain constant in total as the activity level changes.
   B. are fixed per unit as the activity level changes.
   C. increase per unit as the activity level increases.
   D. are always a product cost.

3. Mixed costs:

   A. decrease per unit as the activity level decreases.
   B. are fixed per unit as the activity level changes.
   C. remain constant in total as the activity level changes.
   D. must be separated into their variable and fixed elements before they can be used in CVP analysis.

4. Contribution margin is equal to:

   A. revenue less variable costs.
   B. fixed costs plus profit before tax.
   C. contribution margin per unit times number of units sold.
   D. all of the above.

5. The contribution margin ratio:

   A. indicates what proportion of revenue remains after fixed costs have been covered.
   B. can only be calculated on a per-unit basis.
   C. is equal to 100 percent minus the variable cost ratio.
   D. none of the above.

6. In which of the following economic sectors is CVP analysis applicable?

   A. manufacturing
   B. retailing
   C. service industries
   D. all of the above

7. On a profit-volume graph, the horizontal axis represents:

   A. fixed costs.
   B. sales in units.
   C. sales in dollars.
   D. total costs.

8. Which of the following statements about a breakeven graph is false?

    A. The x-axis represents volume and the y-axis represents dollars.
    B. The slope of the variable cost line is equal to total variable cost per unit.
    C. The area between the total cost and revenue lines represents total contribution margin at each level of volume.
    D. The breakeven point is located where the revenue and total cost lines intersect.

9. The margin of safety is expressed as:

    A. units.
    B. dollars.
    C. a percentage.
    D. all of the above.

10. The margin of safety in units is equal to:

    A. revenue less variable costs.
    B. estimated units less breakeven units.
    C. fixed costs divided by contribution margin per unit.
    D. contribution margin divided by profit before tax.

11. Companies with high operating leverage:

    A. have a cost structure which includes high variable costs and low fixed costs.
    B. have a relatively low breakeven point.
    C. are highly capital-intensive.
    D. can show a profit even when they experience wide swings in volume levels.

12. Other things being equal, replacement of hourly paid assembly line workers with an automated assembly line will result in:

    A. an increase in the breakeven point.
    B. a decrease in the margin of safety.
    C. an increase in the degree of operating leverage.
    D. all of the above.

13. Luther Company sells one product for $200. Variable costs are $130 per unit. Fixed costs are $63,000. How many units will Luther Company have to sell for profit before taxes to equal 10 percent of sales revenue?

    A.   90
    B.  700
    C.  900
    D. 1,260

14.  Rey Company has a contribution margin ratio of 32 percent. Fixed costs are $90,000.  What will the sales revenue be if profit before taxes equals 12 percent of sales?

    A.  $ 54,000
    B.  $144,000
    C.  $200,000
    D.  $450,000

15.  Hall Company sells one product for $8 per unit.  Variable costs are $3 per unit.  Fixed costs total $120,000. How many units must Hall Company sell to break even?

    A.  15,000
    B.  24,000
    C.  40,000
    D.  600,000

16.  Rogers Company sells one product for $24 per unit.  Variable costs are $16 per unit.  Fixed costs total $120,000.  What is the breakeven point in sales dollars?

    A.  $360,000
    B.  $240,000
    C.  $180,000
    D.  $120,000

17.  Jones Company sells one product for $12 per unit.  Variable costs are $4 per unit.  Fixed costs are $48,000. How many units must Jones sell to have a $64,000 profit before taxes?

    A.  6,000
    B.  7,000
    C.  8,000
    D.  14,000

18.  Ussery Company has a contribution margin ratio of 80 percent. Variable costs are $4 per unit.  At the breakeven point, sales are $500,000.  How many units would Ussery sell if the profit before taxes is $80,000?

    A.  11,250
    B.  24,000
    C.  30,000
    D.  36,250

19.  Boley Company sells one product for $90 per unit.  Variable costs are $30 per unit.  The marketing manager has proposed a new advertising campaign that would increase fixed costs by $360,000.  How many additional units must Boley sell to pay for the advertising campaign?

    A.  3,000
    B.  4,000
    C.  6,000
    D.  12,000

20. Wilson Company sells two products--widgets and gizmos. The sales mix (in dollar volume, not in units) is 70 percent widgets and 30 percent gizmos. Widgets sell for $50 and have variable costs of $30. Gizmos sell for $40 and have variable costs of $20. Fixed costs total $860,000. What is the total sales revenue at the breakeven point?

    A. $ 860,000
    B. $1,010,500
    C. $2,000,000
    D. $2,021,000

21. Gibson Company sells one product for $50 per unit. Variable costs are $20 per unit. Fixed costs total $839,000. The tax rate is 40 percent. How many units must Gibson sell to have a $780,000 profit after tax?

    A. 26,000
    B. 53,967
    C. 65,000
    D. 71,300

22. Alpha Company has a contribution margin ratio of 36 percent. Fixed costs are $220,000. The tax rate is 40 percent. What will the sales revenue be if profit after taxes equals 15 percent of sales?

    A. $2,000,000
    B. $1,047,619
    C. $ 628,571
    D. $ 419,048

23. The following is a contribution format income statement for the month of March:

| | |
|---|---|
| Sales (12,000 units) | $1,200,000 |
| Less: variable expenses | 800,000 |
| Contribution margin | $ 400,000 |
| Less: fixed expenses | 300,000 |
| Net income | $ 100,000 |

    What is the company's margin of safety in dollars?

    A. $100,000
    B. $300,000
    C. $400,000
    D. $900,000

24. Last month, West Company reported sales of 12,000 units. Unit contribution margin is $40. Fixed expenses are $250,000. What is the company's margin of safety percentage to the nearest whole percent?

    A. 48%
    B. 52%
    C. 92%
    D. 109%

25. Grantham Company has sales of 2,500 units at $80 per unit. Variable costs are 25% of the sales price. If total fixed costs are $75,000, the degree of operating leverage is:

    A. 0.375
    B. 0.5
    C. 2
    D. 2.67

## APPENDIX 3A--ABSORPTION AND VARIABLE COSTING

26. Under variable costing, product costs include:

    A. direct materials, direct labour, and variable manufacturing overhead only.
    B. direct materials, direct labour, variable manufacturing overhead, and fixed manufacturing overhead only.
    C. direct materials, direct labour, and fixed manufacturing overhead only.
    D. direct materials, direct labour, variable manufacturing overhead, fixed manufacturing overhead, and selling, general, and administrative costs.

27. Which costing method(s) treat(s) variable selling expenses as a product cost?

    A. absorption costing only
    B. variable costing only
    C. variable costing and absorption costing
    D. neither variable costing nor absorption costing

USE THE FOLLOWING INFORMATION TO ANSWER QUESTIONS 28 AND 29

Bradshaw Company's costs incurred in making and selling its one product are as follows:

Manufacturing costs:
    Variable cost per unit:
        Direct materials                              $    14
        Direct labour                                      13
        Variable manufacturing overhead                     8
    Fixed manufacturing overhead costs (total)        360,000

Selling and administrative costs:
        Variable cost per unit                        $     6
        Fixed (total)                                 100,000

During the year, the company produced 40,000 units and sold 38,000 units. There was no beginning inventory.

28. What is the cost of a single unit under absorption costing?

    A. $35
    B. $41
    C. $44
    D. $50

29. What is the cost of a single unit under variable costing?

    A. $35
    B. $41
    C. $44
    D. $50

30. In the current year, Raleigh Corporation produced 100,000 widgets. Unfortunately, demand for widgets was lower than expected, and the company sold only 60,000 units. What will be the difference in net income between variable costing and absorption costing?

    A. There will be no difference in net income.
    B. Net income computed using variable costing will be higher.
    C. The difference in net income cannot be determined from the information given.
    D. Net income computed using variable costing will be lower.


ESSAY QUESTIONS AND PROBLEMS

1. What does the breakeven point represent? How is it computed?

2. What are mixed costs? What must managers do to mixed costs before using them in CVP analysis?

3. What are the steps that a manager must take to prepare a breakeven graph?

4.  What are the steps that a manager must take to prepare a profit-volume graph?

5.  What are the underlying assumptions of cost-volume-profit analysis?

6.  Explain why on a per-unit basis fixed costs are variable and variable costs are fixed.

7.  What does the margin of safety represent?  Why would a manager of a company with a low margin of safety be more risk averse?

8.  The management team of Brady Company decides to outsource their accounting department in order to reduce fixed costs.  Other things being equal, how would this decision impact Brady's degree of operating leverage?

9.  Jones Company produces one product that sells for $1,200.  Variable costs are $840 per unit.  Fixed costs are $720,000.  The tax rate is 40 percent.

(A)  Compute the breakeven point in units and in sales revenue.

(B)  How many units would Jones have to sell to earn a profit before taxes of $900,000?

(C)  How much would the sales revenue have to be for Jones to have a profit after taxes of $1,080,000?

(D)  How many units would Jones have to sell to have a profit before taxes equal to 10 percent of sales revenue?

10.  Rasputin Company produces one product that presently sells for $1,800.  Current annual sales volume is 1,000 units.  Variable costs are $1,200 per unit.  Fixed costs are $640,000.

(A)  The company is considering upgrading some of its production equipment.  The upgrade would result in an increase in fixed costs of $200,000.  If the new equipment is purchased, the variable cost of the product would decrease by $80 per unit because of production efficiencies.  Should the company upgrade the production equipment?

(B)  Assume that the company decides not to proceed with the equipment upgrade.  An alternative strategy that Rasputin is considering is improving the product packaging and marketing their product as a "prestige" item.  No changes would be made to the product itself.  Improvements to the packaging would cost $15 per unit.  The marketing department has advised management that the market for a "prestige" product is smaller; however, consumers are willing to pay a considerably higher price.  Current estimates are for annual sales of 600 units at a sales price of $2,400.  Should Rasputin pursue this alternative strategy?

11.  Vethan Company sells two products.  The regular model sells for $100 per unit.  The deluxe model sells for $200 per unit. Other information is as follows:

|  | Regular | Deluxe | Total |
|---|---|---|---|
| Sales | $900,000 | $100,000 | $1,000,000 |
| Variable costs | 600,000 | 50,000 | 650,000 |
| Contribution margin | $300,000 | $ 50,000 | $ 350,000 |
| Fixed costs |  |  | 204,000 |
| Profit before taxes |  |  | $ 146,000 |

Calculate the total sales revenue, the sales revenue from the regular model, and the sales revenue from the deluxe model if profit before taxes is $510,000.  Assume a constant sales mix in terms of sales revenue.

12.  The following is a contribution format income statement for Alexander Company:

| Sales (150,000 units) | $412,500 |
|---|---|
| Less:  variable expenses | 195,000 |
| Contribution margin | $217,500 |
| Less:  fixed expenses | 145,000 |
| Net income | $ 72,500 |

(A)  Compute the margin of safety in units and in dollars.

(B)  Compute the margin of safety percentage.

13. Gibson Industries has prepared the following income statement using a contribution margin approach:

Gibson Industries
Projected Income Statement
For the Year Ending December 31, 20XX

| | |
|---|---:|
| Sales (100,000 units) | $750,000 |
| Variable expenses | 400,000 |
| Contribution margin | $350,000 |
| Fixed expenses | 210,000 |
| Net income | $140,000 |

(A) Compute the degree of operating leverage at a sales level of $750,000.

(B) What would be the change in net income if sales decrease by 9%?

## APPENDIX 3A--ABSORPTION AND VARIABLE COSTING

USE THE FOLLOWING INFORMATION TO ANSWER QUESTIONS 14 AND 15

Baker Company produced 60,000 units and sold 50,000 units during the calendar year. There was no beginning or ending work in process inventory. There was no volume variance. Other information is as follows:

| | |
|---|---:|
| Sales | $2,500,000 |
| Beginning finished goods inventory | 0 |
| Variable manufacturing costs | 1,200,000 |
| Fixed manufacturing overhead | 180,000 |
| Ending finished goods inventory | ??? |
| Variable selling expenses | 200,000 |
| Fixed selling expenses | 50,000 |
| Fixed administrative expenses | 80,000 |

14. Prepare an income statement using variable costing.

15. Prepare an income statement using absorption costing.

## SELF TEST ANSWERS

### TRUE/FALSE

| | | | | | | | | | |
|---|---|---|---|---|---|---|---|---|---|
| 1. | T | 4. | F | 7. | T | 10. | T | 13. | F |
| 2. | T | 5. | T | 8. | F | 11. | F | 14. | T |
| 3. | F | 6. | T | 9. | F | 12. | T | 15. | T |

### MULTIPLE CHOICE

| | | | | | | | | | | | |
|---|---|---|---|---|---|---|---|---|---|---|---|
| 1. | A | 7. | B | 13. | D | 19. | C | 25. | C |
| 2. | A | 8. | C | 14. | D | 20. | C | 26. | A |
| 3. | D | 9. | D | 15. | B | 21. | D | 27. | D |
| 4. | D | 10. | B | 16. | A | 22. | A | 28. | C |
| 5. | C | 11. | C | 17. | D | 23. | B | 29. | A |
| 6. | D | 12. | D | 18. | C | 24. | A | 30. | D |

### ESSAY QUESTIONS AND PROBLEMS

1.      The breakeven point is the level of activity, in units or dollars, at which total revenues equal total costs. The breakeven point in units is equal to total fixed cost divided by contribution margin per unit.  The breakeven point in sales dollars is equal to total fixed cost divided by the contribution margin ratio.

2.      Mixed costs are costs that have a fixed cost element and a variable cost element. They increase in total when volume increases because of their variable cost element.  Mixed costs per unit decrease when volume increases because of their fixed cost element.  Managers must separate mixed costs into their fixed and variable elements before using CVP analysis.   Managers can use techniques such as the high–low method or regression analysis to separate mixed costs.

3.      The first step is to draw the axes and label the x-axis as volume and the y-axis as dollars. Second, plot the variable cost line as a linear function with the slope equal to the variable cost per unit. Third, plot the revenue line with a slope equal to the sales price. The area between the variable cost line and the revenue line represents total contribution margin. Fourth, graph total cost with a line running parallel to the variable cost line. The distance between the total cost line and the variable cost line represents fixed cost. The breakeven point is where the total revenue line intersects the total cost line.

4.      The first step is to draw the axes and label the horizontal axis as unit sales volume and the vertical axis as dollars. Second, plot total fixed costs on the vertical axis (shown as a negative amount). Third, calculate the breakeven point in units and plot it on the horizontal axis. Fourth, draw a line that passes between the two plotted points and extends through the breakeven point. This line can be used to read, from the vertical axis, the amount of profit or loss for any sales volume.

5.      Nine underlying assumptions of CVP analysis are as follows: (1) all variable cost and revenue behaviour patterns are constant per unit and linear within the relevant range; (2) total contribution margin is linear within the relevant range and increases proportionally with volume; (3) total fixed costs are constant within the relevant range; (4) managers can separate mixed costs accurately into their fixed and variable elements; (5) sales and production are equal; (6) no capacity is added during the period under analysis; (7) the sales mix remains constant for a multiproduct company; (8) either no inflation exists or it affects all cost factors equally; and (9) labour productivity, production technology, and market conditions do not change during the period.

6.      Fixed costs remain constant in total as the level of activity changes. The fixed cost per unit is equal to the fixed costs divided by the number of units. Because the numerator remains constant, a change in the denominator will cause the fixed cost per unit to change or vary. Variable costs change in total in proportion to the change in the activity level. Because the numerator (variable costs) changes in proportion to the denominator (the activity level), variable costs per unit remain fixed.

7.      The margin of safety is the excess of a company's estimated or actual sales over its breakeven point. It represents the amount by which sales can drop before losses begin to be incurred. The lower the margin of safety, the more carefully management must watch sales figures and control costs in order that a net loss will not be incurred. At low margins of safety, the risk of suffering a loss is higher. As a result, managers will be more conservative in their actions and will be less likely to take advantage of opportunities that have the potential to send the company into a loss position.

8.      The degree of operating leverage is equal to contribution margin divided by profit before tax. A reduction in fixed costs will cause profit before tax to increase. Other things being equal, contribution margin will remain the same. Because the numerator remains constant, an increase in the denominator (profit before tax) will result in a lower degree of operating leverage. A given percentage change in sales will have a smaller effect on company profits after the outsourcing. If sales decrease, profits will decrease at a slower rate. However, if sales increase, the increase in profits will also be at a slower rate.

9.     (A)     

| | | |
|---|---|---|
| Sales price | $1,200 | 100% |
| Less: Variable costs | 840 | 70 |
| Contribution margin | $ 360 | 30% |

Fixed costs  $720,000 ÷ $360 per unit = 2,000 units

2,000 units x $1,200 per unit = $2,400,000 in sales revenue

Alternatively, the breakeven point in sales revenue could be determined by dividing the fixed costs by the contribution margin ratio:

$720,000 ÷ 0.3 = $2,400,000

The breakeven point in units can be determined by dividing the breakeven point in sales revenue by the sales price per unit:

$2,400,000 ÷ $1,200 per unit = 2,000 units

The tax rate is not relevant for determining the breakeven point.  If the company breaks even, there is no income tax.

(B)     Add the profit before tax to the fixed costs and divide by the unit contribution margin.

($720,000 + $900,000) ÷ $360 per unit =

$1,620,000 ÷ $360 per unit = 4,500 units

(C)     Convert the profit after tax to the profit before tax by dividing the profit after tax by 1 minus the tax rate.

Profit before tax = $1,080,000 ÷ (1 - 0.4)

= $1,080,000 ÷ 0.6 = $1,800,000

Add the profit before tax to the fixed costs and divide by the contribution margin ratio:

($720,000 + $1,800,000) ÷ 0.3

= $2,520,000 ÷ 0.3 = $8,400,000

(D)     If profit before taxes equals 10 percent of sales, the profit before taxes equals $120 ($1,200 x 10%) times the number of units sold.  One can view this $120 as an additional variable cost, then use the breakeven formula to solve for the number of units that Jones must sell.

Units = FC ÷ (CM - $P_uBT$)

= $720,000 ÷ [($1,200 - $840) - $120]
= $720,000 ÷ ($360 - $120)
= $720,000 ÷ $240
= 3,000

10.    (A)    The decrease in variable costs due to production efficiencies will result in an increase of $80 in the unit contribution margin.  The total contribution margin gained from the production efficiencies must at least cover the increased fixed costs of the equipment upgrade.

Increase in CM [1,000 units x $80 per unit]    $  80,000
Less:  Increase in fixed cost                             (200,000)
Equals:  Reduction in profit before taxes        $(120,000)

Based on the above computation, the company will have less profit before taxes than is currently being generated; therefore, the company should not upgrade the production equipment.

(B)    The alternative strategy results in a net increase in the contribution margin of $111,000 and should be pursued.

| | Current Operations | Alternative Strategy | Difference |
|---|---|---|---|
| Revenue: | | | |
| [1,000 units x $1,800 per unit] | $1,800,000 | | |
| [600 units x $2,400 per unit] | | $1,440,000 | $(360,000) |
| Variable costs: | | | |
| [1,000 units x $1,200 per unit] | (1,200,000) | | |
| [600 units x ($1,200 + $15) per unit] | | (729,000) | 471,000 |
| Contribution Margin | $  600,000 | $  711,000 | $ 111,000 |

11.    Calculate the weighted average contribution margin ratio by dividing the total contribution margin by the total sales revenue.

$350,000 ÷ $1,000,000 = 0.35

To calculate the total sales revenue to achieve the target profit before tax, add the target profit to the fixed costs and then divide by the weighted average contribution margin ratio.

($204,000 + $510,000) ÷ 0.35
= $714,000 ÷ 0.35
= $2,040,000 total sales revenue

To calculate the sale revenue of each product, multiply the total sales revenue of $2,040,000 by the sales mix percentage of each product.

$2,040,000 x 90% = $1,836,000 sales of the regular model

$2,040,000 x 10% = $  204,000 sales of the deluxe model

12.      (A)  The first step is to calculate the breakeven point in units and in sales dollars.

Fixed costs $145,000 ÷ ($217,500 ÷ 150,000 units) = 100,000 units

100,000 units x ($412,500 ÷ 150,000) = $275,000

The margin of safety in units is equal to actual units minus breakeven units:

     150,000 – 100,000 = 50,000 units

The margin of safety in dollars is equal to actual sales dollars minus breakeven sales dollars:

     $412,500 - $275,000 = $137,500

      (B)      The margin of safety percentage can be determined by dividing the margin of safety in units by the actual sales in units:

     50,000 ÷ 150,000 = 33.3%

Alternatively, the margin of safety percentage can be determined by dividing the margin of safety in dollars by the actual sales in dollars:

     $137,500 ÷ $412,500 = 33.3%

13.      (A) The degree of operating leverage is equal to contribution margin divided by profit before tax:

     $350,000 ÷ $140,000 = 2.5

      (B) The degree of operating leverage measures how a percentage change in sales affects company profits.  If sales decrease by 9%, the change in net income is calculated as follows:

     9% x 2.5 x $140,000 = $31,500 decrease in net income

14.     Baker Company

Variable Costing Income Statement
For the Year Ended December 31, 20xx

Sales                                                                                    $2,500,000

Cost of goods sold:
    Beginning finished goods inventory          $          0
    Cost of goods manufactured                        1,200,000
    Cost of goods available for sale               $1,200,000
    Ending finished goods inventory                    200,000
    Cost of goods sold                                                            $1,000,000
Product contribution margin                                                        $1,500,000
Variable selling expenses                                                              200,000
Total contribution margin                                                          $1,300,000
Fixed expenses:
    Manufacturing overhead                            $180,000
    Selling                                                         50,000
    Administrative                                                80,000
    Total fixed expenses                                                            310,000
Net income before taxes                                                            $ 990,000

*$1,200,000 ÷ 60,000 units = $20.00 per unit; $20.00 per unit x 10,000 units = $200,000

15.     Baker Company

Absorption Costing Income Statement
For the Year Ended December 31, 20xx

Sales                                                                                    $2,500,000

Cost of goods sold:
    Beginning finished goods inventory          $          0
    Cost of goods manufactured                        1,380,000
    Cost of goods available for sale               $1,380,000
    Ending finished goods inventory*                  230,000
    Cost of goods sold                                                            $1,150,000
Gross margin                                                                           $1,350,000
Operating expenses:
Selling and administrative expenses                                             330,000
Net income before taxes                                                            $1,020,000

*$1,380,000 ÷ 60,000 units = $23.00 per unit; $23.00 per unit x 10,000 units = $230,000

# CHAPTER 4
# COSTING SYSTEMS

## CHAPTER OVERVIEW

Job order costing is used in companies that make a limited quantity of products or provide a limited number of services uniquely tailored to customer specifications.  In a job order costing system, the job is the cost object for which costs are accumulated.  Job costs are accumulated on a job order cost sheet.

Companies that make large quantities of homogeneous products use process costing to assign costs to products.  Many types of manufacturers—including manufacturers of automobiles, steel, food products, appliances, bricks, and paper—use process costing.  Process costing differs in several ways from job order costing.

The two alternative methods of computing unit costs in a process cost system are the weighted average method and the first-in, first-out (FIFO) method.  The weighted average method is discussed in the main part of the chapter and the FIFO method is illustrated in Appendix 4A.  To compute the cost per unit under either method, the company must calculate the equivalent units of production.  Companies use equivalent units of production because using only completed units would not clearly reflect the production achieved during the period.

The basic document in a process cost system is the production and cost report.  This document shows the accounting for whole units in production, the computation of equivalent units of production, the cost per equivalent unit, and the assignment of the production costs.

Appendix 4B discusses spoiled and lost units.  Reducing spoilage and improving quality are becoming more important in the global economy.  Many companies are not aware of the actual cost of spoilage because they use the method of neglect.  Companies are now turning to methods such as statistical process control (SPC) to discover when quality problems are likely to occur.

## CHAPTER STUDY GUIDE

In order to compute the cost of products, a company must decide on (1) the product costing system, and (2) the valuation method to be used.  The two primary costing systems are job order and process.  The three valuation methods that can be used are actual, normal, and standard.

A job order costing system is appropriate when a company is producing a specialized product to order.  Since each order is substantially different from any other order, a method of cost accounting must be used to track the production costs incurred by a particular order.  In a job order cost system, the company accumulates product costs by job.  A job is a unit or group of similar units that the company makes to meet a customer's specifications.  Service firms can also use job order cost systems.

Each job is a cost object.  Costs of different jobs are maintained in separate subsidiary ledger accounts.  Exhibit 4-1 provides an example of the work in process control and subsidiary ledger accounts for a job order product costing system.  The usual production costs of direct materials, direct labour, and manufacturing overhead are accumulated by job.  While actual direct material and actual direct labour costs can be traced to specific jobs in production, manufacturing overhead costs are not usually traceable to specific jobs.  A typical job order costing system uses normal costing as a valuation method.  Under normal costing, the costs assigned to a particular job consist of actual direct materials, actual direct labour, and applied manufacturing overhead (predetermined overhead rates multiplied by some actual cost driver).

Each job can consist of a single unit or multiple similar or dissimilar units. When multiple similar outputs result from a job, the total accumulated job cost is averaged over the number of units produced to determine a cost per unit. If the output consisted of dissimilar units, no cost per unit could be determined.

A job can fall into one of three basic stages of production: (1) agreed-upon but not yet started, (2) in process, and (3) completed. The materials acquired for all jobs, although often separately distinguishable and related to specific jobs, are accounted for in the raw materials inventory control and subsidiary ledger accounts.

A materials requisition form is the source document used to issue raw materials to a job. This form shows the types, quantities, and costs of materials issued to a job. Also, these materials requisition forms transfer responsibility for the materials from the warehouse to the department that issued the requisition. The management accountant transfers the cost of direct materials issued from the raw materials inventory account to work in process. The management accountant would transfer the cost of any indirect materials issued from the raw materials inventory account to manufacturing overhead. Exhibit 4-2 provides an example of a materials requisition form.

The company records costs for each job on a job order cost sheet. It is the primary document in a job order cost system. A job order cost sheet contains information on actual direct materials cost, actual direct labour cost, and applied manufacturing overhead cost. It also identifies the customer and the nature of the job. The job order cost sheets form a work in process subsidiary ledger. Exhibit 4-3 provides an example of a job order cost sheet.

The company uses employee time sheets or time tickets to trace direct labour cost to jobs. An employee time sheet shows what jobs were worked on during the day and the amount of time the employee worked on them. An example of an employee time sheet is provided in Exhibit 4-4. In a highly automated manufacturing plant, a company may wish to track how much time a job spends at each machine. A company can use machine clocks, machine counters, or bar coding to track the time each machine works on each job. Machine times can then be equated to employee-operator time. This tracking also allows the company to charge machine depreciation to specific jobs using a time-based depreciation method.

The time worked on a job multiplied by the employee's wage rate equals the direct labour cost charged to the job for that employee. The sum of all individual employee direct labour costs equals the total direct labour cost charged to the job as shown on the job order cost sheet.

In an actual cost system all costs are actual costs. A company must wait until the end of the period when total actual overhead cost is known before the actual overhead can be applied to jobs. Managers need timely cost information to make good operating decisions. Therefore, many companies use a normal cost system and apply manufacturing overhead to jobs using a predetermined overhead application rate. If predetermined rates are used, overhead is applied at the end of the period or at completion of production, whichever is earlier.

When a job is completed, the total cost of the job is transferred from work in process to the finished goods inventory account. When a job is sold, the total cost of the job is transferred to cost of goods sold.

Managers use job order costing in planning, controlling, decision making and evaluating performance. Knowing the costs of individual jobs allows managers to better estimate future job costs and establish realistic selling prices.

Job order costing is appropriate for companies making products or providing services in limited quantities that conform to customer specifications. Process costing is used by manufacturers that make large quantities of homogeneous products in a continuous mass production environment to accumulate and assign costs to units of production.

In a process costing system, companies accumulate costs by each cost element (direct materials, direct labour, and manufacturing overhead) in each production department. As a company transfers units from one department to another, it also transfers the related unit costs. At the end of production, the company has accumulated and assigned total production cost to all the units that flowed through that department during the period. Exhibit 4-5 shows how costs are accumulated in the accounts during the production process.

A job order cost system and a process cost system differ in two main ways. The first difference is the quantity of production. A process cost system is appropriate for companies that produce large quantities of products. A job order cost system is appropriate for companies that make small quantities of products. The second difference is the cost object. In a process cost system, the company assigns costs to departments and then to products. In a job order cost system, the company assigns costs to specific jobs and then to products.

Process costing accumulates actual direct materials costs and actual direct labour costs. Manufacturing overhead may consist of actual costs or a company may use a predetermined rate to apply manufacturing overhead to production. Exhibit 4-6 illustrates the cost flows and cost assignments using process costing.

A company must introduce some direct material for a production operation to begin. The material added at the beginning of production is 100 percent complete as to materials throughout the production process. A company can add materials at any point during the production process. Exhibit 4-7 illustrates the production flow for a manufacturing process and shows the need for separate cost accumulations for each cost element.

After a company has accumulated production costs by department and by cost element, the company must assign the costs to the units produced during the period of cost accumulation. Process costing uses an averaging process to assign costs to products using equivalent units of production. Equivalent units of production approximate the number of whole units that the company could have made during a period based on actual effort expended during that period. Using only completed units would not fairly reflect the production for the period. The company started some units last period that it will complete in the current period. The company will complete some units next period that it started in the current period. Dividing production costs by the equivalent units of production gives the cost per equivalent unit.

Weighted average and FIFO are the two alternative methods used to compute production costs in the numerator and equivalent units of production in the denominator to compute the cost per equivalent unit. Both methods usually result in approximately the same unit costs. The key difference in the two methods lies in how they treat beginning work in process inventory. Exhibit 4-8 is an important exhibit that illustrates the six steps involved in process costing. These six steps are as follows: (1) calculate the physical units to account for, (2) calculate the physical units accounted for, (3) calculate the equivalent units of production, (4) calculate the total cost to account for, (5) calculate the cost per equivalent unit, and (6) assign the costs to inventories.

The physical units to account for are the sum of the units in the beginning work in process inventory plus units started into production. The department accounts for these units by showing them transferred to another department or to finished goods or as partially completed units in the ending work in process inventory. A company may use either the weighted average method or the FIFO method to compute the equivalent units of production. The total costs to account for include the costs in the beginning work in process inventory plus all current period costs for direct material, direct labour, and overhead. A company uses the same method (weighted average or FIFO) to compute the cost per equivalent unit as it did to compute the equivalent units of production. The department must assign the total costs to account for to another production department, to finished goods, or to the ending work in process inventory. Exhibit 4-9 provides production and cost information the textbook uses to illustrate the six steps in process costing.

If the materials are at the same degree of completion, a company can make one calculation for the equivalent units of production for materials.  If a company uses multiple materials and places them into production at different stages, then it must make multiple equivalent units of production calculations for materials.  If a company applies overhead using direct labour or if these two elements are always at the same stage of completion, then the company can make a single equivalent units of production calculation for conversion cost.  Otherwise, the company will make separate calculations for direct labour and overhead.

The weighted average method assumes that all the units a company completed during the period were also started during the period.  This assumption simplifies the calculations.  Thus, the weighted average method ignores the work done in the prior period on partially completed units.  The weighted average method computes equivalent units of production as follows:  completed units + (units in the ending work in process inventory x percentage of completion).  The production costs in the weighted average method include the beginning inventory cost and the current period cost.  The cost per equivalent unit is the result of the following calculation: production costs divided by the equivalent units of production for each cost element.

Under the weighted average method, the cost per equivalent unit times the units completed gives the cost transferred to another department or charged to finished goods.  The cost per equivalent unit times the equivalent units in the ending work in process inventory gives the cost of the ending work in process inventory.  The total costs assigned must equal the total costs to account for.  Exhibit 4-11 illustrates a cost of production report using the weighted average method.

Most companies have more than one processing department.  When one department completes its work, it transfers the units to the next department.  The department must also transfer the costs incurred to the next department.  The successor department calls these costs transferred-in costs or prior department costs.  Transferred-in costs always have a completion factor of 100 percent.  After the last department finishes its work, the department transfers the cost of completed production to finished goods.  Exhibit 4-12 illustrates a cost of production report for a company with multiple departments.

Exhibit 4-13 presents summary journal entries and T-accounts for the Moulding and Packaging Departments of the Linda Geraldine Chocoholics Ltd. example.  These journal entries assume the use of a perpetual weighted average inventory system.

## APPENDIX 4A--PROCESS COSTING USING FIFO VALUATION

The FIFO method considers that the department did some work on the partially completed units in the beginning work in process inventory during the prior period.  The FIFO method calculates the equivalent units of production as follows:  units in the beginning work in process inventory x (100 percent - percentage of completion) + (units started and completed this period) + (units in the ending work in process inventory x percentage of completion).

The only production costs included in the numerator in computing the cost per equivalent unit under FIFO are the current period costs.  The cost per equivalent unit is the result of the following calculation:  current period production costs divided by the equivalent units of production for each cost element.

Under the FIFO method, the cost assigned to the next production department or charged to finished goods is equal to the sum of (1) the beginning work in process inventory cost, (2) the cost incurred to complete the units in the beginning inventory, and (3) the cost of units started and completed in the current period. The department calculates the cost incurred to complete the units in the beginning work in process inventory using the following formula: the number of whole units in the beginning work in process inventory x (100 percent - percentage of completion at the beginning of the period) x the cost per equivalent unit in the current period. The cost per equivalent unit times the units started and completed gives the cost of the units started and completed during the current period. The department calculates the ending balance in the work in process inventory in the same way as under the weighted average method. The cost per equivalent unit times the equivalent units in the ending work in process inventory gives the cost of the ending work in process inventory. Exhibit 4-14 illustrates a cost of production report using the FIFO method.

Cost assignment is easier under the weighted average method. The FIFO method, however, is more accurate and focuses on current period costs on which companies evaluate managerial performance. The FIFO method provides managers with better information with which to control costs.

## APPENDIX 4B--SPOILED AND LOST UNITS

Most companies produce some spoiled or defective units. Losses in the manufacturing process can be due to either normal spoilage or abnormal spoilage. Normal losses are those that are expected to occur during the production process, while abnormal losses generally arise because of human or machine error during the production process.

The costs of normal continuous losses are calculated using the method of neglect, whereby the spoiled units are excluded in the equivalent units schedule. As a result, a smaller number of equivalent units results and the cost per equivalent unit is higher. Exhibits 4-15 and 4-16 present cost of production reports for cases of normal and abnormal spoilage.

Managers must look for ways to reduce spoilage in the production process. The control aspect of quality implementation requires answers to three questions: (1) What does the spoilage actually cost? (2) Why does the spoilage occur? and (3) How can the company control spoilage?

Many companies are unaware of the actual costs of spoilage because they simply exclude spoiled units in computing the equivalent units of production. In service firms, spoilage is poor service from the customer's viewpoint. Lost revenue from dissatisfied customers is difficult to quantify, and a company does not record it in the accounting records.

Managers may be aware of the causes of spoilage, but they may consider the spoilage to be minimal. Such managers settle for an acceptable quality level. In other situations, managers may believe that the spoilage is not controllable. In most cases, however, the cause of the spoilage is controllable. Companies have often controlled for spoilage by inspecting products. Now, companies are realizing that they should build quality into a process and control it through process control rather than product control.

Companies often use statistical process control (SPC) to analyze their processes for situations that result in defective products. The normal distribution forms the basis for SPC. Some variations from normal occur by chance. When a variation is significantly different from expected, the result can be a defective product. Some companies are eliminating their quality problems with computer-integrated manufacturing systems.

## SELF TEST

### TRUE/FALSE

1.  T  F  A materials requisition form is a source document that indicates the types and quantities of materials to be placed into production or used in performing a service.

2.  T  F  An actual cost system provides overhead cost information during the accounting period.

3.  T  F  Companies that make large quantities of homogeneous products usually assign costs to products using process costing.

4.  T  F  The two alternative methods that companies usually use to calculate unit costs in a process cost system are weighted average and LIFO.

5.  T  F  The basic document in a process cost system is a cost of production report.

6.  T  F  In process costing, a company must convert partially completed units to equivalent whole units through the use of equivalent units of production.

7.  T  F  Material added at the beginning of the production process is 100 percent complete regardless of the percentage of completion of labour and manufacturing overhead.

8.  T  F  The weighted average method of computing equivalent units of production treats partially completed units in the beginning work in process inventory as if the company started and completed them in the current period.

9.  T  F  Most companies have only one processing department.

## APPENDIX 4A--PROCESS COSTING USING FIFO VALUATION

10. T  F  The FIFO method commingles units and costs of the prior period and the current period.

11. T  F  The FIFO method of computing equivalent units of production reflects more realistically the way that most goods flow through the production system.

## APPENDIX 4B--SPOILED AND LOST UNITS

12. T  F  Under the method of neglect, the company excludes the cost of making spoiled units from production costs.

13. T  F  In most production situations, the cause of spoiled goods is uncontrollable.

14. T  F  Lost revenue from dissatisfied customers is easy to quantify, and a company usually records it in the accounting records.

15. T  F  Some companies are eliminating their quality problems with computer-integrated manufacturing systems.

MULTIPLE CHOICE

1. The source document that provides almost all financial information about a job is the:

    A.  material requisition.
    B.  departmental cost report.
    C.  employee time sheet.
    D.  job order cost sheet.

2. Which of the following would most likely use a process cost system?

    A.  a custom print shop
    B.  a law firm
    C.  a food processing company
    D.  all of the above

3. A process cost system is appropriate for a manufacturer of:

    A.  small quantities of homogeneous units.
    B.  large quantities of homogeneous units.
    C.  small quantities of heterogeneous units.
    D.  large quantities of heterogeneous units.

4. What are the two basic methods of calculating unit costs in a process cost system?

    A.  weighted average and LIFO
    B.  weighted average and FIFO
    C.  FIFO and LIFO
    D.  specific identification and LIFO

5. In a process cost system, which costs can a company easily trace to products?

    A.  direct labour and manufacturing overhead
    B.  direct materials and manufacturing overhead
    C.  direct materials and direct labour
    D.  direct materials, direct labour, and manufacturing overhead

6. When can a company add materials to the production process?

    A.  at the beginning
    B.  during the production process
    C.  at the end
    D.  any of the above

7. The total costs to account for equal:

    A.  the costs in the ending inventory plus current period costs.
    B.  the costs in the beginning inventory plus current period costs.
    C.  current period costs minus the costs in the beginning inventory.
    D.  current period costs minus the costs in the ending inventory.

8. What details all manufacturing quantities and costs, shows the computation of cost per EUP, and indicates the cost assignment to goods produced during the period?

    A. cost of production report
    B. job order cost sheet
    C. work in process account
    D. general ledger

9. What does a company use in the numerator to calculate the cost per equivalent unit using the weighted average method?

    A. current period costs only
    B. current period costs minus beginning work in process
    C. current period costs plus beginning work in process
    D. current period costs minus ending work in process

USE THE FOLLOWING INFORMATION TO ANSWER QUESTIONS 10 AND 11.

Jasperson Company had beginning work in process of 40,000 units that were 30 percent complete. During the period, 250,000 units were started. The ending work in process consisted of 30,000 units that were 60 percent complete.

10. How many units did Jasperson transfer to finished goods?

    A. 250,000
    B. 260,000
    C. 280,000
    D. 290,000

11. What are Jasperson's equivalent units of production using the weighted average method?

    A. 266,000
    B. 278,000
    C. 296,000
    D. 308,000

12. Brown Company uses a weighted average process cost system. The cost per equivalent unit was $8.00. The beginning work in process inventory was $24,000. Costs added during the period were $320,000. What were the equivalent units of production?

    A. 37,000
    B. 40,000
    C. 43,000
    D. cannot be calculated from the information given

USE THE FOLLOWING INFORMATION TO ANSWER QUESTIONS 13 THROUGH 15.

Hennigan Company uses the weighted average method of cost flows. The beginning balance in work in process was $80,000. Hennigan incurred $640,000 of production costs during the period. The beginning work in process inventory consisted of 20,000 units that were 90 percent complete. Hennigan completed a total of 58,000 units during the period. The ending inventory consisted of 10,000 units that were 20 percent complete.

13. What is the cost per equivalent unit?

    A. $10.67
    B. $12.00
    C. $15.24
    D. $17.14

14. What was the cost transferred to finished goods during the period?

    A. $560,000
    B. $640,000
    C. $696,000
    D. $720,000

15. What is the cost of the ending work in process inventory?

    A. $ 24,000
    B. $ 30,480
    C. $ 96,000
    D. $120,000

16. Norris Company had 50,000 units that were 40 percent complete in its beginning work in process. New units started during the period were 426,000. Norris completed 348,000 units during the period. How many units remain in process at the end of the period?

    A. 78,000
    B. 98,000
    C. 108,000
    D. 128,000

17. Doss Company has two processing departments. Processing begins in Department 1 and is completed in Department 2. Department 2 had a beginning work in process balance of $39,500 and an ending balance of $50,900. The cost of goods transferred to finished goods during the period was $487,600. Department 2 added $375,000 in conversion costs but did not add any materials. What cost did Department 1 transfer to Department 2 during the period?

    A. $101,200
    B. $124,000
    C. $386,400
    D. $499,000

## APPENDIX 4A--PROCESS COSTING USING FIFO VALUATION

18. Compared to the weighted average method of determining unit costs, the FIFO method is:

    A. less accurate and less complex.
    B. less accurate and more complex.
    C. more accurate and more complex.
    D. more accurate and less complex.

19. The difference between the weighted average method and the FIFO method of calculating unit costs lies in the treatment of:

    A. beginning inventory.
    B. ending inventory.
    C. direct labour cost for the current period.
    D. manufacturing overhead cost for the current period.

20. In the FIFO method, the number of units started and completed equals:

    A. the total units completed during the period.
    B. the total units completed during the period minus the units in ending inventory.
    C. the total units completed during the period plus the units in the beginning inventory.
    D. the total units completed during the period minus the units in the beginning inventory.

21. The only difference between the weighted average and FIFO methods of computing equivalent units of production (EUP) is that under FIFO:

    A. current period EUP does not include work done on partially completed units in the ending inventory.
    B. a company treats partially completed units in the beginning inventory as if the company started and completed them in the current period.
    C. EUP consists only of units started and completed in the current period.
    D. current period EUP does not include work done in the prior period on beginning inventory.

22. The computation of cost per equivalent unit under FIFO:

    A. ignores prior period costs and uses only costs incurred in the current period.
    B. includes prior period costs and costs incurred in the current period.
    C. includes costs of the prior period but excludes costs incurred in the current period.
    D. includes current period costs only in the denominator.

23. The number of equivalent units of production used to calculate the ending work in process inventory:

    A. will be greater using the FIFO method than under the weighted average method.
    B. will be greater using the weighted average method than under the FIFO method.
    C. will be the same whether a company uses FIFO or weighted average.
    D. may be greater under FIFO or under weighted average depending upon the circumstances.

24. Jasperson Company had beginning work in process of 40,000 units that were 30 percent complete.  During the period, 250,000 units were started.  The ending work in process consisted of 30,000 units that were 60 percent complete.  What are Jasperson's equivalent units of production using the FIFO method?

    A. 266,000
    B. 278,000
    C. 290,000
    D. 308,000

25. Boggs Company uses a FIFO process cost system.  The cost per equivalent unit was $10.00.  The beginning work in process inventory was $46,000.  Costs added during the period were $520,000.  What were the equivalent units of production?

    A. 47,400
    B. 52,000
    C. 56,600
    D. cannot be calculated from the information given

USE THE FOLLOWING INFORMATION TO ANSWER QUESTIONS 26 THROUGH 28.

Peters Company uses the FIFO method of cost flows.  The beginning balance in work in process was $240,000.  Peters incurred $423,000 of production costs during the period.  The beginning work in process inventory consisted of 30,000 units that were 80 percent complete.  Peters completed a total of 64,000 units during the period.  The ending inventory consisted of 10,000 units that were 70 percent complete.

26. What is the cost per equivalent unit?

    A. $6.61
    B. $9.00
    C. $9.34
    D. $14.11

27. What cost did Peters transfer to finished goods during the period?

    A. $423,000
    B. $576,000
    C. $585,000
    D. $600,000

28. What is the cost of the ending work in process inventory?

    A. $27,000
    B. $63,000
    C. $65,380
    D. $90,000

29. Mitchell Company started and completed 92,000 units during the period.  There were 20,000 units that were 10 percent complete in the ending work in process inventory.  There were 120,000 EUP using FIFO.  The units in the beginning work in process inventory were 60 percent complete.  How many whole units were in the beginning work in process inventory?

    A.  8,000
    B.  20,000
    C.  26,000
    D.  65,000

## APPENDIX 4B--SPOILED AND LOST UNITS

30. Treating spoiled units under the method of neglect results in:

    A.  the company excluding the cost of spoiled units from production costs.
    B.  the company excluding the spoiled units from the equivalent units of production.
    C.  the company subtracting the cost of spoiled units from total production costs.
    D.  the company including the spoiled units in the equivalent units of production.

## ESSAY QUESTIONS AND PROBLEMS

1.  For what type of production system is job order costing appropriate?  Give some examples of the kind of companies that use a job order cost system.

2.  For what type of production system is process costing appropriate?  Give some examples of the kind of companies that use a process cost system.

3. What are the two primary differences between a job order cost system and a process cost system?

4. What are equivalent units of production?  Why is calculating the equivalent units of production important?

5. What are the two alternative methods of accounting for cost flows in process costing?  How do these methods differ?

USE THE FOLLOWING INFORMATION TO ANSWER PROBLEMS 6 THROUGH 9.

Freeman Company has two production departments: Cutting and Grinding. Freeman adds all of the direct materials in the Cutting Department. Freeman adds conversion costs in both departments. Freeman first processes the direct materials in the Cutting Department and then transfers them to the Grinding Department. After processing in the Grinding Department, Freeman transfers the goods to finished goods. Freeman Company uses the weighted average method of process costing. Freeman Company provides you with the following information for the Grinding Department:

|                                  | Whole units |
|----------------------------------|-------------|
| Beginning inventory              | 1,000 (40% complete as to conversion cost in grinding) |
| Units transferred in             | 20,000      |
| Units to account for             | 21,000      |
|                                  |             |
| Beginning inventory completed    | 1,000       |
| Units started and completed      | 16,000      |
| Units completed                  | 17,000      |
| Ending inventory                 | 4,000 (70% complete as to conversion cost in grinding) |
|                                  | 21,000      |

|                          | Transferred-in | Conversion | Total in Grinding |
|--------------------------|----------------|------------|-------------------|
| Beginning inventory cost | $ 16,000       | $10,000    | $ 26,000          |
| Current period costs     | 320,000        | 279,080    | 599,080           |
| Total costs              | 336,000        | $289,080   | $625,080          |

6. Compute the equivalent units of production for transferred-in cost and for conversion cost in the Grinding Department.

7. Compute the cost per equivalent unit.

8. Compute the costs transferred to finished goods.

9. Compute the cost of the ending work in process inventory in the Grinding Department.

USE THE FOLLOWING INFORMATION TO ANSWER PROBLEMS 10 THROUGH 13.

Davis Company has only one processing department. It adds all of the direct materials at the very beginning of the production process. The production process is labour intensive. Davis accumulates direct labour cost and overhead cost in one conversion cost pool.

Units:

| | |
|---|---|
| Beginning inventory | 30,000 (70% complete as to conversion cost) |
| Units started | 170,000 |
| | 200,000 |
| Ending inventory | 20,000 (40% complete as to conversion cost) |
| Units completed | 180,000 |

Costs:

| | Materials | Conversion Cost | Total |
|---|---|---|---|
| Beginning inventory | $ 210,000 | $ 420,000 | $ 630,000 |
| Costs added in current period | 1,200,000 | 3,509,200 | 4,709,200 |
| Total costs | $ 1,410,000 | $3,929,200 | $5,339,200 |

10. Assume that Davis Company has a weighted average process cost system. Compute the equivalent units of production and the cost per equivalent unit for materials and for conversion cost.

11. Assume that Davis Company has a weighted average process cost system. Compute the cost transferred to finished goods during the period and the cost of the ending work in process inventory.

## APPENDIX 4A--PROCESS COSTING USING FIFO VALUATION

12.  Assume that Davis Company has a FIFO process cost system.  Compute the equivalent units of production and the cost per equivalent unit for materials and for conversion cost.

13.  Assume that Davis Company has a FIFO process cost system.  Compute the cost transferred to finished goods during the period and the cost of the ending work in process inventory.

## APPENDIX 4B--SPOILED AND LOST UNITS

14.  If a company uses the method of neglect, how does it treat the cost of spoilage?

15.  How have companies traditionally controlled spoilage?  How are companies changing their methods for controlling spoilage?

# SELF TEST ANSWERS

## TRUE/FALSE

| | | | | | | | | | |
|---|---|---|---|---|---|---|---|---|---|
| 1. | T | 4. | F | 7. | T | 10. | F | 13. | F |
| 2. | F | 5. | T | 8. | T | 11. | T | 14. | F |
| 3. | T | 6. | T | 9. | F | 12. | F | 15. | T |

## MULTIPLE CHOICE

| | | | | | | | | | |
|---|---|---|---|---|---|---|---|---|---|
| 1. | D | 7. | B | 13. | B | 19. | A | 25. | B |
| 2. | C | 8. | A | 14. | C | 20. | D | 26. | B |
| 3. | B | 9. | C | 15. | A | 21. | D | 27. | D |
| 4. | B | 10. | B | 16. | D | 22. | A | 28. | B |
| 5. | C | 11. | B | 17. | B | 23. | C | 29. | D |
| 6. | D | 12. | C | 18. | C | 24. | A | 30. | B |

## ESSAY QUESTIONS AND PROBLEMS

1.      A job order cost system is appropriate for companies that make limited quantities of custom-made goods or services that conform to specifications designated by the purchaser. Many manufacturers use job order costing. Examples include print shops and custom-made clothing manufacturers. Job order costing is used by Dell Computer Corporation, in order to price computers configured to meet each customer's needs.

2.      A process cost system is appropriate for companies that make large quantities of homogeneous products. Many manufacturers use process costing. Examples include manufacturers of appliances, automobiles, food products, paper products, oil refineries.

3.      The two primary differences between job order costing and process costing are (1) the quantity of production for which a company accumulates costs at any one time and (2) the cost object to which a company assigns those costs. A job order cost system accumulates costs for a relatively small quantity of production. A process cost system accumulates costs for a relatively large quantity of production. A job order cost system assigns costs to a job and then to individual units. A process cost system assigns costs to departments and then to products.

4.      Equivalent units of production represent the approximate number of complete units that a company could have produced from the actual materials, labour, and manufacturing overhead used during the period. Companies must compute equivalent units of production to calculate a proper unit cost for products. Using only completed units to calculate unit cost would not consider the work accomplished during the period.

5.      The two alternative methods of accounting for cost flows in a process cost system are weighted average and first-in, first-out (FIFO). FIFO is more complex and more accurate. These two methods differ in the treatment of beginning work in process inventory in computing cost per equivalent unit of production. The weighted average method adds the cost of beginning work in process inventory to the current period's production costs to calculate the numerator. The FIFO method uses only costs incurred in the current period. To compute equivalent units of production, the weighted average method treats partially completed units in the beginning inventory as if the company started and completed them in the current period. The FIFO method considers only the work necessary to complete these units in computing equivalent units of production.

6.    Because all transferred-in units are 100 percent complete as to transferred-in costs, the equivalent units of production for transferred-in units is equal to the units in the beginning inventory plus the units transferred in during the current period.  Thus, the equivalent units of production for the transferred-in units are 21,000 (1,000 + 20,000).

Under the weighted average method, the equivalent units of production as to conversion cost is equal to the number of units completed plus the units in the ending inventory times the percentage of completion.  The weighted average method treats the units in the beginning inventory as if they were started and completed in the current period.  Thus, the equivalent units of production as to conversion cost is determined as follows:

| | |
|---|---|
| Units completed | 17,000 |
| Ending inventory (4,000 x 70%) | 2,800 |
| Equivalent units of production | 19,800 |

7.

| | Transferred-in | Conversion | Total in Grinding |
|---|---|---|---|
| Beginning inventory cost | $ 16,000 | $ 10,000 | $ 26,000 |
| Current period costs | 320,000 | 279,080 | 599,080 |
| Total costs | $336,000 | $289,080 | $625,080 |
| Divided by EUP | ÷ 21,000 | ÷ 19,800 | |
| Cost per EUP | $ 16.00 | $ 14.60 | $ 30.60 |

8.

| | |
|---|---|
| Units completed | 17,000 |
| Cost per EUP | x $30.60 |
| Cost transferred to finished goods | $520,200 |

9.

| | |
|---|---|
| Transferred-in cost (4,000 x $16.00) | $ 64,000 |
| Conversion cost (4,000 x 70% x $14.60) | 40,880 |
| Ending work in process inventory | $104,880 |

| | |
|---|---|
| Total costs reconciliation: | |
| Finished goods | $520,200 |
| Ending work in process inventory | 104,880 |
| Total costs | $625,080 |

10.

| | Materials | Conversion Cost |
|---|---|---|
| Units completed | 180,000 | 180,000 |
| Ending inventory 20,000 x 100% = | 20,000 | |
| Ending inventory 20,000 x 40% = | | 8,000 |
| Equivalent units of production | 200,000 | 188,000 |
| Total costs | $1,410,000 | $3,929,200 |
| Divided by equivalent units of production | ÷ 200,000 | ÷ 188,000 |
| Cost per equivalent unit | $7.05 | $20.90 |

11.

| | |
|---|---|
| Units completed | 180,000 |
| Times cost per equivalent unit ($7.05 + $20.90) | x $27.95 |
| Cost transferred to finished goods | $5,031,000 |

| | |
|---|---|
| Materials 20,000 x $7.05 = | $141,000 |
| Conversion cost 20,000 x 40% x $20.90 = | 167,200 |
| Ending work in process inventory | $308,200 |

Total costs reconciliation:

| | |
|---|---|
| Finished goods | $5,031,000 |
| Ending work in process inventory | 308,200 |
| Total costs | $5,339,200 |

12.

| | Materials | Conversion Cost |
|---|---|---|
| To complete beginning inventory: | | |
| 30,000 x (100% - 100%) = | 0 | |
| 30,000 x (100% - 70%) = | | 9,000 |
| Units started and completed: | | |
| 180,000 - 30,000 = | 150,000 | 150,000 |
| Ending inventory 20,000 x 100% = | 20,000 | |
| Ending inventory 20,000 x 40% = | | 8,000 |
| Equivalent units of production | 170,000 | 167,000 |
| | | |
| Costs added in current period | $1,200,000 | $3,509,200 |
| Divided by equivalent units of production | ÷ 170,000 | ÷ 167,000 |
| Cost per equivalent unit | $7.059 | $21.013 |

13.

| | |
|---|---|
| Beginning work in process inventory ($210,000 + $420,000) | $  630,000 |
| Cost to complete: | |
| Conversion cost [30,000 x (100% - 70%) x $21.013] | 189,117 |
| Total cost of units in beginning inventory transferred | $  819,117 |
| Units started and completed [150,000 x ($7.059 + $21.013)] | 4,210,800 |
| Cost transferred to finished goods | $5,029,917 |

| | |
|---|---|
| Materials 20,000 x $7.059 = | $141,180 |
| Conversion cost 20,000 x 40% x $21.013 = | 168,104 |
| Ending work in process inventory | $309,284 |

Total costs reconciliation:

| | |
|---|---|
| Finished goods | $5,029,917 |
| Ending work in process inventory | 309,284 |
| Total costs (off by $1 due to rounding) | $5,339,201 |

14.     Under the method of neglect, a company does not include the spoiled units in computing the equivalent units of production.  The company does include the cost of spoilage in production costs, which increases the cost per equivalent unit for the good units.  The company effectively buries the cost of the spoiled units.  Thus, managers are often not aware of the size of the cost of spoilage.

15.     Traditionally, companies have controlled spoilage through a process of inspecting completed products.  Service firms have attempted to control quality through customer surveys.  Now, more companies are changing to process control as a means to reduce spoilage.  The goal is to build quality into a product and discover defective units before the company incurs additional costs in processing them further.

# CHAPTER 5
# INTRODUCTION TO A STANDARD COST SYSTEM

## CHAPTER OVERVIEW

This chapter discusses a traditional standard cost system, using price and quantity standards for direct materials, direct labour, and manufacturing overhead. The examples in the chapter assume the use of only one direct material and one direct labour category. The chapter explains how companies develop material and labour standards and calculate variances from these standards.

This chapter explains how management can use a standard cost system to help in planning and controlling costs. Management can also use standards to motivate employees and to evaluate their performance. A standard cost is a budgeted cost for one unit of a product. Price and quantity standards for direct materials, direct labour, and manufacturing overhead make up a standard cost. The differences between actual costs and standard costs are variances. Management investigates significant variances to detect the causes and to decide what corrective action, if any, is necessary.

Appendix 5A illustrates the journal entries that a company would make under standard costing. Appendix 5B discusses the use of a standard cost system within a process cost system.

## CHAPTER STUDY GUIDE

Companies can use standard costing with either a job order cost system or with process costing. Companies use standard costs for planning, control, decision making, and for motivating employees and evaluating managerial performance. A standard cost system enables companies to compute variances from standard and correct problems from excess costs or usage. Actual costing systems do not provide these benefits.

The availability of standards equips managers to make more rapid and better decisions, because managers have a predetermined set of expectations upon which to base decisions. Standard costing also simplifies performance evaluation.

The standard cost is the estimated cost to make one unit of a product or to perform a service. Traditionally, companies develop standards for each component of product cost--materials, labour, and overhead. Developing standards requires judgment and practicality in deciding the types, quantities, and prices of materials and labour that a company will use. Overhead standards require that managers classify overhead costs according to cost behaviour, select valid bases for allocation, and specify a reasonable activity level.

A key objective in manufacturing a product or performing a service is to reduce unit cost while achieving certain quality specifications. Companies can make almost any product with a variety of inputs, even after deciding on a quality level. Input choices affect the standards a company sets.

Management establishes the design and manufacturing process and selects the input resources that the company will use to make the desired products. Next management develops quantity and price standards. Representatives from the following areas should help develop the standards: management accounting, product design, industrial engineering, human resources, data processing, purchasing, and production management. Managers should include subordinate managers and employees, whom the managers will evaluate by the standards, in the standards-setting process. This involvement helps to motivate these managers and employees to achieve the standards. Information from suppliers is also helpful in setting materials price standards.

Companies prepare information on the type, quality, and quantity of materials needed to make a product on a document called a bill of materials.  Even companies without a standard cost system will probably prepare a bill of materials for each of their products.  Exhibit 5-1 illustrates a bill of materials.  Next, the company must decide the standard prices for the materials.  The purchasing agent should have input into the setting of materials price standards.

Companies list the labour tasks necessary to make a product and the standard time for each task on an operations flow document.  Management should analyze all listed activities as to their ability to add value to a product.  Management should target non-value-added activities for reduction or elimination.  Exhibit 5-2 illustrates an operations flow document.  The labour rate standards should include the wages and fringe benefits paid to the employees doing the listed tasks.  If the wage rate is different for different employees performing the same task, the company should use a weighted average labour rate.

A company may use a single overhead rate, separate overhead rates for fixed costs and variable costs, or multiple departmental overhead rates.

A standard cost card shows the price and quantity standards for materials, the rate and time standards for labour, and the price or rate and hours or quantities standards for overhead.   Exhibit 5-3 illustrates a standard cost card.

Companies use the standard costs and quantities to assign costs to inventory accounts.  In an actual or normal cost system, companies charge actual material and labour costs to Work in Process Inventory as production occurs.  In most standard cost systems, companies charge standard costs instead of actual costs to Work in Process Inventory.  Any difference between actual and standard costs is a variance.

The most basic variance calculation is the total variance that is the difference between the actual cost and the standard cost.  A company also computes price and quantity variances for each component of product cost.  If a variance is positive, it is unfavourable (U) because the actual costs exceeded the standard costs.  If a variance is negative, one drops the negative sign.  The variance is favourable (F) because the actual costs were less than the standard costs.  If variances are substantial, management will investigate to detect the causes and decide what corrective action to take.

To compute variances, management first computes the standard quantity or hours allowed.  The standard quantity allowed is equal to the standard quantity per unit multiplied by the number of units produced.  For labour and overhead applied based on labour hours, management computes the standard hours allowed by multiplying the standard hours per unit by the number of units produced.

Exhibit 5-4 presents a simple model that one can use to compute price, rate or spending variances, quantity or efficiency variances, and total variances.  One can also compute the total variance by adding the price variance and the quantity variance, taking negative signs, if any, into account.  One can also compute the total variance using the following formula:  (AP)(AQ) - (SP)(SQ).  Another way to calculate price and quantity variances is to use the equations shown at the end of this chapter study guide.  Exhibit 5-5 gives an example of calculating the standard quantities allowed.

The material price variance shows the money spent above or below the standard price for the quantity of materials purchased.  The material quantity variance is the standard price times the difference between the actual quantity of material used and the standard quantity allowed.

Usually, companies use the same quantities or hours to compute the price variance and the quantity variance. For materials, however, there may be a difference between the quantities purchased and the quantities used in production. In such cases, a company should compute the material price variance on the quantities of materials purchased. A company computes the material quantity or usage variance on the quantities of materials used in production. No meaningful total material variance can be derived when a company uses different quantities to compute the price variance and the quantity variance.

Although basing the material price variance on purchases rather than usage allows managers to see the effect of buying decisions quickly, such information is not as relevant in a JIT environment. Management should weigh the benefits of price savings against the additional inventory carrying costs.

The price and usage elements of the total labour variance are the labour rate variance and the labour efficiency variance. The labour rate variance reveals the difference between the actual rate (or weighted average rate) paid to direct labour workers and the standard rate for the actual hours worked. The labour efficiency variance is the standard rate times the difference between the actual hours and the standard hours allowed.

The labour efficiency variance could be misleading if a company fails to consider the number of defective units produced. To correct this problem, companies can use the number of good units produced rather than the number of total units produced in computing the standard hours allowed. A company can compute a quality variance by using the following formula: the number of defective units times the standard hours allowed per unit times the standard rate.

Using separate variable and fixed factory overhead application rates allows a company to compute separate variances for each type of overhead. These separate calculations provide managers with flexibility for control and performance evaluation purposes. Because many companies use different bases for various overhead allocations, such companies may need to compute separate price and usage variances for each cost pool.

The subvariances of the total manufacturing overhead variance are as follows: (1) variable overhead spending variance, (2) variable overhead efficiency variance, (3) fixed overhead spending variance, and (4) fixed overhead volume variance. The variable overhead spending variance is the difference between actual variable overhead and budgeted variable overhead based on actual output. The variable overhead efficiency variance is the difference between budgeted variable manufacturing overhead at the actual input activity and budgeted variable manufacturing overhead at the standard input allowed. The fixed overhead spending variance is the difference between actual and budgeted fixed overhead. The fixed overhead volume variance is the difference between budgeted and applied fixed overhead.

Variance analysis is the process of calculating the differences between actual costs and standard costs, deciding whether the variance is favourable or unfavourable, and searching for the reasons for such differences. The cost control and variance analysis should help managers to learn who is responsible for the variance. If variances reflect poor performance, an early measurement system can help managers to improve operational performance. Learning the cause of a variance becomes more difficult if the system delays reporting it. Material price and labour rate variances are not as controllable at the production or service level as are the material quantity and labour efficiency variances.

The material price variance is normally the responsibility of the purchasing agent. The purchasing agent is not always able to control prices. Nevertheless, the purchasing agent can influence prices by (1) knowing the available suppliers, (2) choosing the suppliers that can supply the proper material in a reasonable time at a reasonable cost, (3) purchasing in quantities that provide for discounts, and (4) negotiating long-term purchase contracts.

The material quantity variance is usually the responsibility of the manager of the production department using the materials. This normal assignment of responsibility does have some exceptions, however. For example, if the purchasing agent buys materials of inferior quality, the production department might use a greater quantity of material. In such a situation, the purchasing agent would bear the responsibility for the material quantity variance.

Management often assigns responsibility for the labour rate and efficiency variances to the person in charge of the production or service area. Such an assignment assumes that the managers can influence the types of labourers used. A common factor can cause multiple variances. For example, the purchase of lower-quality materials could result in a favourable material price variance, an unfavourable material quantity variance, and an unfavourable labour efficiency variance.

The total overhead variance is the difference between the actual overhead and the applied overhead. Companies treat variable and fixed overhead differently for control purposes because of the differences in the type of costs in the two categories and in the abilities of managers to influence those costs. Management controls variable overhead by (1) keeping actual costs consistent with budgeted costs for the actual activity level and
(2) obtaining the planned output yield from the overhead resources used in production.

Price differences often cause variable overhead spending variances. Such differences often happen because the standard rate does not reflect price changes. If managers cannot control prices, then the company should not hold the managers accountable for consequent variances. If managers can influence prices through such methods as long-term purchase contracts, the company should analyze the costs and benefits of such options before changing the standard rates. Waste or spoilage is another possible reason for an unfavourable variable overhead spending variance.

The variable overhead efficiency variance shows the managerial control achieved or needed concerning the output yield. Managers control variable overhead resources by (1) watching and assessing their actual usage compared to standard usage, (2) quickly investigating any variances, and (3) adjusting resource usage when necessary. Managers must analyze each component of variable overhead rather than attempting to analyze and control total variable overhead. If a company applies variable overhead using direct labour hours, the signs of the variable overhead efficiency variance and the labour efficiency variance will be the same. If the company uses other overhead application bases, the signs of these two variances will not necessarily be the same.

Control of fixed overhead costs is quite different from control of variable overhead. Fixed overhead is usually not related to the current activity level. Companies have to commit to incurring fixed overhead costs before a period begins. Thus, managers have only limited ability to control fixed overhead costs in the short run. Control of fixed overhead costs must occur at the time of commitment and not at the time of activity.

The fixed overhead spending variance depicts a variance in the costs of fixed overhead components or a mismanagement of resources. Managers must often control the fixed overhead spending variance on a transaction-by-transaction basis when managers arrange for facilities. The information provided by a total fixed overhead spending variance would not be specific enough to allow managers to decide whether to take corrective action. Managers need to review individual cost variances for each component. Such a review helps managers to detect the causes of and assign responsibility for the various components of the total fixed overhead spending variance.

An unfavourable volume variance shows a less-than-expected use of capacity. If a company is currently using capacity at a level different from anticipated, managers should recognize that difference, examine the reasons for it, and take any appropriate action. Managers should view the extent of capacity use in relation to inventory and sales. If a company overutilizes capacity and inventory is accumulating, managers should decrease capacity utilization. If inventory is not increasing, a favourable volume variance could be due to increased sales only. Then, no adjustment in capacity usage is necessary.

If a company underutilizes its capacity and is not filling its sales orders promptly, managers should attempt to increase capacity utilization. Managers should recognize that underutilization of capacity is desirable sometimes. Companies should not produce additional goods just to add to unneeded inventory. Accumulating excess inventory generates unnecessary costs.

Managers can sometimes affect capacity utilization by (1) changing work schedules, (2) taking measures to ease production constraints, (3) eliminating non-value-added activities, and (4) carefully observing the movement of resources through the production process. Managers should take such actions during the period rather than after the period has ended.

Companies often select expected annual capacity rather than practical or theoretical capacity as the denominator activity level in computing the predetermined fixed manufacturing overhead application rate. Using expected annual capacity ignores unused capacity. Unused capacity creates additional non-value-added organizational costs. The only way to emphasize these costs is to use practical capacity or theoretical capacity to compute the fixed overhead application rate.

Instead of using traditional fixed overhead calculations, companies could compute fixed overhead variances in a way that could provide additional information. Exhibit 5-6 describes this innovative process using practical capacity rather than expected annual capacity. This method allows managers to focus on the cost of unused capacity.

Conversion cost includes direct labour and manufacturing overhead. Traditionally, companies have separated product costs into three categories: direct material, direct labour, and manufacturing overhead. This treatment is appropriate in labour-intensive manufacturing operations. In highly automated factories, direct labour cost is a small part of total product cost.

Many companies are changing their standard cost systems by combining direct labour cost with manufacturing overhead. The sum is conversion cost. This approach is appropriate for companies that have a highly automated production process with little direct labour cost. Companies are likely to separate conversion cost into its fixed and variable elements. Also, companies are likely to classify conversion costs as direct or indirect based on their traceability to a machine rather than to a product. Companies may use a variety of cost drivers to apply conversion costs to products.

Variance analysis for conversion cost usually focuses on the following: (1) spending variances for overhead costs, (2) efficiency variances for machinery and production costs instead of labour costs, and (3) the traditional volume variance for production. Exhibit 5-7 illustrates the calculation of variances under the conversion cost approach.

In setting standards, companies should consider the appropriateness and the attainability of the standards. Appropriateness refers to the basis on which management developed the standards and how long management expects them to last. The attainability of the standards refers to the level of rigour required to achieve the standards. A company should change its standards as its production process changes. To be useful, standards must reflect the current operating environment. Some Japanese companies, especially those emphasizing continuous improvement, change standards often.

Management can use standards to motivate employees.  Expected standards are what a company expects to achieve in the current period.  Practical standards are those standards that management expects employees to reach about 60–70 percent of the time.  Practical standards allow for machine downtime and employees' breaks.  Traditionally, companies have viewed practical standards as the best type of standards for motivating employees.  Theoretical standards do not allow for any inefficiency or any operating delays.  Companies cannot attain theoretical standards, and companies generally have thought that theoretical standards would discourage employees.  This belief, however, has begun to change.

Different acceptable ranges can be used to apply the management by exception principle, depending on the type of standard a company uses.  Management by exception allows managers to set tolerance limits and investigate only the variances that are outside those limits.  To discover the causes of variances, managers must examine problems through observation, inspection, and inquiry.  Accountants and employees in operations are involved in investigating significant variances.  Employees in operations should be aware of variances as they occur and record the reasons for the variances if known.  To be most effective, the standard cost system should report variances in a timely manner so that management can improve operational performance quickly.

As more companies adopt total quality management (TQM) and a just-in-time (JIT) manufacturing system, companies are beginning to question the wisdom of not using theoretical standards.  Both TQM and JIT strive for zero defects, zero inefficiency, and zero downtime.  Under this system, theoretical standards become the expected standards.

To implement theoretical standards, management must prepare to use a four-step migration process.  The first step is to establish teams that will find the current problems and their causes.  If the causes stem from equipment, the facility, or employees, management must take the second step by investing in plant and equipment and employee training.  The third step is for management to give employees the authority to react to quality problems quickly.  Fourth, management must recognize the employees' efforts and provide rewards for achievement.

As business becomes more competitive, companies are more likely to set standards closer to the theoretical level.  If competitors use the highest possible standards, companies must also use such standards to compete on quality and cost objectives.  Higher standards for efficiency reduce costs because of the reduction of non-value-added activities.

Companies have traditionally set standards after a thorough examination of various cost elements.  Companies often retained these standards for a year or longer.  The current business environment changes so rapidly that a standard may not be useful for an entire year.  Management needs to decide whether to change standards in a year in which significant changes occur.

Ignoring the changes is a simplistic concept that means the company will use the same standard all year.  This approach removes any opportunity to control costs or evaluate performance adequately.  Changing the standards to reflect price or quantity changes makes some aspects of control and performance evaluation more effective and others more difficult.  Changing the standards also causes a problem for record keeping and inventory measurement.

Management could use a hybrid approach by comparing plans made using original and new standards.  Any variances would reflect changes in the business environment.  Management could designate these variances as uncontrollable, internally initiated, or internally controllable.

Critics of standard costing question the relevance of traditional variance analysis for cost control and performance appraisal in today's manufacturing and competitive environment.  Nevertheless, standard costing systems continue to be widely used because they provide cost information for many other purposes besides cost control.

Formulas for calculating variances:

Material price variance = AQ(AP - SP)

Material quantity variance = SP(AQ - SQ)

Labour rate variance = AH(AR - SR)

Labour efficiency variance = SR(AH - SH)
If a quality variance is also computed, the SH should be for good units only.

Quality variance = Defective units x SH per unit x SR

Variable overhead spending variance = AH(AR - SR)

Variable overhead efficiency variance = SR(AH - SH)

Fixed overhead spending variance = Actual FOH - Budgeted FOH

Fixed overhead volume variance = Budgeted FOH - Applied FOH

## APPENDIX 5A--STANDARD COST SYSTEM JOURNAL ENTRIES

Exhibit 5-8 illustrates the journal entries for a standard cost system.  Unfavourable variances have debit balances, and favourable variances have credit balances.  Standard costs are useful for internal use.  They are not acceptable for external reporting unless they are substantially equivalent to actual costs.  If a company uses standard costs in its financial reporting system, the company must adjust its accounts at the end of the period to approximate actual costs.  If the variances are not significant, the company closes them to cost of goods sold.  On the other hand, the company closes significant variances to the ending inventories and to cost of goods sold in proportion to their balances.

## APPENDIX 5B--PROCESS COSTING WITH STANDARD COSTS

A company can use a standard cost system within a process cost system.  If a company uses a standard process cost system, the calculation of equivalent units of production is the same as under the FIFO method except that the department uses standard costs instead of actual costs.  The company transfers units out of a department at standard cost.  The use of a standard cost system allows the company to compute variances between actual costs and standard costs.  Management can investigate significant variances to learn their causes.  Management can take remedial action where necessary to control the activities that cause costs.

## SELF TEST

TRUE/FALSE

1.  T  F  A total fixed overhead spending variance usually provides enough information to allow managers to decide whether to take corrective action.

2.  T  F  Companies that use machine hours to apply manufacturing overhead must still use direct labour hours in calculating the variable overhead spending variance.

3.  T  F  A company can use standard costing with a job order cost system or with process costing.

4.  T  F  In the current business environment, companies can usually use the same standards for five years or more.

5.  T  F  Only management accountants should be involved in setting price and quantity standards.

6.  T  F  The estimated cost to manufacture one unit of a product is the standard cost.

7.  T  F  The difference between the total actual costs incurred and the total standard cost for the production of the period is the rate variance.

8.  T  F  Conversion cost includes direct labour and manufacturing overhead.

9.  T  F  When a labour efficiency variance has a negative sign, then the variance is favourable.

10.  T  F  A possible cause of a favourable labour efficiency variance is producing units of poor quality.

11.  T  F  Under the management by exception principle, managers will only investigate      variances that fall outside of tolerance limits.

12.  T  F  The purchase of poor quality raw materials could cause a favourable material price variance, an unfavourable material usage variance, and an unfavourable labour efficiency variance.

13.  T  F  The use of expected standards is an excellent tool for motivating employees.

14.  T  F  Both total quality management and a just-in-time manufacturing system have goals of zero defects, zero inefficiency, and zero downtime.

## APPENDIX 5A--STANDARD COST SYSTEM JOURNAL ENTRIES

15.  T  F  Variance accounts with unfavourable variances will have credit balances.

MULTIPLE CHOICE

1. Overhead standards require that managers:

    A. classify overhead costs according to cost behaviour.
    B. select valid bases for allocation.
    C. specify a reasonable activity level.
    D. all of the above.

2. Standards that provide for no inefficiency of any type are:

    A. theoretical standards.
    B. practical standards.
    C. expected standards.
    D. normal standards.

3. The process of categorizing the nature of the differences between standard costs and actual costs and determining the reasons for those differences is:

    A. cost driver analysis.
    B. standard cost analysis.
    C. variance analysis.
    D. differential cost analysis.

4. The material price variance is usually the responsibility of the:

    A. controller.
    B. president.
    C. purchasing agent.
    D. production manager.

5. What should companies consider in setting standards?

    A. appropriateness only
    B. attainability only
    C. appropriateness and attainability
    D. neither appropriateness nor attainability

6. The estimated cost to manufacture a single unit of product or perform a service is the:

    A. usual cost.
    B. standard cost.
    C. normal cost.
    D. expected cost.

7.  In setting the labour rate standard, what wage rate should a company use when it pays different wages to employees who perform the same tasks?

   A.  the highest wage rate of those employees
   B.  the lowest wage rate of those employees
   C.  a simple average of the wage rates of those employees
   D.  a weighted average of the wage rates of those employees

8.  What document summarizes the standard quantities and standard costs needed to make one unit of a product?

   A.  general ledger
   B.  bill of materials
   C.  standard cost card
   D.  operations flow document

9.  The difference between budgeted and applied fixed overhead is the:

   A.  volume variance.
   B.  spending variance.
   C.  efficiency variance.
   D.  total variance.

10.  Companies usually compute the material price variances at:

   A.  the point of purchase.
   B.  the issuance of the materials into production.
   C.  the time the quarterly financial statements are prepared.
   D.  the time the annual report is prepared.

11.  What variance reflects capacity utilization?

   A.  variable overhead spending variance
   B.  variable overhead efficiency variance
   C.  fixed overhead volume variance
   D.  fixed overhead spending variance

12.  Investigating only significant differences between actual results and standards is an application of what management principle?

   A.  management by objectives
   B.  management by exception
   C.  management by walking around
   D.  span of control

13.  What costs make up conversion cost?

   A.  direct material and direct labour
   B.  direct labour and manufacturing overhead
   C.  direct material and manufacturing overhead
   D.  direct material and indirect labour

14. Breck Company produced 950 good units and 50 defective units. The standard labour rate is $11 per hour. The standard labour hours are 6 hours per unit. What was Breck Company's quality variance?

    A. $ 550 U
    B. $ 3,300 F
    C. $ 3,300 U
    D. $62,700 U

15. Paxon Company had a $1,200 U labour rate variance and a $400 F total labour variance. What was the labour efficiency variance?

    A. $800 U
    B. $800 F
    C. $1,600 U
    D. $1,600 F

16. Truong Company purchased 3,100 litres of materials at a price of $6.80 per litre. The standard price is $6.40 per litre. Truong used 2,700 litres in production. The remaining 400 litres are in the raw materials inventory. What was the material purchase price variance?

    A. $1,080 U
    B. $1,080 F
    C. $1,240 U
    D. $1,240 F

17. Dover Company's standard for raw materials is 5 kilograms per unit. During the year the company produced 950 units and used 4,845 kilograms of materials. What was the standard quantity allowed?

    A.   95 kilograms
    B.  190 kilograms
    C.  969 kilograms
    D. 4,750 kilograms

USE THE FOLLOWING INFORMATION TO ANSWER QUESTIONS 18 THROUGH 26

Lopez Company uses a labour intensive manufacturing process. Lopez applies variable overhead on the basis of direct labour hours. Lopez Company's standard variable costs are as follows:

| | Quantity or Hours | Price or Rate |
|---|---|---|
| Materials (kilograms) | 32 | $15 |
| Direct labour | 8 | $10 |
| Variable overhead | 8 | $ 5 |

During the year, Lopez produced 12,000 units. Lopez purchased and used 382,000 kilograms of materials at an average price of $15.20 per kilogram. Lopez used 97,000 direct labour hours. The total direct labour cost was $921,500. Actual variable overhead cost was $543,200.

18. What was the material price variance?

    A. $400 F
    B. $400 U
    C. $76,400 U
    D. $76,800 U

19. What was the material quantity variance?

    A. $30,000 F
    B. $30,000 U
    C. $30,400 U
    D. $76,800 U

20. What was the total material variance?

    A. $ 30,400 U
    B. $ 46,400 F
    C. $ 46,400 U
    D. $106,400 F

21. What was the labour rate variance?

    A. $10,000 F
    B. $10,000 U
    C. $48,500 F
    D. $48,500 U

22. What was the labour efficiency variance?

    A. $10,000 F
    B. $10,000 U
    C. $48,500 F
    D. $48,500 U

23. What was the total labour variance?

    A. $38,500 F
    B. $38,500 U
    C. $58,500 U
    D. $97,000 U

24. What was the variable overhead spending variance?

    A. $5,000 F
    B. $5,000 U
    C. $58,200 F
    D. $58,200 U

25. What was the variable overhead efficiency variance?

    A. $5,000 F
    B. $5,000 U
    C. $58,200 F
    D. $58,200 U

26. What was the variable overhead total variance?

    A. $53,200 F
    B. $53,200 U
    C. $63,200 F
    D. $63,200 U

## USE THE FOLLOWING INFORMATION TO ANSWER QUESTIONS 27 THROUGH 29

Leah's Company uses a fixed overhead application rate of $8 per machine hour. Actual machine hours were 72,000. Budgeted machine hours were 69,000. Actual fixed overhead cost was $565,800. The standard machine hours allowed were 70,000.

27. What was the fixed overhead spending variance?

    A. $13,800 F
    B. $13,800 U
    C. $24,000 F
    D. $24,000 U

28. What was the fixed overhead volume variance?

    A. $8,000 F
    B. $8,000 U
    C. $13,800 U
    D. $24,000 F

29. What was the fixed overhead total variance?

    A. $5,800 F
    B. $5,800 U
    C. $10,200 F
    D. $19,600 U

## APPENDIX 5A--STANDARD COST SYSTEM JOURNAL ENTRIES

30. At the end of the period, if the balances in the variance accounts are not significant, the company should close the variance accounts to:

    A. work-in process.
    B. cost of goods sold.
    C. manufacturing overhead.
    D. the ending inventories and to cost of goods sold.

ESSAY QUESTIONS AND PROBLEMS

1.  Who should be involved in setting standard costs?

2.  What is variance analysis?  How can variance analysis help management?

3.  Explain why the purchase of poor quality materials could lead to a favourable materials price variance, an unfavourable materials quantity variance, and an unfavourable labour efficiency variance.

4.  Explain how management uses standard cost systems to plan and control costs.

5.  Define expected standards, practical standards, and theoretical standards.  Why are more companies using theoretical standards for quality improvement?

6.  What are some ways that the purchasing manager could influence the prices paid for materials?

7.  How can managers control variable overhead resources?

8.  McAllister Company's standard direct labour hours per unit is 3 and the standard labour rate is $11 per hour. During the month, McAllister produced 4,200 units consisting of 4,000 good units and 200 defective units. McAllister Company used 13,000 direct labour hours at a cost of $140,400.  (A) Compute the labour efficiency variance assuming that McAllister does not compute a quality variance.  (B) Compute the quality variance and the labour efficiency variance assuming that McAllister Company does compute a separate quality variance.

9. Lee Company's standard labour rate is $12 per hour. The company produced 3,000 units last month. The standard for labour hours per unit is 5. The labour efficiency variance was $2,400 U. How many actual labour hours did Lee Company use?

10. Thomas Company applies fixed overhead on the basis of machine hours. The fixed overhead application rate is $6 per machine hour. The budgeted fixed overhead cost was $30,000 based on expected capacity of 5,000 machine hours. The actual fixed overhead cost was $29,340. The actual machine hours used were 5,120. The standard machine hours allowed were 4,900. Calculate the fixed overhead spending variance, the fixed overhead volume variance, and the total fixed overhead variance.

USE THE FOLLOWING INFORMATION TO ANSWER QUESTIONS 11 THROUGH 13

The standard variable cost per unit for a product of Mills Company is as follows:

|  | Quantity or Hours | Price or Rate | Total |
|---|---|---|---|
| Material | 6 kilograms | $ 7.00 | $42.00 |
| Direct labour | 2 hours | 9.50 | 19.00 |
| Variable manufacturing overhead | 2 hours | 15.00 | 30.00 |
|  |  |  | $91.00 |

During the month Mills Company produced 2,000 units. The company used all of the materials that it purchased in production. The quantity of materials purchased was 12,800 kilograms. The total cost of these materials was $88,320. The company used a total of 3,900 direct labour hours. The total direct labour cost was $39,000. The total variable overhead cost was $62,400. Mills Company applies variable overhead cost on the basis of direct labour hours.

11. Calculate the material price variance, the material quantity variance, and the total material variance.

12. Calculate the labour rate variance, the labour efficiency variance, and the total labour variance.

13. Calculate the variable overhead spending variance, the variable overhead efficiency variance, and the total variable overhead variance.

## APPENDIX 5A--STANDARD COST SYSTEM JOURNAL ENTRIES

14. What does a company do with the balances in the variance accounts if the amounts are not significant?

## APPENDIX 5B--PROCESS COSTING WITH STANDARD COSTS

15. Explain how process costing using standard costs differs from process costing using actual costs.

## SELF TEST ANSWERS

### TRUE/FALSE

| | | | | |
|---|---|---|---|---|
| 1. F | 4. F | 7. F | 10. T | 13. F |
| 2. F | 5. F | 8. T | 11. T | 14. T |
| 3. T | 6. T | 9. T | 12. T | 15. F |

### MULTIPLE CHOICE

| | | | | |
|---|---|---|---|---|
| 1. D | 7. D | 13. B | 19. A | 25. B |
| 2. A | 8. C | 14. C | 20. C | 26. D |
| 3. C | 9. A | 15. A | 21. C | 27. B |
| 4. C | 10. A | 16. C | 22. B | 28. A |
| 5. C | 11. C | 17. D | 23. A | 29. B |
| 6. B | 12. B | 18. C | 24. D | 30. B |

## ESSAY QUESTIONS AND PROBLEMS

1.      Management develops quantity and price standards.  Representatives from the following areas, however, should help management develop the standards: management accounting, product design, industrial engineering, human resources, data processing, purchasing, and production management.  Managers should include subordinate managers and employees, whom the managers will evaluate by the standards, in the standards-setting process.  This involvement helps to motivate these managers and employees to achieve the standards. Information from suppliers is also helpful in setting materials price standards.

2.      Variance analysis is the process of calculating the differences between actual costs and standard costs, deciding whether the variance is favourable or unfavourable, and searching for the reasons for such differences. The cost control and variance analysis should help managers to learn who is responsible for the variance.  If variances reflect poor performance, an early measurement system can help managers to improve operational performance.

3.      Companies can usually purchase poor quality materials at a lower cost than materials of a higher quality. Buying materials at a lower price than standard results in a favourable material price variance.  Some of these materials, however, could be of such poor quality that the company cannot use them.  The poor quality materials used can cause more units to be defective.  Thus, the company will use more materials resulting in an unfavourable material quantity variance.  The company will use more labour time to rework defective units, which could lead to an unfavourable labour efficiency variance.

4.      Management determines through research and analysis the standards or norms for the prices and quantities of materials, the number of hours and the wage rate for labour, and the number of units and the price or rate of the variable(s) used to apply overhead.  The variable(s) used to apply overhead could include direct labour hours, machine hours, kilograms of materials, number of setups, and other activities that drive overhead costs. Management uses these norms to plan what a product should cost to manufacture.  Management can use the standards for the components of a single product to plan aggregate costs by simply multiplying the cost per unit times the number of units.

Management uses a standard cost system for control purposes by comparing the actual results with those predicted by the standards. If the variances are significant, management looks for the causes. Once management identifies the causes, management can take remedial action to reduce costs. Management could also decide that no remedial action is necessary and that the company should revise its standards.

5.      Expected standards are the standards that reflect what a company expects to occur in the future period. They incorporate expected waste and inefficiencies. Practical standards are those standards that employees can achieve or slightly exceed 60 to 70 percent of the time. Practical standards allow for normal, unavoidable time problems or delays such as machine downtime. Theoretical standards are those standards that allow for no inefficiencies of any kind. They call for the highest level of rigour and do not allow for normal operating delays or human limitations such as fatigue or boredom.

More companies are adopting theoretical standards as part of their total quality management (TQM) and just-in-time (JIT) systems. Both TQM and JIT allow for zero defects, zero inefficiency, and zero downtime. Companies are improving quality in order to compete in the global economy.

6.      The purchasing agent could influence the prices paid for materials by (1) knowing the available suppliers, (2) choosing the suppliers that can supply the proper material in a reasonable time at a reasonable cost, (3) purchasing in quantities that provide for discounts, and (4) negotiating long-term purchase contracts.

7.      Managers control variable overhead resources by (1) watching and assessing their actual usage compared to standard usage, (2) quickly investigating any variances, and (3) adjusting resource usage when necessary. Managers must analyze each component of variable overhead rather than attempting to analyze and control total variable overhead.

8.      (A) Labour efficiency variance assuming that McAllister does not compute a quality variance:

SR(AH - SH) = $11[13,000 - (4,200 x 3)] = $11(13,000 - 12,600) = $4,400 U

(B) Quality Variance:

200 defective units x  SH per unit x  SR = 200 x  3 x  $11 = $6,600 U
Labour efficiency variance assuming that McAllister does compute a quality variance:

SR (AH - SH) = $11[13,000 - (4,000 x 3)] = $11(13,000 - 12,000) = $11,000 U

9.      The labour efficiency variance is SR (AH - SH). The standard hours allowed were 15,000 (3,000 units x 5 hours per unit). Mathematically, the $2,400 U variance is $2,400. Thus, the formula is $12(AH - 15,000) = $2,400. One solves this equation with algebra as follows:

12(AH - 15,000) = 2,400

12AH - 180,000 = 2,400

12AH = 182,400

AH = 15,200    The actual labour hours used were 15,200.

10.     Fixed overhead spending variance = Actual fixed overhead cost - Budgeted fixed overhead cost
= 29,340 - 6(5,000) = 29,340 - 30,000 = -$660 = $660 F

Fixed overhead volume variance = Budgeted fixed overhead cost - Applied fixed overhead cost
= 6(5,000) - 6(4,900) = $30,000 - $29,400 = $600 = $600 U

Total fixed overhead variance = Actual fixed overhead cost - Applied fixed overhead cost
= 29,340 - 6(4,900) = 29,340 - 29,400 = -$60 = $60 F or -660 + 600 = -$60 = $60 F

11.     Compute the actual price:  $88,320 ÷ 12,800 kilograms = $6.90

Material price variance = AQ(AP - SP)
= 12,800(6.90 - 7.00) = -$1,280  = $1,280 F

Compute the standard quantity allowed:  2,000 units x 6 kilograms per unit = 12,000 kilograms

Material quantity variance = SP(AQ - SQ)
= 7.00(12,800 - 12,000) =  $5,600 U

Material total variance = -$1,280 + $5,600 = $4,320 U or
AQ(AP) - SQ(SP) = 12,800(6.90) - 12,000(7.00) = $4,320 U

12.     Compute the actual rate:  $39,000 ÷ 3,900 hours = $10.00

Labour rate variance = AH(AR - SR)
= 3,900(10.00 - 9.50) = $1,950 U

Compute the standard hours allowed:  2,000 units x 2 hours per unit = 4,000 hours

Labour efficiency variance = SR(AH - SH)
= 9.50(3,900 - 4,000) = -$950 = $950 F

Total labour variance = $10.00(3,900) - 9.50(4,000) = $1,000 U

13.     Compute the actual variable overhead rate:  $62,400 ÷ 3,900 hours = $16.00 per hour

Variable overhead spending variance = AH(AR - SR)
= 3,900($16.00 - $15.00) = $3,900 U

Variable overhead efficiency variance = SR(AH - SH)
= $15.00(3,900 - 4,000) = -$1,500 = $1,500 F

Total variable overhead variance:
= $16.00(3,900) - $15.00(4,000) = $2,400 U

14.     If the amounts in the variance accounts are not significant, a company should close them to cost of goods sold.  The company will credit the variance accounts with a debit balance for the amount of the balance.  The company will then debit cost of goods sold for the same amounts.  The company will debit the variance accounts with a credit balance for the amount of the balance.  The company will then credit cost of goods sold for the same amounts.

15.     Process costing using standard costing is simpler than using actual costing.  Also, the use of standard costs enables the company to compute variances from standard during the period.  Actual costing requires the computation of a new production cost for each period.  However, a company needs to review its standard costs at least annually.  With standard costing, the computation of equivalent units of production is the same as under FIFO using actual costing.

# CHAPTER 6
# ACTIVITY-BASED MANAGEMENT AND COSTING

## CHAPTER OVERVIEW

Companies that make many products need to use multiple predetermined overhead rates to assign overhead costs to the products.  Companies should develop these rates using the underlying cost drivers.  Activity-based costing helps managers obtain the best possible estimates of product and service costs.  ABC is a part of activity-based management (ABM).  This chapter defines ABC and ABM and illustrates the process of analyzing activities and cost drivers.  This chapter also shows how a company can use the results of the analysis to assign overhead costs more accurately to products and services.  Under certain conditions ABC systems will provide better information than traditional overhead allocations.

Activity-based management focuses on the activities involved in the production/performance process as the way to improve the value customers receive and the profit the company realizes.  Activity-based management concepts also emphasize the interrelationships among functional areas.

Managers seek to reduce or eliminate non-value-added activities to reduce non-value added costs.  Product variety and product or process complexity cause some of these non-value-added activities.  Simultaneous engineering can help companies reduce process complexity.  Another method of reducing process complexity is business process reengineering.  Business process reengineering involves radical changes in business processes to reduce complexity and cost.  Through activity-based costing, management can readily see the cause-effect relationship between activities and costs.  Management then makes use of activity-based management techniques to find ways to reduce or eliminate non-value-added activities.  Activity-based management is important as companies strive for continuous improvement to maintain or obtain a competitive advantage.

## CHAPTER STUDY GUIDE

An activity-based costing (ABC) system has three strategic objectives:  (1) to report accurate costs that can be used to identify the source of firm profits, (2) to identify the cost of activities so that more efficient ways to perform them can be identified, and (3) to identify the future need for resources so that they can be acquired more efficiently.  ABC systems model the way that resources are consumed.

Managers need product or service cost information for three reasons:  (1) to provide information for financial reporting purposes, (2) to make decisions such as pricing and product line expansions or deletions, and (3) to monitor and control operations.  The financial reporting requirements have too often dictated the form that cost information takes for management accounting purposes.  There are two main reasons why the financial reporting requirement has dominated management accounting.  First, generally accepted accounting principles as promulgated by organizations such as the CICA include rules for computing product cost.  Second, companies find that using one product costing system for all three purposes is easier than using multiple product costing systems.

Often, cost information adapted from the financial reporting system does not provide relevant information for managerial decision making.  The financial reporting system requires the cost of inventories and cost of goods sold be reported on an aggregate basis.  Managers need timely and reliable cost information on each product.

Although calculating exact product costs is impossible, managers need the best estimate of how much a product costs.  The best estimate results when the company can trace the largest production or service costs directly to the products or services produced.  Direct tracing requires the use of cost drivers--what causes resource consumption.  Traditionally, companies have traced only direct materials and direct labour to products.  Companies have usually allocated overhead costs to products using volume-based measures such as direct labour hours.  This method was reasonable when manufacturing was more labour intensive.

The modern manufacturing environment, however, is highly machine intensive.  Direct labour costs have fallen while overhead costs have increased.  Using direct labour hours or direct labour cost to allocate overhead costs in the modern manufacturing environment can lead to significant cost distortions.

In a more machine-intensive manufacturing environment, machine hours may be more useful in assigning overhead costs to products.  Using machine hours alone may be inadequate.  The reason is that product variety, product complexity, and other non-volume-based drivers create overhead costs.  Obtaining more accurate product costs requires the use of multiple allocation bases.  Computers and other technological advances have made the processing of cost information much easier.  Exhibit 6-1 illustrates cost distortions in a machine-intensive environment.

Although the accounting department develops product or service costs, these costs have an impact on corporate strategy.  Thus, product costs affect decisions made in the marketing, production, and finance departments.  ABC traces costs to the products that cause them, providing a much more accurate picture.

Theoretically, product costs would not matter as long as customers would pay the price set by the company, which would provide an acceptable profit.  This concept presents two problems.  First, customers buy a product or service only if they believe that the value provided by the product or service justifies its cost.  Second, competitive forces in the market decide prices.  Companies attempt to provide a quality product along with good service to increase the perception of the product's value to customers.  Since the market decides prices, management must be concerned about controlling costs to ensure an adequate profit.

Managers can use activity-based management (ABM) to help them increase the customer value of a product or service and increase the resulting profit.  ABM helps to increase the company's efficiency and effectiveness and compute more accurate costs.  Activity-based management is closely related to total quality management and business process reengineering.  Exhibit 6-2 lists some concepts that come under the umbrella of activity-based management.  The company should incorporate activity-based management with strategic planning and the company's cost management system.  Management should view the concepts under the ABM umbrella as integral parts of the company's customer focus and long-run financial success.  Exhibit 6-3 illustrates process-driven improvement.

Activity-based management requires an analysis of the company's activities.  Activities are the actions, movements, or work sequences that a company performs to fulfill business functions.  A company can use a process map to detail all activities involved in a specific process.  Some process maps are value charts because they show the time spent in each activity and assess the value of each activity.  Exhibit 6-4 illustrates a value chart.

Companies can classify activities as value-added activities, business-value-added activities, or non-value-added activities.  Activities are value-added if they increase the worth of a product or service in the eyes of customers.  The time spent in value-added activities is the value-added processing or service time.

Non-value-added activities add to the time spent in making and delivering a product, but they do not increase the worth of the product to customers. Non-value-added activities are wasteful and cause unnecessary costs. Non-value-added activities include transfer time, idle time, and inspection time. By reducing or even eliminating non-value-added activities, managers can reduce their costs while providing products that customers want.

Some non-value-added activities, however, are essential to the company's operations, but customers would not willingly pay for such activities. These activities are business-value-added activities. A required audit is an example of a business-value-added activity.

Cycle time or lead time is the time from the receipt of an order to its completion (or possibly delivery). Cycle time is equal to value-added processing time plus non-value-added time. Manufacturing cycle efficiency is equal to value-added processing time divided by cycle time.

A typical company has a manufacturing cycle efficiency of only 10 percent. Thus, companies have the potential for increasing their efficiency and reducing costs by reducing non-value-added activities. The use of a just-in-time manufacturing system is one way to reduce idle time and increase manufacturing cycle efficiency. A just-in-time system attempts to eliminate excess inventory and waste.

For a retail company, cycle time refers to the time from a customer's order to the sale. Non-value-added activities include the shipping time from the supplier, delays in counting the products in the receiving department, and storage time. In a service firm, cycle time is the time between the service order and the completion of the service. All activities other than the actual performance of the service are non-value-added.

Non-value-added activities are attributable to systemic, physical, and human factors. Managers should focus on all these factors and direct their efforts to reducing the non-value-added activities that cause the most unnecessary costs. Exhibit 6-5 shows various opportunities for improving activities.

A measure of an activity that directly causes the company to incur a cost is a cost driver. In controlling costs, managers should identify a reasonable number of cost drivers. Also, managers should ensure that the additional benefits of more accurate costs exceed the cost of measuring the selected cost drivers. Also, the cost drivers selected should be easy to understand, directly related to the activity performed, and appropriate for performance measurement.

As compared to traditional cost accounting methodology, ABC provides the ability to more directly observe where, how, and why costs are incurred. With traditional costing, departmental expenses are typically allocated directly to products. With ABC, costs are first traced to the activities associated with them and are then assigned to products.

The three underlying elements of ABC are as follows: (1) accumulating costs into related cost pools, (2) knowing that various activity and cost levels exist, and (3) using multiple cost drivers to assign costs to products and services. Activity-based costing is an accounting system that uses activities to collect costs by examining the underlying nature and extent of those activities. ABC assigns costs to products and services based on the activities used to make, perform, distribute, or support products and services. Exhibit 6-6 illustrates the relationship between ABM and ABC.

In a traditional cost system, companies accumulate overhead costs into one or two cost pools. Then the company uses only volume-based measures such as direct labour hours to assign overhead costs to products. The ABC method of collecting costs allows a more detailed understanding of how the company can control costs. Exhibit 6-7 compares the traditional and the ABM focus on sales order department activities.

To reflect more complex environments, companies must recognize that they incur costs at different levels and revise their accounting systems accordingly.  There are four levels of costs:  (1) unit level costs, (2) batch level costs, (3) product or process level costs, and (4) organizational or facility level costs.  Unit-level costs result from the production or acquisition of one unit of product or the delivery of one unit of a service.  Batch-level costs occur when a company makes, handles, or processes a group of similar products simultaneously.  Activities such as developing products, processing engineering change orders, and maintaining production specifications create product- or process-level costs.  Costs incurred to support and sustain a business unit are organizational- or facility-level costs.

Traditionally, companies treated costs that did not vary with units as fixed costs.  Activity-based management recognizes that a company incurs some of its costs at the three higher levels.  Activity-based systems often refer to fixed costs as long-term variable costs.  Long-term variable costs are basically step fixed costs.  Companies should assign costs in the first three levels to products.  Although assigning organizational- or facility-level costs to products is generally not appropriate, some companies do assign these costs to products on some arbitrary basis.  Exhibit 6-8 defines these four levels of costs and gives examples of each.  In addition, Exhibit 6-9 illustrates how companies can assign costs at each of the first three levels to products and that companies should usually not assign organizational- or facility-level costs to products.

In an activity-based cost system, companies accumulate costs in activity center cost pools.  An activity center is a segment for which managers want a cost report.  Companies accumulate costs with the same driver in pools based on the level of cost incurrence.  If the company can reduce or eliminate the driver, then it will also reduce or eliminate its corresponding cost.  In addition, accumulating costs in activity center cost pools allows managers to see the cross-functional activities involved in cost incurrence.  Exhibit 6-10 illustrates the horizontal flow of work activities.

After the company accumulates costs in activity center cost pools, the company assigns the costs to products using an activity cost driver. Exhibit 6-11 shows typical activity drivers for various activity centers.  The company will assign unit-level costs to products using a volume-based cost driver.  The company will charge costs incurred at higher levels to products using volume-based cost drivers, but the volume measure should include only those units related to the batch or product/process and not total production.  Exhibit 6-12 illustrates how an activity-based costing system traces costs to products.

The textbook provides a detailed illustration of activity-based costing.  Table 6-1 provides a breakdown of manufacturing costs for Abbott Cosmetics Ltd.  Table 6-2 provides annual production information for the three products produced.  Table 6-3 presents the unit cost for each product under traditional costing.

ABC requires an investigation of each production department to determine (a) how much time personnel actually spend on each product and (b) what factor drives costs in that department.  Table 6-4 provides the activity-based cost information for Abbott Cosmetics Ltd.  Table 6-5 presents the unit cost for each product under activity-based costing and compares it to the unit cost for each product under traditional costing.  This comparison shows how traditional cost systems distort product costs.

Biased product cost information may lead to poor strategic decisions by management.  Table 6-5 provides a price and markup analysis.  A forward-looking attribute of ABC is that it yields better information for setting appropriate prices and determining the cost and profit impact of different product mixes.  With traditional costing, a company may inappropriately assume that a particular product is contributing more profit than it actually is.

Although activity-based costing is a useful cost system, it may not be appropriate for all companies. Traditional, volume-based cost systems provide accurate and useful information for some companies. Two key underlying assumptions of ABC are (1) homogeneous activities in each cost pool drive the costs, and (2) the costs in each cost pool are proportional to the activity. If these assumptions are valid, then ABC will be beneficial under the following conditions: (1) product/service variety or complexity is significant; (2) a lack of commonality characterizes the creation and use of overhead; (3) problems exist with current cost allocations; and (4) the environment in which the company operates has changed considerably. Exhibit 6-13 presents a comparison of the allocation of overhead costs to standard, moderate, and premium products using a traditional method and using ABC.

Two factors often associated with a need to consider an ABC system are product/service variety and complexity. Product variety refers to the number of different products that the company makes. Service variety refers to the number of different types of services provided. Exhibit 6-14 illustrates the potential additional overhead costs with an increase in product variety. Changes in overhead costs caused by increased product variety show costs that are apparently fixed are in fact long-term variable costs.

Some companies are using flexible manufacturing systems to provide mass customization of products to customers at a low cost. Mass customization has several potential problems: (1) customers have too many choices; (2) a tremendous opportunity for errors exists; and (3) customers often make selections from a small percentage of the available choices.

Another important factor to consider is product complexity. Product complexity refers to the number of components, operations, or processes used in making a particular product. Management can reduce product complexity by standardizing the company's products and processes and reducing the number of different components, tools, and processes required. Management should ask whether the company can use common parts without reducing quality. If so, the company can reduce complexity by using common parts. If not, management should ask whether customers are willing to pay a premium price to cover the higher costs of using low-volume components.

Process complexity may develop over time or be due to inadequate planning in product development. Process complexity involves many non-value-added activities and thus reflects significant non-value-added costs. A process is complex if it creates difficulties for the people performing production operations or using manufacturing machinery.

A company can use simultaneous (or concurrent) engineering to reduce both product complexity and process complexity. Simultaneous engineering refers to the continuous involvement of all primary functions and personnel from the beginning of a project. Design for manufacturability occurs when a multifunctional team considers customer requirements, vendor capabilities, common parts, and production process compatibility in the design of a product.

Although a company may use simultaneous engineering, process complexity can still develop over time. Business process reengineering or process innovation and redesign is one way to overcome process complexity. Business process reengineering includes making drastic changes in production processes to realize significant cost, service, or time reductions.

Unlike traditional cost systems, activity-based cost systems account for the number of different parts used in making a product. Activity-based cost systems provide important information concerning cost drivers and relationships among activities to those involved in reengineering efforts. Thus, reengineering efforts can focus on the primary causes of process complexity and those activities that create the greatest amount of waste.

Another cause of significant overhead costs is a variety of support services.  Examples of these support services include advertising, distribution channels, and the use of high-technology machinery.

Distortions in product costs occur when a company uses only one or two cost pools to allocate overhead costs.  A company would allocate overhead costs related to a specific product among all products.  This practice leads to higher costs for products that are not responsible for such costs.  The distortion is not usually significant if production volumes for all products are fairly similar.  When production volumes are significantly different, greater cost distortion will occur.

A company should consider setting up an activity-based cost system when any of the following occurs: (1) the use of automation increases in the production process, (2) the competitive environment changes, and (3) management strategies change.

As companies use more automation in production, cost systems based on direct labour become less valid. Using a cost system based on direct labour, a company would charge too little overhead to products made with automated equipment and charge too much overhead to products made with a large amount of direct labour.

When competition increases, management needs accurate product costs to know whether prices can be adjusted while maintaining adequate profit margins.  Competition may increase because of three reasons:  (1) other companies recognize the profit potential of a particular product or service; (2) the product or service has become cost effective to produce; and (3) government has deregulated the industry.

The need for more accurate product costs may accompany changes in management strategies. Management may want to know the effects of their decisions on product costs.  For example, if management wants to start new operations, the cost system needs to provide information on how costs will change.  The traditional separation of costs into fixed or variable may not provide accurate information.

Another problem with traditional cost systems is that they often ignore period costs and place too much emphasis on product costs.  Activity-based costing recognizes that companies can trace some period costs to particular products.

An activity-based cost system can help in a company's quest for continuous improvement.  An activity-based cost system shows the relationship between cost drivers and costs.  Management can use this information to reduce or eliminate non-value-added activities.  Reducing non-value-added activities reduces costs, eliminates waste, and increases profits.  The increase in profits may not be immediate; lower costs do not occur until management reduces or redeploys excess resources.  If management is unable to make changes based on ABC information, then the company will not realize the benefits from ABC information.

The number of companies using activity-based costing is growing.  Technologies such as personal computers, bar coding, and software packages have made ABC systems feasible for many companies.  Most companies that use ABC employ it to make operational and strategic decisions.

ABC is as applicable to the service sector as it is to the manufacturing sector.  Within the service sector, managers need to make decisions on proper resource allocation and product offering mix and diversity, as well as evaluate client profitability.

One difference between service organizations and manufacturing organizations is that there tends to be a much higher use of time-related or duration cost drivers as opposed to transaction-based cost drivers such as the number of setups or inspections.

Although activity-based costing provides better cost information, it does not provide exact product costs or solve all of management's problems.  In addition, several problems accompany the implementation of an activity-based cost system.

Activity-based cost systems require a large investment in time and money.  Implementation requires substantial support throughout the organization.  The company must overcome individual, organizational, and environmental barriers to change for the implementation to be successful.  Individual barriers often relate to (1) fear of the unknown, (2) a possible loss of status, and (3) the need to learn new skills.  Organizational barriers could be associated with territorial, hierarchical, or corporate culture issues.  Employee groups such as unions, regulatory agencies, or other stakeholders may raise environmental barriers.

Management must recognize the barriers, investigate their causes, and communicate information about activity-based costing to the concerned parties.  Commitment to the implementation process by top management is imperative.  The company must educate managers and other employees about the new terminology, concepts, and performance measures accompanying the ABC implementation.  The company will need more time to analyze the activities, trace costs to those activities, and determine the cost drivers.

Another problem with an activity-based cost system is that costs reported under ABC do not conform specifically with generally accepted accounting principles (GAAP).  Exhibit 6-15 shows differences between inventoriable indirect costs in GAAP and ABC.  Consequently, most companies with an ABC system use it in addition to their cost systems for financial reporting purposes.

Another criticism of ABC is that it does not support total quality management and continuous improvement.  This criticism has merit only if companies view ABC as a panacea for all their problems.  Companies can use ABM and ABC, however, as companions to such world-class methodologies as total quality management, just-in-time systems, and business process reengineering.  Activity-based costing and activity-based management can promote continuous improvement, reduce lead times, and enhance flexible manufacturing by helping managers do the following:  (1) recognize and monitor major technology costs, (2) trace many technology costs to products, (3) increase market share through target costing, (4) identify cost drivers, (5) identify non-value-added activities, (6) understand the effect of new technologies on all aspects of performance, (7) translate company goals into activity goals, (8) analyze performance of activities across business functions, (9) analyze performance problems, and (10) foster standards of excellence.  Activity-based costing is one tool that managers can use to compete successfully in the global economy.

## SELF TEST

TRUE/FALSE

1.  T  F  In most cases, cost information extracted from the financial accounting system will provide relevant information for managerial decision making.

2.  T  F  Product variety and product complexity often cause overhead costs.

3.  T  F  Activities are repetitive actions, movements, or work sequences performed to fulfill a business function.

4.  T  F  Value-added activities increase a product's perceived worth in the view of the customer.

5.  T  F  Moving products from one place to another during production is considered to be a value-added activity.

6.  T  F  Determining exact product costs is easy with activity-based costing.

7.  T  F  A cost caused by the development, production, or acquisition of a type of product is a unit-level cost.

8.  T  F  The time taken to move products or components from one place to another is called idle time.

9.  T  F  Business process reengineering involves radical changes and innovations in business processes.

10.  T  F  Costs reported under an activity-based costing system usually do not conform strictly to generally accepted accounting principles.

11.  T  F  Customers are willing to pay for business-value-added activities.

12.  T  F  Mass customization involves the use of flexible manufacturing systems to produce customized products at relatively low cost.

13.  T  F  Only a few small companies have implemented activity-based costing systems.

14.  T  F  Activity-based costing recognizes that companies should trace some period costs to particular products for internal purposes.

15.  T  F  Historically, managers have considered long-term variable costs as fixed costs.


MULTIPLE CHOICE

1.  What is the philosophy that deals with performing production, purchasing, or delivery on an as-needed basis?

      A.  activity-based management
      B.  activity-based costing
      C.  just-in-time
      D.  concurrent engineering

2.  A measure of the demands placed on activities and the resources consumed by products and services is called a(n):

      A.  activity object.
      B.  activity cost driver.
      C.  activity centre.
      D.  value chart

3.  Which of the following is a value-added activity?

      A.  inspection time
      B.  idle time
      C.  processing time
      D.  transfer time

4. The time from the receipt of an order to the completion of a product or service is:

    A.  cycle time.
    B.  processing time.
    C.  idle time.
    D.  transfer time.

5. Cycle time equals value-added production time:

    A.  minus non-value-added time.
    B.  plus non-value-added time.
    C.  plus value-added time.
    D.  minus value-added time.

6. What is the highest manufacturing cycle efficiency (MCE) achieved at most companies?

    A.  10%
    B.  20%
    C.  50%
    D.  80%

7. Costs created when a company makes, handles, or processes a group of things at a single time are:

    A.  unit-level costs.
    B.  batch-level costs.
    C.  product-level costs.
    D.  organizational-level costs.

8. Another term for simultaneous engineering is:

    A.  business process engineering.
    B.  reverse engineering.
    C.  concurrent engineering.
    D.  just-in-time.

9. In the second stage of cost allocation in an activity-based cost system, a company assigns costs to:

    A.  products and services.
    B.  activity centre cost pools.
    C.  paid in capital.
    D.  retained earnings.

10. Many people have come to view fixed costs as:

    A.  not worthy of management's attention.
    B.  short-term variable cost.
    C.  long-term mixed costs.
    D.  long-term variable costs.

11. In a perfect environment, manufacturing cycle efficiency would be:

    A. 0%.
    B. 20%.
    C. 80%.
    D. 100%.

12. The use of automation:

    A. increases direct labour cost and decreases overhead cost.
    B. increases direct labour cost and increases overhead cost.
    C. decreases direct labour cost and decreases overhead cost.
    D. decreases direct labour cost and increases overhead cost.

13. Activity-based costing allows managers to recognize the _____ flow of products and services through an organization.

    A. upward
    B. diagonal
    C. horizontal
    D. downward

14. Companies use activity-based costing primarily for:

    A. preparing the financial statements for external users.
    B. preparing the tax return.
    C. managerial decision making.
    D. all of the above.

15. Which of the following defines process innovation and redesign aimed at finding and implementing radical changes in how the company makes products or performs tasks to achieve significant cost, service, or time reductions?

    A. activity-based management
    B. activity-based costing
    C. simultaneous engineering
    D. business process reengineering

16. Increased competition may occur because:

    A. other companies recognize a product's profit potential.
    B. the product is cost-feasible to produce.
    C. the industry has been deregulated.
    D. all of the above.

17. Which of the following is a unit-level cost?

    A. direct materials
    B. machine setup
    C. plant depreciation
    D. product design

18.  A cost caused by the development, production, or acquisition of a type of product is a(n):

    A.  unit-level cost.
    B.  batch-level cost.
    C.  product-level cost.
    D.  organizational-level cost.

19.  Which of the following is a batch-level cost?

    A.  engineering change orders
    B.  inspection
    C.  plant manager's salary
    D.  direct labour

20.  What highlights value-added and non-value added activities and the time spent in those activities from the beginning of a process to its end?

    A.  value chart
    B.  process map
    C.  simultaneous engineering report
    D.  cost driver analysis

21.  After initial recording, a company using an ABC system assigns costs to:

    A.  activity centre cost pools.
    B.  functional departments.
    C.  investment centres.
    D.  products and services.

22.  Companies need product cost information to:

    A.  report to external parties.
    B.  help in product decisions.
    C.  allow managerial control over operations.
    D.  all of the above.

23.  The concept of _____ focuses on the activities performed during the production/performance process as the way to improve value received by customers and the resulting profit to the company.

    A.  flexible manufacturing
    B.  activity-based management
    C.  concurrent engineering
    D.  process maps

24.  Activity-based costing and activity-based management can be useful for:

    A.  long-term decisions only.
    B.  short-term decisions only.
    C.  long-term and short-term decisions.
    D.  preparation of external financial statements only.

25.  Which of the following is an integrated approach toward the continuous involvement of all the primary business functions and personnel that contribute toward a product's design and production?

    A.  business-process reengineering
    B.  simultaneous engineering
    C.  activity-based management
    D.  business-value-added activities

26.  Mass customization is the production at a relatively low cost of a variety of products made to customers' specifications using:

    A.  flexible manufacturing systems.
    B.  reverse engineering.
    C.  activity-based management.
    D.  business process engineering.

27.  Who mandates how companies should develop product costs for product decisions and managerial control over operations?

    A.  the Canadian Institute of Chartered Accountants
    B.  the Society of Management Accountants of Canada
    C.  the Canada Customs and Revenue Agency
    D.  no one

28.  In analyzing activities, managers should prepare a _____ that indicates the activities performed in making or doing something.

    A.  cost of good manufactured statement
    B.  value chart
    C.  process map
    D.  product complexity report

29. Waterhouse Company completed production of an order for a customer five days after receiving the order. The five days consisted of the equivalent of one day of value-added production time and four days of non-value added time. What was the manufacturing cycle efficiency for this order?

    A.  20%
    B.  25%
    C.  80%
    D.  500%

30.  Sisung Company produces three products. Each of its 400 units of gizmos produced costs $14.00 in direct materials and $6.50 in direct labour. Total setup costs for 10 setups for all three products were $2,000. Of these 10 setups, gizmos required 2 setups. Other overhead costs for all products made by Sisung Company relate to the usage of machines. These overhead costs total $30,000 for all three products. Sisung used 6,000 machine hours in making all three of its products. Each gizmo requires two machine hours to make. What is the per-unit cost for gizmos using activity-based costing?

    A.  $20.50
    B.  $26.50
    C.  $31.17
    D.  $31.50

## ESSAY QUESTIONS AND PROBLEMS

1.  Why do managers need product or service cost information?

2.  Define value-added activities, non-value-added activities, and business-value-added activities. Give examples of each.

3.  To what factors can management attribute non-value-added activities? What should be the focus of reducing non-value-added activities?

4.  What factors should management consider in determining the cost drivers the company should use in allocating overhead in an activity-based cost system?

5.  Define the four different levels of costs in an activity-based costing system.  Give examples of each.

6.  Under what conditions could an activity-based costing system be beneficial to a company?

7.  Explain how activity-based costing and activity-based management can be useful for making short-term decisions.

8.  Explain how simultaneous engineering and business process reengineering can reduce process complexity.

9.  What are the three underlying elements of activity-based costing?

10.  What is mass customization? What are some potential problems with mass customization?

11.  Define product complexity and process complexity.

12.  How can activity-based management and activity-based costing encourage product improvement, reduce lead times, and enhance flexible manufacturing?

13. Veller Company took 10 days from the receipt of a customer's order to ship the order. Veller Company spent those 10 days as follows:

value-added production time: 2.5 days
transfer time: 3.5 days
idle time: 1 day
inspection time: 3 days

Calculate Veller Company's manufacturing cycle efficiency for this order.

## USE THE FOLLOWING INFORMATION TO ANSWER PROBLEMS 14 AND 15

Allen Company produces two versions of its product – the regular model and the premium model. Allen produces the regular model on a regular basis. However, Allen produces the premium model only upon customer request. Production costs and other information are as follows:

|  | Regular | Premium |
|---|---|---|
| Direct materials and direct labour | $105,000 | $20,000 |
| | | |
| Number of setups | 70 | 50 |
| Machine hours | 25,000 | 5,000 |
| Direct labour hours | 5,000 | 600 |
| Total number of units produced | 10,000 | 1,000 |

| Overhead Costs: | Both Products |
|---|---|
| Machine setup cost | $ 33,600 |
| Machine processing costs | 168,000 |
| Total overhead costs | $201,600 |

14. If Allen uses direct labour hours to allocate all overhead costs, what will be the total production costs charged to each product? What will be the total per-unit cost for each product?

15.  If Allen uses the number of setups to allocate machine setup costs and machine hours to allocate machine processing costs, what will be the total production costs charged to each product? What will be the total per-unit cost for each product?

## SELF TEST ANSWERS

### TRUE/FALSE

| 1. | F | 4. | T | 7. | F | 10. | T | 13. | F |
|----|---|----|---|----|---|-----|---|-----|---|
| 2. | T | 5. | F | 8. | F | 11. | F | 14. | T |
| 3. | T | 6. | F | 9. | T | 12. | T | 15. | T |

### MULTIPLE CHOICE

| 1. | C | 7. | B | 13. | C | 19. | B | 25. | B |
|----|---|----|---|-----|---|-----|---|-----|---|
| 2. | B | 8. | C | 14. | C | 20. | A | 26. | A |
| 3. | C | 9. | A | 15. | D | 21. | A | 27. | D |
| 4. | A | 11. | D | 16. | D | 22. | D | 28. | C |
| 5. | B | 11. | D | 17. | A | 23. | B | 29. | A |
| 6. | A | 12. | D | 18. | C | 24. | C | 30. | D |

## ESSAY QUESTIONS AND PROBLEMS

1.      Managers need product or service cost information for three reasons: (1) to provide information for financial reporting to shareholders and regulatory bodies, (2) to make decisions such as pricing and product line expansions or deletions, and (3) to monitor and control operations.

2.      An activity is a value-added activity if it increases the worth of the product or service in the eyes of the customer. Because the customer perceives the value of the activity, the customer is willing to pay for it. The time spent actually producing a product or providing a service is usually a value-added activity. Activities that do not add to the product's worth in the eyes of the customer are non-value added activities. Inspecting the product and moving it between work stations are examples of non-value-added activities. Business-value-added activities are activities that are essential to the company's operations even though customers are not willing to pay for such activities. An example of a business-value-added activity is the preparation of a bill to send to the customer.

3.      Management can attribute non-value-added activities to systemic, physical, and human factors. Systemic factors relate to the requirements of the system. Physical factors often relate to the layout of the plant. Human factors can contribute to non-value-added activities because of poor skills, poor training, poor morale, or the need to be sociable. Companies should focus on the non-value-added activities that cause the most unnecessary costs. Non-value-added activities are wasteful. Reducing waste leads to higher profits.

4.　　　Management should keep the number of cost drivers used to a reasonable number. The cost of measuring the cost driver should be reasonable. The system may already generate some cost driver information. If so, these may be preferable to similar cost drivers that the accounting system does not produce. Cost drivers should be understandable, directly related to the activities they measure, and useful for performance evaluation.

5.　　　Four levels of costs characterize an activity-based costing system: (1) unit-level costs, (2) batch-level costs, (3) product- or process-level costs, and (4) organizational- or facility-level costs. Unit-level costs result from the production or acquisition of one unit of product or the delivery of one unit of a service. Examples include direct materials and direct labour. Batch-level costs occur when a company makes, handles, or processes a group of similar products at the same time. Examples are machine setup and movement of work in processes. Activities such as developing products, processing engineering change orders, and maintaining production specifications create product- or process-level costs. Examples include engineering change orders, maintenance, and product development. Costs incurred to support and sustain a business unit are organizational- or facility-level costs. Examples include the plant manager's salary and depreciation on the building.

6.　　　An activity-based costing system may be beneficial to a company under the following conditions: (1) product/service variety or complexity is significant; (2) a lack of commonality characterizes the creation and use of overhead; (3) problems exist with current costs allocations; and (4) the environment in which the company operates has changed considerably. Two factors often associated with a need to consider an ABC system are product/service variety and complexity.

7.　　　Activity-based costing and activity-based management provide management with the cost of activities. Management can see how reducing non-value-added activities can reduce costs. Managers can implement programs to reduce or eliminate non-value-added activities and thereby reduce costs and waste.

8.　　　Simultaneous engineering refers to the continuous involvement of all primary functions and personnel from the beginning of a project. Design for manufacturability occurs when a multifunctional team considers customer requirements, vendor capabilities, common parts, and production process compatibility in the design of a product.

　　　Although a company may use simultaneous engineering, process complexity can still develop over time. Business process reengineering, or process innovation and redesign, is one way to overcome process complexity. Business process reengineering includes making drastic changes in production processes to realize significant cost, service, or time reductions. Business process reengineering ignores the way the company currently performs processes and asks how the company should perform them.

9.　　　The three underlying elements of ABC are as follows: (1) accumulating costs into related cost pools, (2) knowing that various activity and cost levels exist, and (3) using multiple cost drivers to assign costs to products and services.

10.　　　Mass customization is providing mass production of relatively low-cost products tailored to the specifications of individual customers. Companies use flexible manufacturing systems to effect mass customization. Mass customization has a number of potential problems: (1) customers have too many choices; (2) a tremendous opportunity for errors exists; and (3) customers often make selections from a small percentage of the available choices.

11.　　　Product complexity refers to the number of components, operations, or processes used in making a particular product. Process complexity may develop over time or be due to inadequate planning in product development. Process complexity involves numerous non-value-added activities and thus reflects significant non-value-added costs. A process is complex if it creates difficulties for the people performing production operations or using manufacturing machinery.

12.     Activity-based management and activity-based costing can promote continuous improvement, reduce lead times, and enhance flexible manufacturing by helping managers do the following: (1) recognize and monitor major technology costs, (2) trace many technology costs to products, (3) increase market share through target costing, (4) identify cost drivers, (5) identify non-value-added activities, (6) understand the effect of new technologies on all aspects of performance, (7) translate company goals into activity goals, (8) analyze performance of activities across business functions, (9) analyze performance problems, and (10) foster standards of excellence.

13.     Manufacturing cycle efficiency is equal to value-added production time divided by cycle time. Cycle time is the time that elapses from the receipt of an order until its shipment. Thus, the cycle time is 10 days for this order. Transfer time, idle time, and inspection time are not value-added. Thus, the manufacturing cycle efficiency for Veller Company for this order was 25 percent (2.5 days ÷ 10 days).

14.

| | Regular | Premium |
|---|---|---|
| Direct materials and direct labour | $ 105,000 | $20,000 |
| Overhead costs: | | |
| $201,600 ÷ 5,600 DLH = $36.00 per DLH | | |
| $36.00 per DLH x 5,000 DLH | 108,000 | |
| $36.00 per DLH x   600 DLH | | 21,600 |
| Total Production Costs | $285,000 | $41,660 |
| Divided by the number of units | 10,000 | 1, 000 |
| Per-unit cost | $  28.50 | $  41.66 |

15.

| | Regular | Premium |
|---|---|---|
| Direct materials and direct labour | $105,000 | $20,000 |
| Overhead costs: | | |
| Machine setup: | | |
| $33,600 ÷ 120 setups = $280 per setup | | |
| $280 per setup x 70 setups | 19,600 | |
| $280 per setup x 50 setups | | 14,000 |
| Machine processing: | | |
| $168,000 ÷ 30,000 MH = $5.60 per MH | | |
| $5.60 per MH x 25,000 MH | 140,000 | |
| $5.60 per MH x  5,000 HM | | 28,000 |
| Total production costs | $264,600 | $62,000 |
| Divided by the number of units | 10,000 | 1,000 |
| Per-unit cost | $  26.46 | $62.00 |

# CHAPTER 7
# CONTROLLING COSTS

## CHAPTER OVERVIEW

Companies need to generate revenues and control all costs. Effective cost control encompasses efforts before, during, and after a cost is incurred. A cost control system is used to analyze and control costs.

Companies are seeking to reduce their costs of buying and producing inventory to be more competitive in today's marketplace. The investment in inventory causes carrying costs and provides no return until the company sells the goods.

Companies have developed several techniques to reduce their investment in inventory and its associated costs. These techniques include ABC inventory analysis, economic order quantity (EOQ), materials requirement planning (MRP), manufacturing resource planning (MRP II), and just-in-time (JIT) systems. This chapter discusses each of these techniques. This chapter also discusses the traditional ideas of order point and safety stock. Backflush costing is illustrated and described. The chapter also discusses cost control issues arising from the product life cycle.

Target costing and value engineering are specific tools that drive interorganizational information sharing in designing new products. These tools facilitate cost management across the value creation chain in the life cycle design stage.

## CHAPTER STUDY GUIDE

A cost control system must perform at three points: (1) before an event, (2) during an event, and (3) after an event. An event could be a time period, production or sale of a product, or the performance of a service. Exhibit 7-1 lists the methods that a cost control system uses to fulfill its functions. Cost control is a continual process that requires the support of all employees at all times. Thus, as shown in Exhibit 7-2, a good cost control system includes cost consciousness, which is the attitude of all employees regarding cost understanding, cost containment, cost avoidance, and cost reduction.

The first exercise in cost control is the development of an expectation for that cost. Expectations provide standards against which management can compare actual costs. Effective cost control and expectation development require management understanding of the reasons why actual costs differed from expected costs.

Several reasons account for changes in costs. For example, total variable costs and mixed costs change with changes in the activity level. Three other reasons for changes in costs are (1) different-from-expected quantities purchased, (2) inflation or deflation, and (3) changes in supply or supplier cost adjustments.

Changes in quantities purchased can affect unit costs because of changes in quantity discounts. Inflation or deflation reflects changes in the general price level. Inflation or deflation affects prices for almost all goods and services. Some companies, especially those with long production times, include provisions in contracts that increase prices to compensate for inflation before delivery. Changes in supply or the price charged for specific goods may change due to changes in demand and technology. Other reasons for changes in the cost of goods and services are taxes, the cost of complying with government regulations, and the number of suppliers of a product or service. Managers must understand the reasons for a change in costs to control costs effectively.

Price fixing occurs when companies unethically agree to keep prices at a certain level. The two basic types of price fixing are vertical price fixing and horizontal price fixing. Vertical price fixing (resale price maintenance) occurs when a company and its distributors agree to control the prices charged to consumers. Vertical price fixing is against the law. Horizontal price fixing occurs when competitors attempt to control prices or the quantity of goods produced or offered for sale.

Cost containment is a method of cost control that attempts to minimize the increases in per-unit variable costs and total fixed costs from one period to the next. Cost containment is difficult for cost changes stemming from inflation, tax and regulatory changes, and supply and demand adjustments because these factors are outside the company's control.

Increased costs due to reduced competition among suppliers, seasonality, and quantities purchased are subject to cost containment activities. A company should look for ways to limit increases in costs because of these factors. Purchasing agents may choose alternative suppliers that have lower costs, but they should consider other factors besides price.

If cost containment is not possible, the company could probably control costs through cost avoidance. Cost avoidance is finding acceptable alternatives to high-cost items and not spending money on unnecessary goods or services. Avoiding one cost may require that a company incur a lower, alternative cost.

Another tool for cost control is cost reduction. Cost reduction means lowering current costs especially unnecessary costs. Cost reduction efforts focus on eliminating or reducing non-value-added activities.

Many companies think that cost reduction always means labour reduction. Reducing a company's labour force can sometimes create other problems. If the terminated employees were performing a value-added task, a company may reduce its ability to do important tasks. Companies are starting to see their personnel needs from a strategic staffing perspective, which requires that departments analyze their personnel needs by considering long-term objectives and determining a specific combination of employees that will best meet those needs. Companies can hire temporaries for peak periods, special projects, and specific expertise. Companies also hire temporaries to work until they find appropriate permanent employees.

Companies can also reduce costs by outsourcing certain activities or services instead of maintaining internal departments. Information technology, internal auditing, legal and travel services, and accounting are good candidates for outsourcing. Companies should not outsource core competencies or activities needed for competitive advantage.

Exhibit 7-3 shows five steps in implementing a cost control system. These five steps require that managers do the following: (1) understand the types of costs that the organization incurs, (2) communicate the need for cost consciousness to all employees, (3) motivate employees by education and incentives to engage in cost control, (4) generate reports that compare actual results to budget, and (5) view the cost control system as a long-run process not as a short-run solution.

Management needs to maximize its attention to the most important inventory items and minimize the attention given to the least important items. One way management can do this is through ABC analysis (not to be confused with activity-based costing). ABC analysis separates inventory into three categories based on annual cost-to-volume usage. Management designates items with the highest dollar volume as A, items with moderate dollar volume as B, and items with the lowest dollar volume as C. The degree of control management exerts over the inventory items depends on their classification. Management exerts the most control over A items and often accounts for them using a perpetual inventory system. C items receive the least control. Exhibit 7-4 gives the results of a typical ABC inventory analysis.

Management may use simple techniques for managing items in the C category. Two such techniques are the two-bin system and the red-line system. Under a two-bin system, when the first bin or container for the item is empty, the company begins using the second bin and places an order or produces enough to fill the first container. Under the red-line system, a company uses a single container. A red line painted on the container shows the reorder point. When the inventory of the item drops below the red line, the company places an order or produces enough to fill the container.

For items in the B category, the level of control will depend on management's judgment. Such judgment will depend on how crucial the item is in the production process, how rapidly suppliers respond to orders, and a comparison of the costs and benefits of additional controls. Advances in technology have reduced the costs of inventory controls.

The three basic costs associated with inventory are (1) purchase or production, (2) ordering or setup, (3) carrying or not carrying goods in stock. Exhibit 7-5 shows the elements of each of these costs. The company records the purchase or production cost in the inventory account.

Purchase costs include the contract purchase price plus shipping and insurance charges while the items are in transit and net of any discounts. Production costs for a manufacturing company include costs for direct materials, direct labour, traceable manufacturing overhead, and allocated fixed manufacturing overhead. Ordering costs are the incremental costs incurred for preparing, receiving, and paying for an order. Carrying costs include costs for storage, insurance, property taxes, handling, losses from obsolescence or theft, and the opportunity cost for capital invested in inventory. A manufacturing company's setup costs include labour, machine downtime, and other costs incurred to set up a production run.

Excess inventory generates costs as does a fully depleted inventory. A company incurs stockout cost when it does not have the inventory available to satisfy a customer's demand. Stockout cost includes lost customer goodwill, lost contribution margin, and the ordering and shipping costs incurred to fill special orders. Because stockout cost is an opportunity cost, companies do not record it in their books. Companies also often ignore the opportunity cost resulting from any possible loss from inventory obsolescence or damage.

A purchasing manager has to make three decisions in purchasing inventory: (1) from whom, (2) how much, and (3) when. The supplier with the lowest price is not necessarily the best supplier for the long run. A purchasing manager should also consider quality and reliability when selecting suppliers. Many companies are now viewing suppliers as partners rather than as adversaries. Moving to the partnership view requires time and effort as well as trust in the supplier or the purchaser. A company works with its vendors to assure quality, improve service, and reduce costs.

Vendors (suppliers) must be willing to make frequent deliveries in small quantities. Long-term contracts with vendors help to keep prices low and to ensure a reliable supply source. A sharing of information about each entity's processes is also necessary. To build worthwhile relationships, purchasers should help vendors improve their processes to reduce costs.

Once a company has selected its suppliers, management can then use the economic order quantity (EOQ) model to calculate how many units to order each time. The EOQ equals the square root of [(2 x Estimated Annual Quantity Used in units x Estimated Ordering Cost per Order) ÷ Estimated Annual Carrying Cost per Unit]. The EOQ model minimizes the sum of ordering costs and carrying costs. Under the EOQ, this sum reaches a minimum when ordering costs equal carrying costs. A manufacturing company can change the EOQ model into an economic production run (EPR) formula by changing ordering costs to setup costs. Exhibit 7-6 provides information used later to calculate the economic order quantity.

The EOQ model assumes that an order arrives when the inventory on hand is zero. The average inventory is half of the order size (EOQ ÷ 2). The average inventory in units times the carrying cost per unit equals the annual carrying cost. The estimated annual quantity of units divided by the EOQ equals the number of times the company will place an order. The number of orders times the ordering cost per order equals the annual ordering cost. Exhibit 7-7 presents the graphic solution to economic order size.

A deficiency of the EOQ model is that the result may not be realistic. For example, suppliers often specify minimum order quantities. Also, there is no such thing as a fraction of an order. Other factors that management must consider include cash availability and storage space limitations.

Companies are decreasing their ordering costs significantly through electronic data interchange (EDI) and open purchase ordering. A company using open purchase ordering prepares one purchase order that authorizes a supplier to provide a large quantity of one or more items according to the buyer's specifications in smaller quantities as the buyer needs them over an extended time. Companies are also raising their estimates of carrying costs because they are more aware of the high cost of non-value-added activities such as move time and storage time for excess inventory.

The order point is the inventory level at which the company places an order or produces more items. The rate of usage, the lead time, and the safety stock are the factors that affect the order point. If the company does not maintain a safety stock, the formula for the order point is as follows: Average Daily Usage x Lead Time = Order Point. To allow for variations in the rate of usage and delays in receiving orders, companies may keep extra inventory as a buffer. This extra inventory is safety stock. A company should base the size of safety stock for a particular item on how critical the item is to the business, the cost of the item, and the uncertainty as to usage and lead time. When the company maintains a safety stock, the formula for the order point is as follows: (Average Daily Usage x Lead Time) + Safety Stock = Order Point. The formula for maximum safety stock is (Maximum Daily Usage - Average Daily Usage) x Lead Time. Another way to compute the order point using a maximum safety stock is as follows: Maximum Daily Usage x Lead Time = Order Point.

The EOQ model has three major problems. First, identifying all the relevant inventory costs, especially carrying costs, is difficult. Second, the model does not give managers any guidance for controlling individual types of purchasing and carrying costs. Third, the EOQ model ignores relationships among inventory items. The most significant shortcoming of EOQ is the assumption that there is some optimal level of inventory; that assumption is contrary to the just-in-time approach to inventory.

A company can overcome the third major problem of the EOQ model with the use of materials requirement planning (MRP) or manufacturing resource planning (MRP II). MRP is a computer simulation system that answers the questions of what, how many, and when the company needs items. MRP coordinates future production output requirements with individual production input needs using a master production schedule (MPS). MRP then uses the bill of materials to determine all production components, any purchases needed, and the lead times for those purchases. MRP then prepares a time-sequenced schedule for purchases and production component needs. MRP identifies potential bottlenecks or resource constraints. Management then changes input factors and runs MRP again until the schedule compensates for all potential bottlenecks.

MRP II uses MRP but MRP II also includes other resource needs besides purchases and production components. MRP II computes resource needs such as labour and machine hours. MRP II includes manufacturing, marketing, and finance in preparing the master production schedule.

MRP and MRP II are extensions of the EOQ model. They are push systems of production control in which a company may purchase or produce unneeded inventory. Exhibit 7-8 illustrates a push system of production control.

A just-in-time (JIT) system is a pull system in which a company purchases or produces inventory or performs an operation only as the company needs it. Manufacturing companies, wholesale and retail trade companies, and service organizations can use JIT. The basic purpose of JIT is to eliminate or reduce waste to reduce total costs. The three primary goals of a JIT system are (1) elimination of production processes or operations that do not add value to the product or service, (2) continuous improvement in production or performance efficiency, and (3) reduction in the total cost of production or performance while increasing quality. Exhibit 7-9 lists the elements of the JIT philosophy.

In addition to buying materials and producing inventory only as needed, a JIT system attempts to reduce defective products, reduce lead times and setup times. Traditional push systems seek to maintain smooth production to maintain a steady workforce and continuous machine use. Smooth production often results in the accumulation of excess inventory. The inventory can, however, be a buffer that prevents a company from discovering inefficiencies in the purchase and/or production process. Exhibit 7-10 compares traditional and JIT production philosophies and portrays these inefficiencies as rocks in high water. High water represents excess inventory. Once a company removes the high water under the JIT system, the inefficiencies become visible and the company can correct them.

Other names for JIT include zero-inventory production system (ZIPS), material as needed (MAN), and kanban (the Japanese word for card). The JIT system began in Japan from the use of cards to control the flow of materials between work centers.

Unlike the traditional push systems, JIT is a demand pull system. In a pull system of production control, parts are not delivered or made until the work center that needs them demands them. Exhibit 7-11 illustrates a pull system of production control. A JIT system is highly dependent on accurate market data because of the tight linkage between production and sales. The sales forecast is the force that controls production.

Adequate time is necessary to realize the most benefits from a JIT system. A company normally receives the most impressive benefits only after the system has been in place for five to ten years. Exhibit 7-12 lists some benefits realized by one company over a four-year period after implementing a JIT system.

A company wanting to achieve JIT goals must change most of its organizational functions. Companies must consider developing partnership-type arrangements with suppliers. Manufacturers must address product design, product processing, plant layout, and employee empowerment.

In a JIT system, one objective is to reduce setup time. Reducing setup time allows processing to shift more quickly among the different types of units. It helps to make the manufacturing process more flexible. The savings resulting from reduced setup time are often much greater than the costs incurred.

JIT also emphasizes quality with a goal of zero defects. Companies select vendors based not on price only, but also based on quality and reliability. Poor quality can lead to downtime and additional costs for scrap, rework, repair work under warranties, and lost customer goodwill. JIT provides no excess inventory to act as a buffer when a defect occurs in production. Companies using JIT assess quality continually rather than at quality checkpoints only. Identifying defective units before the company does additional work on them reduces costs. Companies can improve their quality by using modern production equipment that often relies on computerized technology to schedule, control, and monitor production processes.

The company designs its plant layout to reduce lead time from one process to another.  Often the company arranges machines in a U-shaped grouping known as manufacturing cells.  Manufacturing cells improve materials handling and control, increase communication among workers, improve quality control, and increase use of machines.  Exhibit 7-13 depicts a U-shaped manufacturing cell.

Manufacturing cells provide an opportunity to cross-train employees.  Cross-training broadens employees' skills and increases their involvement in the workplace.  Nonmanufacturing companies can also develop multiple skills in their employees.  Training costs are large, and employees often oppose change.  Nevertheless, eventually training results in employers having a workforce that is more highly skilled.  Employees often realize increased job satisfaction.  As employees increase their understanding of a process as a whole, they can provide helpful suggestions for process improvement.

An underlying concept of a JIT system is employee empowerment.  A company can empower employees only if they have the abilities, tools, and training to perform tasks well and are involved in organizational planning.  In addition, employees must be able to trust management and be trusted by management.  Cross-training is a part of employee empowerment.  Empowerment means that management grants decision-making authority and responsibility to the lowest reasonable level in the company.  Good relationships with employees are vital to a successful implementation of a JIT system.  Exhibit 7-14 lists seven steps in implementing JIT.

Every company has suppliers and customers.  Real opportunities for improvement exist in a company's relationships with its suppliers and customers.  Through better cooperation and communication, these entities can treat each other as extensions of themselves.  By doing so, they can realize gains in quality, throughput, and cost efficiency.  The same holds true within a company. Within each company each employee or work center has an upstream supplier and a downstream customer.  When employees see their internal suppliers and customers as extensions of themselves, they foster the spirit of teamwork to reduce defects, increase productivity, and reduce costs.

Accounting in a JIT system focuses on throughput (output).  All costs should be at standard because employees notice variations and correct them almost immediately.  Daily accounting for the individual costs of production is not necessary.  Companies allocate fewer costs arbitrarily to products.  Companies can trace more costs directly to products by using manufacturing cells to make a particular product or family of products.

Backflush costing is a streamlined cost accounting method that speeds up and simplifies the accounting process.  A company using backflush costing records purchases of raw materials and actual conversion costs.  At the completion of production or upon sale of the goods, the company makes a journal entry to allocate the total costs incurred to Cost of Goods Sold and to Finished Goods using standard production costs.  Exhibit 7-15 illustrates backflush costing.

Three alternatives are possible in recording the cost information presented in Exhibit 7-15.  If the production time is short, the company might not record raw material purchases until the completion of production.  If the company ships goods to customers upon completion of production, the company could record the cost of goods sold and any unsold finished goods simultaneously.  Another alternative is to charge the accounts Raw and In Process Inventory, Finished Goods, and Cost of Goods Sold only at the end of the period.

**Chapter 7  Controlling Costs**

The product life cycle is a major factor in executing a company's planning and control of costs. A product's stage in the product life cycle affects is sales volume, price, and unit production cost. A product's revenues and costs change as the product goes through the development, introduction, growth, maturity, and harvest stages. Some products have short life cycles and other products remain popular for many years. Exhibit 7-16 shows the relative sales levels for products in the different stages of the product life cycle.

In the development stage, costs are high and revenues are nonexistent. A company also incurs high costs in the introduction stage as sales begin. Profits, if any, are small. Unit costs level off during the remaining three stages as production becomes routine. Total sales increase through growth, level off in maturity, and decline during the harvest stage.

If a company designs its products well, the products should require few engineering changes after production begins. Each time a company makes an engineering change it incurs additional costs due to one or more problems. These additional costs include having to reprint the operations flow document, employees learning new tasks, changing machine dies or setups, and parts in inventory or under order becoming obsolete. Exhibit 7-17 shows that design changes must be made early in the process so that costs and time to market are not affected.

Companies need to design products using the fewest number of parts. As much as possible, a company should use standardized parts. Customers demand variety, but an excessive number of different parts causes unnecessary costs. Although a company can make design changes after production has begun, any cost savings resulting from such changes will be significantly less than if the company had made the changes early in the design/development process.

Decisions made during the development stage are especially important. They can affect the sales, design, costs, and quality of the product for the remainder of its life cycle. Studies indicate that decisions made before production begins determine 80 to 90 percent of a product's life cycle costs.

In the introduction stage, sales are low and the prices of substitute products affect the price of the new product. A company incurs substantial costs for product design, market research, advertising, and promotion.

The growth stage begins when the product breaks even. In the growth stage the product gains market acceptance and profits increase. Quality may improve because of competition, and prices are stable.

In the maturity stage, sales begin to stabilize or slowly decrease. Price is an important competitive factor. Costs are often at their lowest level, and companies may realize high profits.

The harvest stage reflects declining sales. Companies often reduce prices to stimulate business. Management normally tries to generate as much short-term profits and cash flow as possible during this stage.

Companies should be concerned about maximizing the profits of a product or service over its life cycle. To be profitable, a product or service must generate revenues that exceed total life cycle costs. Each stage of the product life cycle affects sales and costs differently. Thus, each stage requires its own budgetary focus. As a company implements its plans, it needs a monitoring system in place so that it can compare actual results with the expectation for each stage in the life cycle. Monitoring activities will provide feedback to managers so that they can direct activities to achieve desired objectives throughout each stage of the product life cycle.

Exhibit 7-18 lists ways that a company can substantially reduce product costs and improve performance.

133

Target costing is a process of computing an allowable cost for a product or component, by estimating a market price for the product and subtracting the required profit margin. Target costing, which originated in Japan, is a customer-driven analysis because the estimated market price depends on the customer's valuation of the value creation chain's output. The target cost includes the cost of developing, designing, manufacturing, marketing, distributing , and servicing the product.

In bringing products to the market, Western companies have traditionally used a different approach with the following sequence: (1) the company designs a product; (2) the company determines the product's costs; and (3) the company decides a selling price based in part on the costs incurred. If the market will not bear the selling price, the company either accepts a lower profit or attempts to reduce production costs. The left side of Exhibit 7-19 illustrates this process.

As shown on the right side of Exhibit 7-19, a company that applies target costing first begins with market research to estimate what the market will pay for a product with specific features. Although the market price of a product may change over its life cycle, the sales price should reflect future market conditions and the best forecasting efforts. After subtracting the required profit margin to find the target cost, the company compares the target cost with the expected product cost. If the target cost is less than the expected cost, the company has several alternatives. First, the company could alter the product design or process to reduce costs. Cost tables aid in making these decisions. Cost tables are databases that provide information about how the use of different input resources, manufacturing processes, and design specifications affects product costs. Second, the company could accept a lower profit margin. Third, the company can decide not to enter the particular product market at the time.

To reduce estimated costs, companies should examine production processes and production components. For the components that the company produces internally, the company could consider outsourcing them if they are available at a lower cost. For those parts purchased externally, the company could negotiate for price concessions from vendors. Another option is for vendors to help in redesigning the product to reduce the cost of parts or conversion processes.

The type of product affects the extent to which companies use target costing. As product cost and complexity increase and the production stage of the product life cycle becomes shorter, target costing becomes more important because proper design can significantly reduce costs.

Value engineering is a tool that companies use to manage the relationships among product design, product price, and target cost. To apply value engineering, a company must break down the value of the product into its various functions that deliver value to the customer. The sum of the values of the various functions equals the value of the product.

Once a company has assigned a value to each function, the company must estimate the cost of each function. The cost of each function includes the costs of making or buying the component parts plus the costs of assembly and installation. Management can use the estimates of the value and cost of each function to identify and eliminate or improve functions that have poor value-to-cost relationships. Management will subject these functions to more scrutiny in the product design process to improve the value-to-cost relationship and realize the target profit.

By forcing the cost analysis down to the function level, management can examine the design and conversion processes required for individual product components. Accountants use techniques such as activity-based costing and cost driver analysis to compute the cost of individual functions.

Value engineering leads to exchanges of information among the company, its vendors, and its customers.  Customer input is required to identify the value of functions; vendors must be involved to learn the cost of purchased components, to generate ideas on alternative product and component designs, and to identify engineering constraints.  For supplier/customer companies that have long-term relationships, developing more formal information systems that combine information from both companies may be feasible.

Exhibit 7-20 presents the survival triplet which consists of the three dimensions that define a product: cost/price, quality, and functionality.

## SELF TEST

### TRUE/FALSE

1.  T  F  The first exercise in cost control is the preparation of an expectation.

2.  T  F  Cost control requires the support and attention of management only.

3.  T  F  Vertical price fixing involves agreements by companies and their distributors to     control the prices at which they may sell products to consumers.

4.  T  F  Inventory carrying costs include costs for storage, insurance, property taxes, losses for obsolescence or theft, and the opportunity cost of capital invested in inventory.

5.  T  F  The costs of preparing, receiving, and paying for an order are ordering costs.

6.  T  F  In an ABC inventory management system, management exerts the most control  over C items.

7.  T  F  A stockout can lead to lost sales and lost customer goodwill.

8.  T  F  The economic order quantity (EOQ) includes purchase cost in the numerator.

9.  T  F  One problem with the EOQ model is that it ignores relationships among inventory items.

10.  T  F  Materials requirement planning (MRP) is a computer simulation system that calculates the future availability of raw materials, parts, and subassemblies based on a master production schedule.

11.  T  F  Manufacturing resource planning (MRP II) plans production jobs using MRP methods and also calculates other resource needs such as labour and machine hours.

12.  T  F  Just-in-time (JIT) manufacturing is a push system.

13.  T  F  In backflush costing, daily accounting for the individual costs of production is extremely important.

14.  T  F  Research indicates that decisions made before production often determine 80 to 90 percent of a product's life cycle costs.

15.  T  F  Value engineering is a tool used to manage the relationship between product design, product price, and target cost.

## MULTIPLE CHOICE

1. Finding acceptable alternatives to high cost items and not spending money for unnecessary goods or services is:

   A. cost containment.
   B. cost avoidance.
   C. cost consciousness.
   D. cost reduction.

2. A company-wide employee attitude about cost understanding, cost containment, cost avoidance, and cost reduction is:

   A. cost control.
   B. cost consciousness.
   C. cost efficiency.
   D. cost effectiveness.

3. As a general rule, if the technology of producing a good or service advances, the cost of that good or service:

   A. increases slightly.
   B. increases greatly.
   C. declines.
   D. does not change.

4. As taxes and the number of regulations increase, costs will:

   A. decline slightly.
   B. decline greatly.
   C. increase.
   D. not change.

5. Management should view the cost control system as:

   A. a short-run solution to complex problems.
   B. a long-run process, not a short-run solution.
   C. a way to exert their authority over employees.
   D. a way to satisfy government regulations.

6. Which costs would a manufacturing company incur instead of ordering costs?

   A. stockout costs
   B. carrying costs
   C. setup costs
   D. selling costs

7.  The economic order quantity (EOQ) model computes the optimal balance between:

    A. ordering costs and carrying costs.
    B. purchase costs and stockout costs.
    C. ordering costs and stockout costs.
    D. carrying costs and stockout costs.

8.  Carrying costs should include:

    A. the shipping charges on purchased items.
    B. the cost of receiving an order.
    C. the opportunity cost of capital invested in inventory.
    D. the cost of lost customer goodwill.

9.  The economic order quantity does not include:

    A. the cost of placing an order.
    B. the estimated annual quantity needed in units.
    C. the purchase cost.
    D. the cost of carrying one unit in stock for one year.

10.  The economic order quantity (EOQ) model assumes that when an order arrives the inventory on hand will be equal to:

    A. zero.
    B. one fourth of the order size.
    C. one half of the order size.
    D. the order size.

11.  The basic economic order quantity (EOQ) model does not consider:

    A. the annual cost of carrying an item for one year.
    B. relationships among inventory items.
    C. the estimated annual quantity needed in units.
    D. the cost to place one order.

12.  Which inventory management technique plans production jobs and calculates resource needs such as labour and machine hours using a computer simulation model?

    A. materials requirement planning (MRP)
    B. manufacturing resource planning (MRP II)
    C. just-in-time manufacturing (JIT)
    D. economic order quantity (EOQ)

13.  Stockout cost is a(n):

    A. production cost.
    B. purchase cost.
    C. ordering cost.
    D. opportunity cost.

14. Just-in-time manufacturing emphasizes:

    A. high quality.
    B. long lead times.
    C. many vendors.
    D. buying in large quantities.

15. When does a company using a JIT system assess quality?

    A. only at the completion of production
    B. only at quality control checkpoints
    C. on a continual basis
    D. only when the company receives materials

16. One way to reduce cycle time in a plant is to establish U-shaped groupings of employees and machines known as:

    A. U-control groups.
    B. manufacturing cells.
    C. ABC cells.
    D. a focused factory.

17. A traditional inventory system is:

    A. a pull system.
    B. very similar to JIT.
    C. a push system.
    D. not concerned with storing inventory.

18. Which of the following is a deficiency of the economic order quantity (EOQ) model?

    A. It may not be realistic because of minimum order quantities.
    B. It ignores carrying costs.
    C. It ignores ordering costs.
    D. It ignores the opportunity cost of the investment in inventory.

19. Which of the following is a primary goal of a just-in-time manufacturing system?

    A. elimination of non-value-added processes or operations
    B. continuous improvement in production efficiency
    C. reduction in the total cost of production
    D. all of the above

20. The basic purpose of JIT is to eliminate:

    A. waste.
    B. inventory.
    C. the economic order quantity model.
    D. materials requirement planning.

21. What method of controlling inventory separates inventory into three groups based upon relative cost-to-volume usage?

    A. 1-2-3
    B. ABC
    C. JIT
    D. XYZ

22. Which of the following is a pull type of production system?

    A. EOQ
    B. MRP
    C. MRP II
    D. JIT

23. The time from placing an order until the goods arrive is:

    A. safety time.
    B. just-in-time.
    C. lead time.
    D. order time.

24. Ussery Company computed its economic order quantity to be 2,000 units. Ussery sells an average of 200 units a day. The lead time is 4 days and the desired safety stock is 450 units. What is the order point?

    A.    500 units
    B.    800 units
    C.    950 units
    D. 1,250 units

25. Gray Company sells a maximum of 600 units a day. The average sales are 520 units a day. The lead time is 6 days. What is the maximum safety stock that Gray needs?

    A.    80 units
    B.    480 units
    C. 3,120 units
    D. 3,600 units

26. Eibert Company estimates that it will buy 60,000 units of a component each year. The cost to place an order is $300. The cost to carry one unit of the component in inventory for a year is $4. What is the economic order quantity?

    A.    40
    B.    200
    C.    3,000
    D. 15,000

27. What type of costing focuses on throughput and works backwards through the system to allocate costs between cost of goods sold and inventory?

    A. backflush costing
    B. throughput costing
    C. backwards costing
    D. variance costing

28. In the development stage of the product life cycle:

    A. costs are low and revenues are high.
    B. costs are low and revenues are nonexistent.
    C. costs are high and revenues are nonexistent.
    D. costs are high and revenues are relatively low.

29. A process of calculating an allowable cost for a product inferred from projecting a market price for the product and subtracting a required profit margin is:

    A. business process reengineering.
    B. target costing.
    C. standard costing.
    D. kaizen costing.

30. A tool that companies use to manage the relationship among product design, product price, and target cost is:

    A. target costing.
    B. value engineering.
    C. the theory of constraints.
    D. open-book management.

## ESSAY QUESTIONS AND PROBLEMS

1. List the three functions of a cost control system and explain the reasons for each function.

2. Define cost containment.  What causes of cost changes are subject to cost containment?  What causes of cost changes are not subject to cost containment?

3. What are the five steps that management should use in implementing a cost control system?

4. List and explain the elements of the three basic costs associated with inventory.

5. Define materials requirement planning (MRP).  What deficiency in the EOQ model does MRP overcome?

6. Explain how manufacturing resource planning (MRP II) differs from MRP.

7. What is the basic purpose of a just-in-time (JIT) system? What are the three primary goals of a JIT system?

8. Explain how a JIT system differs from a traditional inventory system.

9. Explain why high quality is so important to a successful JIT system. How does a company assure quality in a JIT system?

10. Datz Company uses 240,000 units per year. The cost to place one order is $50. The cost to carry one unit in inventory for a year is $6. Compute (A) the economic order quantity, (B) the number of orders that Datz will make during the year, (C) the annual cost of placing orders, (D) the average inventory that Datz will have during the year, and (E) the annual carrying cost for the average inventory.

11. Highfill Company sells a maximum of 770 units per day. The average sales are 700 units per day. The lead time is 8 days. Determine (A) the order point assuming no safety stock, (B) the maximum safety stock that Highfill needs to carry, and (C) the order point assuming that Highfill carries the maximum safety stock.

12. Describe how a backflush accounting system is a simplified cost system.

13. Why is understanding the product life cycle important in controlling costs?

14. What is target costing?  How do companies apply target costing concepts?

15. What is value engineering?  How do companies use value engineering to earn a target profit?

## SELF TEST ANSWERS

### TRUE/FALSE

| | | | | |
|---|---|---|---|---|
| 1.  T | 4.  T | 7.  T | 10.  T | 13.  F |
| 2.  F | 5.  T | 8.  F | 11.  T | 14.  T |
| 3.  T | 6.  F | 9.  T | 12.  F | 15.  T |

### MULTIPLE CHOICE

| | | | | |
|---|---|---|---|---|
| 1.  B | 7.  A | 13.  D | 19.  D | 25.  B |
| 2.  B | 8.  C | 14.  A | 20.  A | 26.  C |
| 3.  C | 9.  C | 15.  C | 21.  B | 27.  A |
| 4.  C | 10.  A | 16.  B | 22.  D | 28.  C |
| 5.  B | 11.  B | 17.  C | 23.  C | 29.  B |
| 6.  C | 12.  B | 18.  A | 24.  D | 30.  B |

### ESSAY QUESTIONS AND PROBLEMS

1.      The three functions of a cost control system are (1) control before an event, (2) control during an event, and (3) control after an event.  The reason for control before an event is to plan the costs that the company expects to incur and to prevent unnecessary costs.  The purpose for control during an event is to correct problems as they occur to minimize unnecessary costs.  The reason for control after an event is to diagnose the causes of costs and to guide future actions to reduce non-value-added costs.

2.      Cost containment is minimizing increases in per-unit variable costs and total fixed costs from one period to the next.  Cost increases arising from reduced competition, seasonality, and quantities purchased are subject to cost containment.  Cost changes arising from inflation, technology, supply and demand adjustments, and increases in taxes and regulations are not subject to cost containment.  These changes are not subject to cost containment because they are due to factors outside the organization.

3.      The five steps that management should use in implementing a cost control system are
(1) understand the types of costs that the organization incurs, (2) communicate the need for cost
consciousness to all employees, (3) motivate employees by education and incentives to engage in cost control,
(4) generate reports that compare actual results to expectations, and (5) view the cost control system as a long-
run process not as a short-run solution.

4.      The three basic costs associated with inventory are (1) purchase or production costs,
(2) ordering or setup costs, and (3) carrying costs, including costs of not carrying sufficient inventory
(stockout costs).  Purchase costs include the quoted price plus shipping costs less discounts.  Production costs
for a manufacturing company include direct materials cost (taking shipping charges and discounts into
account), direct labour, traceable overhead, and allocated overhead.  Ordering costs include costs for invoice
preparation, receiving and inspection reports, clerical processing, and payment.  Setup costs for a
manufacturing company include labour and machine downtime costs.  Carrying costs are those costs incurred
to carry inventory in stock.  They include storage, handling, insurance, property taxes, losses from
obsolescence, damage, and theft, and the opportunity costs of capital invested in inventory.  Stockout costs
are the costs a company incurs for not having inventory on hand.  They include lost contribution margin from
lost sales, lost customer goodwill, and increased ordering or setup costs for filling special orders.

5.      Materials requirement planning (MRP) is a computer simulation model that helps a company to
decide what items it needs, how many it needs, and when it needs them.  MRP calculates the future
availability of materials, subassemblies, and finished products based on the master production schedule.
MRP decides whether the company needs to make purchases and prepares a time-sequenced schedule for
purchases and production components.  The EOQ model is deficient in that it ignores the relationships among
inventory items.  MRP overcomes this deficiency.

6.      Manufacturing resource planning (MRP II) plans production using MRP methods.  MRP II calculates
needs for resources other than purchases and production components.  MRP II determines the needs such as
labour and machine hours.  MRP II includes manufacturing, marketing, and finance in preparing the master
production schedule.

7.      Although many people often regard a just-in-time (JIT) system as a system to eliminate inventory, the
basic purpose of a JIT system is to eliminate or at least minimize wasted activities and excess costs.  The three
primary goals of a JIT system are (1) to eliminate any production process or operation that does not add value
to products or services, (2) to strive for continuous improvement in production or performance efficiency, and
(3) to reduce the total cost of production or performance.

8.      A traditional inventory system maintains inventory not only to reduce stockout costs but also to act as
a buffer when production problems arise.  Inefficient operations often cause these production problems.  A
traditional inventory system is a push system that encourages smooth production.  Traditional systems often
create excess inventory and make detecting and correcting operating problems more difficult.  A JIT system is
a pull system in which parts are delivered only as a particular work center needs them.  Forecasted sales is the
variable that pulls production through a JIT system.  Like a traditional system, JIT strives to maintain a steady
production schedule.  In JIT the goal is to avoid accumulating unnecessary inventory.  When the company
does not need current production, production employees perform maintenance on the machines or receive
additional training.  Quality is much more important in a JIT system.  Good relationships with suppliers and
employees are essential to a successful JIT system.

9.      Quality is important in JIT systems because little if any inventory is available to act as a buffer if the company has to rework or scrap defective units.  Poor quality leads to higher costs in the form of downtime, rework, scrap, warranty costs, and lost sales.  JIT assures quality by purchasing from only a small number of vendors that produce high quality materials.  The company chooses vendors based on quality and reliability in addition to price.  After the company chooses a vendor, the company monitors the vendor to ensure that the vendor maintains high quality.  JIT also assures quality by assessing quality continually rather than at quality checkpoints only.  The company finds defective units before the company incurs additional costs.  Thus, the company reduces the costs of poor quality.

10.     (A) EOQ = Square Root of [(2 x $50 x 240,000) ÷ $6]
                = Square Root of ($24,000,000 ÷ $6)
                = Square Root of 4,000,000
                = 2,000

        (B) 240,000 units ÷ 2,000 units per order = 120 orders per year

        (C) 120 orders per year x $50 per order = $6,000

        (D) (2,000 + 0) units ÷ 2 = 1,000 units

        (E) 1,000 units x $6 per unit = $6,000

11.     (A) 700 units per day x 8 days = 5,600 units

        (B) Maximum usage          770 units per day
            Average usage          700 units per day
            Difference              70 units per day
            Lead time              x 8 days
            Maximum safety stock   560 units

        (C) 5,600 units + 560 units = 6,160 units OR
            770 units per day x 8 days = 6,160 units

12.     Backflush accounting focuses on the throughput and works backwards to allocate costs between cost of goods sold and inventory.  Accounting in a JIT system focuses on throughput (output).  Backflush costing differs from traditional costing systems in that it is a streamlined cost accounting method that speeds up and simplifies the accounting process.  A company using backflush costing records purchases of raw materials and actual conversion costs.  At the completion of production or upon sale of the goods, the company makes a journal entry to allocate the total costs incurred to Cost of Goods Sold and to Finished Goods using standard production costs.

13.     The product life cycle is a major factor in executing a company's planning and control of costs.  A product's stage in the product life cycle affects its sales volume, price, and unit production cost.  A product's revenues and costs change as the product goes through the development, introduction, growth, maturity, and harvest stages.  Some products have short life cycles, and other products remain popular for many years.

14.     Target costing is a process of computing an allowable cost for a product or component by estimating a market price for the product and subtracting the required profit margin. The target cost includes the cost of developing, designing, manufacturing, marketing, distributing, and servicing the product.

A company applies target costing concepts by first conducting market research to estimate what the market will pay for a product with specific features.  Although the market price of a product may change over its life cycle, the sales price should reflect future market conditions and the best forecasting efforts.  After subtracting the required profit margin to find the target cost, the company compares the target cost with the expected product cost.  If the target cost is less than the expected cost, the company has several alternatives.  First, the company could alter the product design or process to reduce costs.  Cost tables aid in making these decisions.  Cost tables are databases that provide information about how the use of different input resources, manufacturing processes, and design specifications affects product costs.  Second, the company could accept a lower profit margin.  Third, the company can decide not to enter the particular product market at the time.

15.     Value engineering is a tool that companies use to manage the relationship among product design, product price, and target cost.  To apply value engineering, a company must break down the value of the product into its various functions that deliver value to the customer.  The sum of the values of the various functions equals the value of the product.

Once a company has assigned a value to each function, the company must estimate the cost of each function.  The cost of each function includes the costs of making or buying the component parts plus the costs of assembly and installation.  Management can use the estimates of the value and cost of each function to identify functions that have poor value-to-cost relationships.  Management will subject these functions to more scrutiny in the product design process to improve the value-to-cost relationship and realize the target profit.

# CHAPTER 8
# RELEVANT COSTING

## CHAPTER OVERVIEW

One function of management is decision making. Managers use cost information in making many types of decisions. To be useful, the costs must be relevant. Relevant costs are those costs that are logically associated with a particular decision. Relevant costs are future costs that differ across the alternatives under consideration. Besides the relevant costs, managers must consider the qualitative aspects of the decisions.

Relevant costing is essential in many decision-making situations, including those related to further processing of a product, make-or-buy alternatives, scarce resource allocations, sales mix distributions, and retentions or eliminations or product lines.

## CHAPTER STUDY GUIDE

Accounting information can help managers to make better decisions. Managers make many of these decisions based on incremental analysis. This analysis includes the idea of relevant costing. Relevant costing focuses on relevant facts and disregards needless data. Managers use relevant costing to make decisions such as making or buying a product or part, allocating scarce resources, and deciding the proper sales or production mix.

Managers often choose from alternatives that are feasible solutions to problems or feasible ways to achieve objectives. In doing so, they must weigh the relevant costs and benefits associated with each alternative. Relevant costs are logically related to a specific problem or decision and differ between alternatives.

Information is relevant when it relates to a decision about the future. Relevant costing considers differential revenues, incremental revenues, differential costs, and incremental costs of the decision alternatives. Differential revenues are the revenues that differ between or among alternatives. Differential costs are the costs that differ between or among alternatives. Incremental revenues are the additional revenues that would result if a company makes a contemplated sale of a product or service. Incremental costs are the additional costs of producing or selling a contemplated output.

Incremental costs can be fixed or variable. Most variable costs are relevant while most fixed costs are not relevant. Incremental fixed costs, however, are relevant. The difference between the incremental revenues and incremental costs is the positive or negative incremental benefit of that alternative. Managers should choose the alternative with the most positive incremental benefit or in cost minimization decisions the alternative with the least negative incremental benefit.

Managers should remember to include opportunity costs in decisions involving relevant costs. Opportunity costs are the benefits foregone from choosing one alternative over another. Although the accounting system does not include opportunity costs, managers should remember to include them even if managers must estimate the opportunity costs.

When choosing from alternatives, management sometimes chooses the "change nothing" alternative. The change nothing alternative may be the best choice, or management may select it because it is easier than making changes. Management could choose the change nothing alternative because of inadequate information. Managers could view the lack of information as making change more risky than maintaining the status quo. The change nothing option has a zero incremental benefit. The change nothing option is not available for certain laws and government regulations.

Management's need for specific information depends on the importance of the information to management's objectives.  Generally, management prefers information to be as precise as possible.  Managers sometimes have to weigh the importance of the information against its precision.

Information is relevant only if it relates to the future and differs between or among the alternatives.  The company can define the future as short run or long run.  Management can use historical information to help predict the future.  Costs already incurred, however, are not relevant because management cannot change them.  These costs are sunk costs.

A common error is trying to use a sunk cost to make a current decision.  Current costs represent relevant information and should be considered in the decision-making process.  In contrast, sunk costs are not recoverable and cannot be changed, regardless of what current circumstances exist or what future course of action is taken.

In industries such as refineries, lumber mills, and food, chemical, and cosmetics manufacturers, multiple products are produced from a single process.  A joint process is a process in which one product cannot be manufactured without others being produced.

A joint production process generates outputs known as joint products, which are two or more products that have relatively significant sales values and are not separately identifiable as individual products until the split off point.  By-products and scrap are incidental outputs of a joint process.  Both are saleable, but their sales values alone would not be enough for management to justify undertaking the joint process.  A final output from a joint process is waste, which is a residual output that has no sales value.  Exhibit 8-1 provides an illustration of joint process output.

The split-off point is the point at which the outputs of a joint process are first identifiable as individual products.  Output may be sold at the split-off point or some or all of the products may be processed further after exiting the joint process.

The costs incurred for materials, labour, and overhead up to the split-off point represent the joint cost of the production process.  After the joint process cost has been incurred, it is a sunk cost.  At the split-off point, the joint cost is allocated only to the joint products and not to any resulting by-products, scrap, or waste.  Allocation may be made on the basis of a physical or a monetary measure.

If any of the joint process outputs are processed after the split-off point, additional costs will be incurred.  Costs incurred after split-off are assigned to the separate products for which those costs are incurred.  A joint product should be processed further only if the incremental revenue exceeds the incremental cost of further processing.  If the incremental cost of further processing exceeds the incremental revenue, the joint product should be sold at the split-off point.  The joint cost is not considered in this decision process.

Managers routinely make decisions on alternatives that have been identified as feasible solutions to problems or feasible methods for the attainment of objectives.  In doing so, managers should select the alternative that provides the highest incremental benefit to the company.

Asset replacement decisions require the use of relevant cost information.  Decisions must be made about whether to keep or dispose of an old asset and, if disposed, whether to replace it.  Exhibit 8-2 presents data that are used to demonstrate an equipment replacement decision.  Exhibit 8-3 presents the relevant costs related to the equipment replacement decision.

The relevant factors in making an equipment replacement decision are (1) the cost of the new equipment, (2) the current resale value of the old equipment, and (3) the annual savings, if any, of the new equipment and the number of years that the savings would be enjoyed.

A concern in manufacturing is whether components of the right quality will be available at the right time and at a reasonable price. Some companies assure the availability of a component by manufacturing it themselves. Other companies prefer to outsource, or purchase some or all components from external parties.

The make-or-buy decision should be made only after proper analysis. Managers should compare the cost of internally manufacturing a product component with the cost of purchasing it from outside suppliers. Relevant information for a make-or-buy decision includes both quantitative and qualitative factors. Exhibit 8-4 lists some relevant quantitative and qualitative considerations for a make-or-buy decision.

In a make-or-buy decision, relevant costs are those costs that are germane and avoidable, whether they are fixed or variable. Variable production costs are relevant. Fixed costs may be relevant if a company can avoid them by ceasing production. Fixed costs which continue under either alternative are not relevant. Exhibit 8-5 presents data that are used to demonstrate a make-or-buy decision.

If an alternative use of the facilities used to make a component exists, management must consider the opportunity cost of shifting the capacity to the alternative use. Exhibit 8-6 considers opportunity cost in a make-or-buy decision.

Management should consider qualitative factors such as product quality, on-time delivery, and the stability of the supplier. Although management often views outsourcing decisions as short-run decisions, these additional considerations reveal that outsourcing decisions have potential long-run effects. Companies are viewing outsourcing decisions with a long-range perspective.

Make-or-buy decisions must also be made by many service organizations. In the case of a service organization, a decision must be made regarding provision of an in-house service versus reliance on an external source to provide the service.

Managers often must make the best use of scarce resources that place constraints on producing products or providing services. When one resource is scarce and management wants to maximize total contribution margin, management should produce the product that has the highest contribution margin per unit of the scarce resource. Exhibit 8-7 provides an example of maximizing total contribution margin given a scarce resource. Management should also consider qualitative factors in making production mix decisions. For example, two products may be complementary. By not making one product, the company could lose sales of the other product.

The relative combination of the quantities sold of a company's products is its sales mix. Factors that affect a company's sales mix include prices, salesforce compensation, and advertising expenditures. If a company changes one or all of these factors, its sales mix could change also. Exhibit 8-8 provides information used in later exhibits to illustrate the effects of sales mix decisions.

Managers must always observe the selling prices of their company's products in relation to each other and to competitors' prices. This process may provide information that causes management to change one or more selling prices. In making price changes a manager should consider (1) changes in demand, (2) production distribution costs, (3) economic conditions, and (4) competition.

Managers should consider unit contribution margin and sales volume together in evaluating profitability. Exhibit 8-9 illustrates the relationship between contribution margin and sales volume. The sales volume of a product or service is usually directly related to its selling price. If demand is elastic with respect to price and the company raises the selling price, the quantity demanded will decrease by a greater percentage than the percentage price increase. Exhibit 8-10 illustrates the relationship between sales price and demand.

In making decisions to change prices, management should consider the following relevant quantitative factors: (1) new contribution margin per unit, (2) short-term and long-term changes in product demand and production volume, and (3) the best use of any scarce resources. The manager should also consider the following qualitative factors: (1) the effect on customer goodwill, (2) customer loyalty toward the company's products, and (3) competitors' reactions.

Sometimes a company will receive an order for a product or service that is outside the company's normal business. In making pricing decisions for such special orders, the price should be high enough to cover all variable costs, any incremental fixed costs, and the desired profit on the special order. Special order situations include jobs requiring a bid, special orders received during slack periods, or products made to a particular customer's specifications. Setting a price for special orders requires knowledge of the relevant costs related to the specific problem or decision

Sometimes a company may decide to sell a special order even below variable costs to acquire profitable future business from a new customer. Special pricing of this nature may provide work for a period of time but cannot be continued in the long run. In the long run, a company must set selling prices that cover total variable costs and an appropriate amount of fixed, selling, or administrative costs, and provide a reasonable profit margin.

Special pricing concessions may be justified when a company produces related or complementary products, when orders are of an unusual nature, or when products are being tailor-made to customer specifications. Special pricing can also be used when producing goods for a one-time job.

Management must consider the qualitative issues as well as the quantitative ones when setting a special order price. Qualitative issues include the impact of a low bid price on future prices, the additional burdens placed on management and employees by the activity, and the impact of special order sales on normal sales.

Many companies compensate their salespeople by paying a fixed commission rate on gross sales dollars. Under this type of commission structure, sales personnel will be motivated to sell the product with the highest selling price. Emphasizing sales of the product with the highest selling price may not help the company to achieve its profit maximization objective if this product doesn't also have the highest contribution margin.

As an alternative, a company could compensate their salespeople by paying a fixed commission rate on product contribution margin. Under this type of commission structure, sales personnel will be motivated to sell the product with the highest contribution margin. This will help the company to achieve its profit maximization objective. Exhibit 8-11 illustrates the impact of a change in the commission structure. Exhibit 8-12 illustrates the total effect of changing sales commissions.

Changes in advertising expenditures can cause a shift in the sales mix or the number of units sold. Managers should compare the increase in expected contribution margin to the increase in advertising cost. The advertising is cost effective if the increase in contribution margin is greater than the increase in advertising cost. Exhibit 8-13 illustrates the effect of an increase in advertising cost.

Exhibit 8-14 illustrates a product line income statement that reflects a mixture of relevant and irrelevant information in its presentation.  This mixture occurs because the statement shows an allocation of all fixed costs to the individual product lines.  Three categories of fixed costs shown in Exhibit 8-14 are (1) avoidable fixed expenses,
(2) unavoidable fixed expenses, and (3) allocated common costs.  Avoidable fixed expenses are those fixed costs that the company could avoid by eliminating the product line.  The company cannot eliminate unavoidable fixed expenses associated with the product line by ending the product line.  Allocated common costs are fixed costs associated with the division as a whole.  Unavoidable fixed expenses and allocated common costs are not relevant to the decision concerning whether to delete a product line.

The contribution margin of a product line less its avoidable direct fixed expenses is its product margin.  Managers should use the product margin to make decisions about the elimination of a product line.  Using the information from Exhibit 8-14, Exhibit 8-15 shows the product line income statement in its proper format.

If the product margin is negative, management should consider making changes to make the product line profitable.  If necessary changes are not possible, the company will usually increase its profits by dropping the product line.

Another decision concerning product lines is extension or expansion.  Expansion is the introduction of completely new products.  Extension is an augmentation of current products because the company believes that it should segment the market further.  Extensions could be due to competitive pressure and could focus on such things as price, size, or flavour.

Companies have often seen extensions as costing little especially if a company has excess capacity.  Sometimes unforeseen incremental costs of expansions and extensions are necessary.  These incremental costs include market research, product and packaging development, product introduction, and advertising.


**SELF TEST**

TRUE/FALSE

1.  T  F  Sunk costs are always relevant costs.

2.  T  F  Opportunity costs are relevant, quantifiable, and are an integral part of the accounting system.

3.  T  F  By-products are viewed as having a higher sales value than scrap.

4.  T  F  At the split-off point, the joint cost is allocated only to the joint products and not to any resulting by-products, scrap, or waste.

5.  T  F  The joint cost is relevant to the decision to sell or process a particular joint output further.

6.  T  F  When evaluating alternative courses of action, managers should select the alternative that provides the highest incremental benefit to the company.

7.  T  F  In an equipment replacement decision, the acquisition cost of the old equipment is relevant to the decision process.

8.  T  F  Relevant information for a make-or-buy decision includes both quantitative and qualitative factors.

9.  T  F  In a make-or-buy decision, fixed production costs are irrelevant.

10.  T  F  Besides costs, control over product quality and on-time delivery are two important factors in a make-or-buy decision.

11.  T  F  Making the best use of a scarce resource is a long-run problem.

12.  T  F  If management wants to maximize contribution margin, the best use of a scarce resource is to produce and sell the product that has the highest contribution margin per unit of the scarce resource.

13.  T  F  A company refers to the relative combination of the quantities sold of its products        as its contribution mix.

14.  T  F  When selling price is increased and demand is elastic with respect to price, demand for that product decreases.

15.  T  F  Product margin equals product contribution margin less avoidable fixed expenses.


MULTIPLE CHOICE

1.  Those costs that are pertinent to or logically associated with a specific problem or decision are:

    A.  sunk costs.
    B.  relevant costs.
    C.  opportunity costs.
    D.  joint costs.

2.  The additional revenue resulting from a contemplated sale or provision of a service is:

    A.  gross margin.
    B.  incremental revenue.
    C.  product margin.
    D.  a sunk cost.

3.  Historical costs that a company incurred to purchase an asset or resource are:

    A.  sunk costs.
    B.  opportunity costs.
    C.  incremental costs.
    D.  relevant costs.

4.  Costs that differ between or among the alternatives under consideration are:

    A.  opportunity costs.
    B.  sunk costs.
    C.  differential costs.
    D.  incremental costs.

5. The additional costs of producing or selling a contemplated quantity of output are:

    A. opportunity costs.
    B. sunk costs.
    C. differential costs.
    D. incremental costs.

6. The benefits foregone because a company chooses one course of action over another are:

    A. opportunity costs.
    B. sunk costs.
    C. differential costs.
    D. incremental costs.

7. If a company chooses the change nothing alternative while its competitors upgrade processes, that company:

    A. risks nothing.
    B. will maximize profits.
    C. risks losing its market.
    D. has no opportunity cost.

8. Which of the following outputs from a joint production process has substantial revenue-generating ability?

    A. joint products
    B. by-products
    C. scrap
    D. waste

9. At the split-off point, the joint cost is allocated to:

    A. the joint products only.
    B. the joint products and the by-products.
    C. the joint products, by-products, and scrap.
    D. the joint products, by-products, scrap, and waste.

10. Which of the following is not a relevant factor in the equipment replacement decision?

    A. the cost of the new equipment
    B. the cost of the old equipment
    C. the current resale value of the old equipment
    D. the annual savings of the new equipment and the number of years that the savings would be enjoyed

11. Contracting with external vendors to provide necessary parts or services rather than producing them internally is:

    A. outsourcing.
    B. insourcing.
    C. horizontally intregrating.
    D. value creation chain analysis.

12. Which qualitative factor should management consider in outsourcing decisions?

    A. product quality
    B. on-time delivery
    C. stability of the supplier
    D. all of the above

13. Which of the following statements regarding the make-or-buy decision is false?

    A. Relevant information for a make-or-buy decision includes both quantitative and qualitative factors.
    B. A company must consider the long-run effects of the make-or-buy decision.
    C. The make-or-buy decision applies only to a manufacturing company.
    D. All of the above statements regarding the make-or-buy decision are true.

14. Which of the following is not a relevant cost in a make-or-buy decision?

    A. variable costs of production
    B. avoidable fixed production costs
    C. common fixed production costs
    D. all of the above costs are relevant in a make-or-buy decision

15. If management's objective is to maximize profits, the best use of a scarce resource is to produce and sell the product with the:

    A. highest price.
    B. highest contribution margin.
    C. lowest use of the scarce resource.
    D. highest contribution margin per unit of the scarce resource.

16. Which of the following factors can cause a company's sales mix to change?

    A. selling prices
    B. advertising
    C. both of the above
    D. none of the above

17. Factors that might influence price changes include:

    A. fluctuations in demand.
    B. economic conditions.
    C. competition.
    D. all of the above.

18. Which of the following are not relevant costs in a special order pricing decision?

    A. direct materials, direct labour, and variable manufacturing overhead costs.
    B. fixed manufacturing overhead costs that are not expected to increase because of the sale.
    C. incremental fixed costs caused by the job.
    D. all of the above costs are relevant in a special order pricing decision.

19. Which of the following is not a qualitative factor involved in decisions regarding price changes?

    A. short-term and long-term changes in product demand and production volume caused by the price increase or decrease.
    B. influence on customer goodwill.
    C. customer product loyalty
    D. competitors' reactions to the firm's new pricing structure.

20. Product contribution margin less avoidable fixed expenses equals:

    A. product margin.
    B. gross margin.
    C. variable costs.
    D. net income.

21. Incremental costs of product expansion or extension include:

    A. market research.
    B. product and packaging development.
    C. advertising.
    D. all of the above.

22. Last year, Jennings Aerospace purchased some production equipment. Due to technological advances, the company is considering replacing the production equipment with the latest technology. Data on the existing and the proposed equipment follow:

|  | Old Equipment | New Equipment |
|---|---|---|
| Remaining life | 5 years | 5 years |
| Original cost | $20,000 | $10,000 |
| Current market value | $5,000 | $10,000 |
| Salvage value in 3 years | $0 | $0 |
| Annual cash operating costs | $6,000 | $4,500 |

What is the incremental cost/benefit in the equipment replacement decision?

    A. $2,500 benefit
    B. $7,500 benefit
    C. $7,500 cost
    D. $12,500 cost

23. Williams Company is considering outsourcing one of the components used in its main product.  Williams Company incurs the following unit costs to make the component:

| | |
|---|---|
| Direct materials | $ 4.00 |
| Direct labour | 2.00 |
| Variable manufacturing overhead | 3.00 |
| Fixed manufacturing overhead | 5.00 |
| | $14.00 |

The fixed manufacturing overhead includes $1.00 of avoidable costs and $4.00 of allocated costs.  Williams Company has no alternative use for the facilities used to make the component.

With respect to the make-or-buy decision, what are the relevant costs that Williams Company incurs to make the product?

    A. $6.00
    B. $9.00
    C. $10.00
    D. $14.00

## USE THE FOLLOWING INFORMATION TO ANSWER QUESTIONS 24 AND 25

North Company has only 18,000 machine hours available for the month.  North can produce two products.  Product X has a contribution margin of $28 per unit and requires 4 machine hours to make.  Product Y has a contribution margin of $30 per unit and requires 5 machine hours to make.  North can sell all that it produces of either product.

24.  North wants to maximize total contribution margin for the month.  North should make:

    A.  Product X.
    B.  Product Y.
    C.  Some of Product X and some of Product Y.
    D.  Either product because it makes no difference.

25.  If North made only Product X, the total contribution margin would be _____ than if North made only Product Y.

    A.  $18,000 more
    B.  $18,000 less
    C.  $36,000 more
    D.  $90,000 more

26. Better Homes Products is a retailer of kitchen appliances.  The product information for three types of kitchen appliances is as follows:

|  | Blender | Food Processor | Microwave Oven |
|---|---|---|---|
| Unit selling price | $50.00 | $65.00 | $105.00 |
| Variable unit costs | 19.00 | 27.50 | 95.00 |
| Unit contribution margin | $31.00 | $37.50 | $ 10.00 |

The company presently compensates their salespeople by paying a commission equal to 10% of gross sales dollars.  Management is considering a new policy of paying salespeople a commission of 20% on product contribution margin rather than 10% on sales price.

Which of the following statements is (are) true?

A. Under the existing policy, sales personnel will be motivated to sell microwave ovens.
B. Under the new policy, sales personnel will be motivated to sell food processors.
C. Emphasizing sales of food processors will help the company achieve its profit maximization objective.
D. All of the above.

USE THE FOLLOWING INFORMATION TO ANSWER QUESTIONS 27 AND 28

Vaughn Company produces a product with the following unit cost:

| Direct materials | $ 5.50 |
|---|---|
| Direct labour | 2.50 |
| Variable overhead | 8.00 |
| Fixed overhead | 5.00 |
| Unit cost | $21.00 |

Fixed selling costs are $600,000 per year and variable selling costs are $2.50 per unit sold.

Production capacity is 1,000,000 units per year.  However, the company expects to produce only 800,000 units next year.  The product normally sells for $30 per unit.  A customer has offered to buy 150,000 units for $20 each.  The units would be sold in an area outside the market area currently served.

27. The incremental cost per unit associated with the special order is:

A. $16.00.
B. $16.75.
C. $18.50.
D. $19.25.

28. If the company accepts the special order, the effect on income would be:

A. $525,000 decrease.
B. $112,500 increase.
C. $225,000 increase.
D. $600,000 increase.

29. Bristow Industries Inc. is considering closing down SD-6, one of its divisions. The division presently has a contribution margin of $375,000. Overhead allocated to the division is $1,125,000, of which $125,000 cannot be eliminated. If this division were discontinued, by what amount would Bristow's pretax income increase?

    A. $125,000
    B. $375,000
    C. $625,000
    D. $750,000

30. Last year the deluxe model of Nova Industries, Inc., had sales of $905,000, variable production costs of $502,000, variable selling costs of $90,500, avoidable fixed expenses of $113,000, and allocated corporate fixed expenses of $140,000. What was the product margin for the deluxe model?

    A. $ 59,500
    B. $199,500
    C. $312,500
    D. $403,000

## ESSAY QUESTIONS AND PROBLEMS

1. Define sunk costs and explain why they are not relevant costs.

2. What are opportunity costs? Why are opportunity costs relevant costs?

3. What are differential costs and incremental costs?

4.  What cost elements make up the joint cost in a joint production process?  How is the joint cost allocated?

5.  What are the relevant quantitative and qualitative factors for a make-or-buy decision?

6.  What are the relevant costs in a make-or-buy decision?

7.  What are the relevant quantitative and qualitative factors involved in a decision to raise or lower prices?

8.  In what situations might a company depart from its typical price-setting routine?

9.  What are the qualitative factors involved in a decision to set a special order price?

10.  Define product margin and explain why it is the appropriate figure on which to base a decision to continue or eliminate a product.

11.  What is the difference between product line expansion and product line extension?  What are some of the incremental costs of expansions and extensions?

12. Chapman Company has a high degree of vertical integration and makes a component used in making its final product. An outside manufacturer has offered to sell Chapman Company the component at a cost of $20.00 per unit. Chapman Company's costs to manufacture the component are as follows:

| | |
|---|---|
| Direct materials | $ 6.00 |
| Direct labour | 3.00 |
| Variable manufacturing overhead | 5.00 |
| Fixed manufacturing overhead | 8.00 |
| Total | $22.00 |

The fixed manufacturing overhead consists of $2.00 in avoidable fixed overhead costs related to the production supervisor's salary and $6.00 of allocated costs. Assume that the quality of the outside manufacturer's components is not different from the quality of Chapman Company's components. Also, assume that the outside manufacturer can deliver all the components that Chapman Company needs when it needs them. Chapman Company has no alternative use of the facilities it uses to make the component. Should Chapman Company make or buy the component? Prove your answer with a cost analysis.

13. Adams Company has only 70,000 kilograms of raw materials for the next month. Due to a shortage, Adams Company can purchase no more raw materials. Adams can make product A, product B, or a combination of each. Product A has a contribution margin of $35 per unit and uses 7 kilograms of raw materials. Product B has a contribution margin of $30 per unit and uses 5 kilograms of raw materials. Adams Company can sell all of the output that it can produce. Calculate the number of units of product A and the number of units of product B that Adams Company should make if Adams Company wants to maximize its contribution margin.

14. Morris Company sells its product for $75 per unit. The variable costs incurred to make the product are $40 per unit. Morris allocates to each unit $5 of fixed manufacturing overhead costs. Variable selling expenses are $15 per unit. A new customer has offered to buy 5,000 units from Morris at $60 per unit. Morris has sufficient idle capacity and the sale to this new customer would not affect sales to current customers. Also, Morris would avoid $10 in variable selling expenses usually incurred. Calculate the net benefit or detriment that Morris would realize if Morris accepts the special order. Should Morris accept the special order?

15. The economy model of Brown Company is not performing according to management's expectations. The income statement for the economy model for the previous year is as follows:

| | |
|---|---|
| Sales | $800,000 |
| Variable costs | 450,000 |
| Contribution margin | $350,000 |
| Fixed costs | 600,000 |
| Net income (loss) before taxes | ($250,000) |

The fixed costs include the $60,000 salary for the manager of the economy model and other expenses of $140,000 associated with the economy model. Included in the $140,000 of these other fixed costs is $30,000 in depreciation on equipment that has no resale value. The remaining fixed costs represent corporate overhead costs that Brown Company has allocated to the economy model based on relative sales.

The president wants to drop the economy model, but he wants to see your analysis first. Prepare an income statement in a more useful format for the economy model. What would be the effect on the net income before taxes if Brown Company drops the economy model?

## SELF TEST ANSWERS

### TRUE/FALSE

| | | | | | | | | | |
|---|---|---|---|---|---|---|---|---|---|
| 1. | F | 4. | T | 7. | F | 10. | T | 13. | F |
| 2. | F | 5. | F | 8. | T | 11. | F | 14. | T |
| 3. | T | 6. | T | 9. | F | 12. | T | 15. | T |

### MULTIPLE CHOICE

| | | | | | | | | | | | |
|---|---|---|---|---|---|---|---|---|---|---|---|
| 1. | B | 7. | C | 13. | C | 19. | A | 25. | A |
| 2. | B | 8. | A | 14. | C | 20. | A | 26. | D |
| 3. | A | 9. | A | 15. | D | 21. | D | 27. | C |
| 4. | C | 10. | B | 16. | C | 22. | A | 28. | C |
| 5. | D | 11. | A | 17. | D | 23. | C | 29. | C |
| 6. | A | 12. | D | 18. | B | 24. | A | 30. | B |

## ESSAY QUESTIONS AND PROBLEMS

1.      Sunk costs are costs a company incurred in the past to acquire an asset or resource.  A sunk cost is not relevant to a decision because a company has already incurred the cost and cannot change it by any decision now or in the future.

2.      Opportunity costs are the benefits foregone when a company chooses one course of action over another.  Companies do not record opportunity costs in the accounting records.  Companies may not be able to quantify opportunity costs with precision.  Nevertheless, opportunity costs are relevant costs that managers should take into account when making decisions.  Opportunity costs relate to future endeavors and differ between alternatives.  Thus, opportunity costs are relevant costs.

3.      Differential costs are costs that differ between or among alternatives.  Incremental costs are the additional costs of producing or selling a quantity of output under consideration.  Both differential costs and incremental costs are relevant costs in decision making.  Differential costs and incremental costs may be variable or fixed.

4.      The joint cost of a joint production process consists of the costs incurred for materials, labour, and overhead up to the split-off point.  At the split-off point, the joint cost is allocated only to the joint products and not to any resulting by-products, scrap, or waste.  Allocation may be made on the basis of a physical measure (such as kilograms or units) or a monetary measure (such as final sales value).

5.      The relevant quantitative factors are:  (1) incremental production costs for each unit; (2) unit cost of purchasing from outside supplier; (3) availability of production capacity to manufacture components; (4) opportunity costs of using facilities for production rather than for other purposes; and (5) availability of storage space for units and raw materials.

        The relevant qualitative factors are: (1) relative net advantage given uncertainty of estimates; (2) reliability of source(s) of supply; (3) ability to assure quality when units are purchased from outside; (4) nature of the work to be subcontracted; (5) number of available suppliers; (6) impact on customers and markets; (7) future bargaining position with supplier(s); (8) perceptions regarding possible future price changes; (9) perceptions about current product prices; and (10) strategic and competitive importance of component to long-run organizational success.

6.      In a make-or-buy decision, variable costs of production are relevant. Fixed production costs may be relevant if they can be avoided by discontinuance of production. The opportunity costs associated with the facilities being used for production may also be relevant.

7.      In making decisions to raise or lower prices, the relevant quantitative factors include (1) prospective or new contribution margin per unit of product, (2) both short-term and long-term changes in product demand and production volume caused by the price increase or decrease, and (3) best use of any scarce resources. Some relevant qualitative factors involved in decisions regarding price changes are (1) influence on customer goodwill, (2) customer product loyalty, and (3) competitors' reactions to the firm's new pricing structure.

8.      There are situations in which a company will depart from its typical price-setting routine. For example, a company may "low-ball" bid some jobs in order to obtain the job in an effort to introduce company products or services to a particular market segment. Special pricing concessions may also be justified when orders are of an unusual nature (because of the quantity, method of delivery, or packaging) or because the products are being tailor-made to customer specifications. Further, special pricing can be used when producing goods for a one-time job, such as an overseas order that will not affect domestic sales.

9.      When setting a special order price, management must consider the qualitative issues as well as the quantitative ones. For instance, will a low bid price cause this customer (or others) to feel that a precedent has been established for future prices? Will the contribution margin on a bid set low enough to acquire the job earn an amount sufficient to justify the additional burdens placed on management or employees by this activity? How, if at all, will special order sales affect the company's normal sales? If the job is taking place during a period of low business activity (off-season or recession), is management willing to take the business at a lower contribution or profit margin simply to keep a trained workforce employed?

10.     Product margin is the excess of a product's revenues over both its direct variable expenses and any avoidable fixed expenses related to the product. It is the amount remaining to cover unavoidable direct fixed expenses and common costs and then to provide profits. The product margin is the appropriate figure on which to base a decision to continue or eliminate a product, since that figure measures the product's ability to help cover indirect and unavoidable costs.

11.     Product line expansion refers to the introduction of totally new products. Product line extension refers to the introduction of "offshoots" of current products because the company decides that the market needs to be more highly segmented. The segmentation might focus on price, size, operating costs, or aesthetics issues; alternatively, extensions may be necessary to meet competitive pressures. Incremental costs of expansions and extensions (other than the variable costs of the product) include market research, product and packaging development, product introductions, and advertising.

12.     Chapman Company should continue to make the component because the relevant costs to make the component are $16.00. The $6.00 in allocated fixed overhead costs is not relevant. Thus, Chapman Company saves $4.00 ($20.00 - $16.00) per unit by continuing to make the component.

Relevant costs to make:
| | |
|---|---|
| Direct materials | $ 6.00 |
| Direct labour | 3.00 |
| Variable manufacturing overhead | 5.00 |
| Fixed manufacturing overhead | 2.00 |
| Total | $16.00 |

13. 

| Product | A | B |
|---|---|---|
| Contribution margin per unit | $35 | $30 |
| Divided by kilograms of raw materials used | 7 | 5 |
| Contribution margin per kilogram of raw materials | $ 5 | $ 6 |

Adams should not produce any units of product A. To maximize its contribution margin, Adams should produce 14,000 units of product B only. The contribution margin is $70,000 greater from producing product B rather than product A. Although product A has a higher contribution margin per unit, product B has a higher contribution margin per kilogram of raw materials.

$\dfrac{70,000 \text{ kilograms of raw materials}}{7 \text{ kilograms of raw materials per unit of A}}$ = 10,000 units of product A

10,000 units of A x $35 per unit = $350,000 contribution margin, or
70,000 kilograms x $5 per kilogram =  $350,000 contribution margin

$\dfrac{70,000 \text{ kilograms of raw materials}}{5 \text{ kilograms of raw materials per unit of B}}$ = 14,000 units of product B

14,000 units of B x $30 per unit = $420,000 contribution margin, or
70,000 kilograms x $6 per kilogram =  $420,000 contribution margin

Advantage of producing product B:  $420,000 - $350,000 = $70,000,
or 70,000 kilograms x ($6 - $5) per kilogram = $70,000

14. 

| | | |
|---|---|---|
| Sales price | | $60 |
| Variable manufacturing costs | $40 | |
| Variable selling expenses ($15 - $10) | 5 | |
| Total relevant costs | | 45 |
| Net benefit per unit | | 15 |
| Number of units | | x 5,000 |
| Net benefit | | $75,000 |

Morris should accept the special order since it provides a net benefit of $75,000. Allocated fixed costs are not relevant to the decision.

15. 

| | | |
|---|---|---|
| Sales | | $800,000 |
| Variable costs | | 450,000 |
| Product contribution margin | | $350,000 |
| Less: Avoidable fixed costs | [$60,000 + ($140,000 - $30,000)] | 170,000 |
| Product margin | | $180,000 |

The corporate overhead costs are common fixed costs and are not relevant. These common fixed costs will remain the same and be allocated to other products if Brown Company drops the economy model. The depreciation expense of $30,000 is a direct fixed cost, but it is not relevant because it is an allocation of a sunk cost. Thus, Brown Company's net income before taxes would be $180,000 lower if it drops the economy model.

# CHAPTER 9
# THE BUDGETING PROCESS

## CHAPTER OVERVIEW

All types of organizations prepare and use budgets for planning and control.  This chapter covers some of the managerial aspects of budgeting, the quantitative aspects of the budgeting process, and the preparation of a master budget.  The master budget is the set of all budgetary schedules and pro forma financial statements.  The master budget consists of operating budgets and financial budgets.  The capital budget is an important budget, but companies do not include it in the master budget.

The sales budget is the first budget that a company must prepare.  The budgeted sales affect the sales budget and all other budgets.  These other budgets include the production budget, the direct materials purchases budget, the direct labour budget, the manufacturing overhead budget, the selling, general, and administrative expenses budget, the cash budget, and the pro forma financial statements.  This chapter illustrates each of these budgets.  The chapter includes helpful solution strategies immediately following the glossary.

## CHAPTER STUDY GUIDE

Budgeting is the process of developing a financial plan for an organization's future operations.  Budgeting is a management function, not an accounting function.  Organizations can use budgets to indicate direction and priorities, measure performance, encourage achievement and continuous improvement, and identify areas of concern.

Organizations can perform the budgeting process in a variety of ways:  (1) top-down, (2) bottom-up, or (3) a combination of the two.  Exhibit 9-1 provides a flowchart of the budgeting process.

Budgeting helps managers to choose a specific direction.  The chosen path generally focuses on achieving some financial measure of performance.  Management can compare actual results to the budget and compute the variances.  Budgets help to identify potential problems and plan ways to solve them.  Budgets communicate objectives, constraints, and expectations to everyone in the organization.  Participation of managers and employees in the budgeting process motivates greater commitment to the budget.  Also, such participation fosters a spirit of teamwork and cooperation.  Employee participation is also important to obtain necessary information.

Management usually expresses budgets in financial terms.  The budgeting and planning processes, however, are concerned with all of the organization's resources.  Management can view these processes from either a short-term or a long-term perspective.

When managers plan on a long-term basis (5 to 10 years), they are engaged in strategic planning.  Strategic planning is generally performed only by top-level management.  The result of the process is a statement of long-range goals for the organization and of the strategies and policies that will help in the achievement of those goals.

Managers engaging in strategic planning should identify key variables, or critical factors believed potentially to be direct causes of the achievement or nonachievement of organizational goals and objectives.  Exhibit 9-2 lists the external factors considered to be the most critical in determining the strategic plans of manufacturing companies.

The process of determining the specific objectives and means by which strategic plans will be achieved is called tactical (or operational) planning. Most tactical plans are short-term (1 to 18 months). The annual budget is an example of a single use tactical plan. Exhibit 9-3 illustrates the relationships among strategic planning, tactical planning, and budgeting.

Both strategic and tactical planning require that information regarding the economy, environment, technological developments, and available resources be incorporated into the setting of goals and objectives.

Management should begin budgeting activity after evaluating the operating environment and relevant product life cycles and deciding on the company's strategic plan. The budgeting process requires a careful integration of a complex set of facts and estimates with human relationships and attitudes. Thus, no single budgeting system is right for all organizations.

Nevertheless, the two basic ways of preparing budgets are from the top down (imposed budgets) and from the bottom up (participatory budgets). Exhibit 9-4 lists the advantages and disadvantages of imposed budgets. Exhibit 9-5 likewise lists the advantages and disadvantages of participatory budgets.

The degree of participation in the budgeting process falls somewhere along a spectrum. At one end is the right to comment on the budgets before their implementation. At the opposite end is the right to set the budgets. Neither extreme is usually appropriate. The right to comment on imposed budgets reflects little participation, and the right to set budgets ignores the cooperation and communication among areas crucial to the operation of a cohesive organization.

A participatory budget is a budget that top management and operating personnel have developed through a process of joint decision making. The degree to which top management allows lower-level managers to participate in budget development generally depends on two factors: (1) top management's awareness of the advantages of the participation process and (2) its confidence in those advantages.

A potential disadvantage of participatory budgets is budget slack. Budget slack does not usually exist in imposed budgets. Budget slack is the deliberate underestimation of revenues and/or overestimation of expenses. Budget slack allows managers to achieve their budget targets with less effort than they would otherwise expend. Budget slack can also cause operational problems. Underestimated sales may lead to inadequate resources in production.

To reduce the possibility of budget slack, management can choose to base the budget on activities rather than on costs. Activity-based budgets require an analysis of cost drivers and tracing the budget line items to the activities performed. Activity-based budgets provide answers to questions about the processes, activities, and resources of the organization.

Most budgets have some characteristics of imposed budgets and some characteristics of participatory budgets. Typically, budgeting involves a coordinated effort of input from operating personnel followed by revisions from top management. Top management sets the strategic objectives for lower-level management. Next lower-level managers propose and justify performance targets for their operations. Then top management combines all component budgets, evaluates the results, and provides feedback on any needed changes to lower-level managers.

Management has a responsibility to review the completed budget before approving it. This review is necessary to ascertain (1) whether the assumptions underlying the budget are reasonable, and (2) whether the budgeted results are realistic and acceptable.

Companies normally prepare budgets on an annual basis.  Companies generally divide the annual budget into quarterly and monthly budgets.  Budgeting should occur at least two to three months before the period the budget covers.  Participatory budgets take longer to develop than do imposed budgets.  Also, the larger and more complex the company is, the longer the budgeting process will take.

Some companies use a continuous or rolling budget.  A continuous budget always covers a twelve-month period.  As the current month expires, management adds one more month to the continuous budget period.  Exhibit 9-6 illustrates the period covered by a continuous  budget.  Continuous budgets provide for a smoother planning process.  Also, continuous budgets have more of a long-range focus to minimize surprises at the end of the year.  The use of a detailed budget manual can also help in minimizing surprises within the budgeting process.

The use of electronic spreadsheets greatly aids in the budgeting process.  Electronic spreadsheets allow organizations to analyze possible scenarios quickly and inexpensively.  They allow mangers to adjust interrelated budgets to reflect internal or environmental changes.  Electronic spreadsheets also help a company to maintain a continuous budget.

A budget manual also facilitates the budgeting process.  A budget manual should include (1) statements of the budgeting purpose and the desired results, (2) budgetary activities to be performed, (3) a calendar of scheduled budgetary activities, (4) sample budget forms, and (5) original, revised, and approved budgets.

After a budget is prepared and accepted, it is implemented.  Budget implementation means that the budget is now considered a standard against which performance can be measured.  Once the budget is implemented, the control phase begins.  Control includes making actual-to-budget comparisons, determining variances, providing feedback to operating managers, investigating the causes of the variances, and taking any necessary corrective action.  Exhibit 9-7 diagrams the nature of the budgeting process.

Managers hold subordinates responsible for the revenues and costs over which they have control.  The difference between actual results and budgeted results is a variance.

The difference between actual sales revenue and budgeted sales revenue is the total revenue variance.  Management can break down the total revenue variance into the sales price variance and the sales volume variance.  The sales price variance is the difference between the actual sales price and the budgeted sales price multiplied by the actual sales volume.  The sales volume variance is the difference between the actual sales volume and the budgeted sales volume multiplied by the budgeted sales price.

If these revenue variances are positive, they are favourable (F).  If they are negative, one drops the negative sign and the variance is unfavourable (U).

After revenue variances have been explained, managers can focus on analyzing cost variances.  Costs must be analyzed in relation to the actual volume of sales rather than the budgeted volume of sales.  Comparing actual expenses to budgeted expenses that were calculated at a different level of sales will not provide valid information on how well costs were controlled during the period.  Flexible budgets and flexible budget formulas look at costs and revenues at different sales and production levels and are used to analyze cost variances.

In addition to determining whether costs were controlled, managers need to analyze the ways in which money was spent.  Spending analysis should focus on individual line items, not just totals, and on spending within categories.

Variances should be calculated as early as possible and the causes of the variances should be investigated.  Management should also consider the effects that current changes in conditions may have on future operations and on the types and extent of future budgetary variances.  Exhibit 9-8 indicates some possible problems and causes of poor actual-to-budget performance.

Under certain circumstances, management may decide to revise the budget.  If actual performance is substantially less or substantially better than was expected, the budget may or may not be adjusted depending on the causes of the variances.  For example, if the cost of inputs increases, management may decide to revise budget estimates upward to reflect costs more realistically.

The budget is often used to evaluate performance.  If revised budgets are prepared, top management may want to compare performance to both the original and the revised budgets and then use multiple evaluation tools to judge the quality as well as the quantity of performance.

The possibility exists that operating managers may attempt to introduce budgetary slack into their budgets.  Top management can try to reduce slack by evaluating actual performance against budgeted performance through a bonus system.

In addition to including budget slack in the process, managers may play other "budget games."  Some of these games are discussed in Exhibit 9-9.

If budgets are to be used in effectively evaluating performance, they should be challenging but achievable.  The advantages of using achievable budget targets include the following:  (1) managers' commitment to achieving the budget targets is increased, (2) managers' confidence remains high, (3) organizational control costs decrease, (4) the risk of managers engaging in harmful short-term "income-management" practices is reduced, (5) effective managers are allowed greater operating flexibility, (6) the corporation is somewhat protected against the costs of optimistic projections, such as overproduction and warehousing, and (7) the predictability of corporate earnings is increased because the probability of target achievement is high.

Participatory budgeting is essential for multinational companies.  Multinational companies face a large number of external factors, including foreign currency exchange rates, that can affect the planning process.  The company may need to prepare separate budgets for each international market served in addition to an overall budget.  A list of underlying assumptions should support the budget for each foreign operation.

After management implements the budget, the control phase begins.  Budgets are standards against which to measure performance.  Managers are held responsible for the revenues and costs over which they have control.  In many cases, determining the underlying causes of budget variations is difficult because of the effects of noncontrollable factors, which include competitive maneuvers, economic conditions, and government regulations.

In an international organization, the supporting list of assumptions is critical if the organization uses the budget for control and evaluation purposes.  Top management should not hold lower-level managers and employees responsible for not achieving budget objectives if the causes are due to unforeseen factors.  These factors include new import or export restrictions, exchange rate fluctuations, and market disturbances created by economic adjustments in a foreign country.  Top management should hold lower-level managers responsible, however, for taking advantage of new opportunities these factors create.

The master budget is a comprehensive set of an organization's budgetary schedules and pro forma financial statements.  The master budget consists of operating budgets and financial budgets.  Operating budgets contain information both in units and in dollars.  Financial budgets include information expressed in dollars only.  Financial budgets include the cash budget and the pro forma financial statements.  The capital budget is also a financial budget although the master budget does not include it.

Management prepares the master budget for a specific period.  The master budget is static rather than flexible.  Management chooses the most likely level of activity in preparing the master budget.  The predicted level of unit sales used in the preparation of the master budget affects all the components of the organization.  All components of the organization must interact in a coordinated manner because a budget developed in one department is usually an essential element in preparing another department's budget.  Exhibit 9-10 illustrates the budgetary process in a manufacturing company.

Assuming that a company uses participatory budgeting, each department involved in the budgeting process will either prepare its own budget or submit information for inclusion in the budget.  The budgeting process begins with the sales department's estimate of the types, quantities, and timing of the demand for the company's products.  The production department and the accounts receivable department then use this information.  The production department needs sales estimates to prepare the production budget.  The accounts receivable department needs sales estimates to estimate the amounts and timing of cash flows.  Certain information must flow back into the department in which it originated.  For example, the sales department needs information on finished goods inventory levels to ensure that products are available for sale.  Exhibit 9-11 provides an overview of the sequence and component budgets in the preparation of the master budget.

Organizations usually prepare the master budget for an annual period and then subdivide it into quarterly and monthly periods.  The process of preparing the master budget is the same regardless of the time period that it covers.  The budgeting process must begin well ahead of the period the master budget covers.  An estimated balance sheet at the end of the period preceding the period the master budget covers (the same as the beginning of the period the master budget covers) provides account balance information used to prepare the master budget.  Exhibit 9-12 illustrates an estimated balance sheet.  The budget committee reviews and approves the master budget after making any necessary adjustments.  The budget committee usually includes top management and the chief financial officer (CFO).

The sales budget shows expected sales in units and in dollars.  The sales in dollars equal the sales in units times the price of the product.  Exhibit 9-13 illustrates a sales budget.

After management prepares the sales budget, management then prepares the production budget.  Exhibit 9-14 illustrates a production budget.  The units to be produced are equal to the budgeted sales in units (obtained from the sales budget) plus the desired ending inventory, less the beginning inventory.  This example shows budgeted production by month for the first quarter of the year and for the first quarter as a whole.

The ending inventory for the quarter as a whole is equal to the ending inventory for the last month in the quarter (March in this example).  March 31 is the end of the month and also the end of the quarter.  Thus the ending inventories are the same.  One should avoid the temptation to add the ending inventories for the months in the quarter across to obtain the ending inventory for the quarter.  Doing so will lead to an incorrect result.  If the company bases its ending inventory for the last month of the quarter on budgeted sales for the next month, the company will need to estimate the next month's budgeted sales figure to compute the ending inventory.

Also, the beginning inventory for the quarter as a whole is equal to the beginning inventory for the first month in the quarter. The beginning inventory for the first month in the quarter is the same as the ending inventory for the preceding period. In this example, January 1 is the beginning of the month of January and it is also the beginning of the first quarter. Thus, the beginning inventories are the same. Again, one should avoid the temptation to add the beginning inventories across to obtain the beginning inventory for the quarter. That method might seem correct, but it is not. The ending inventory for one month becomes the beginning inventory for the next month. A good way to check the accuracy of the production budget is to add the units to be produced for each month in the quarter. They should equal the units to be produced for the quarter as a whole.

Management usually decides the company's inventory policy. The desired ending inventory is a function of the quantity and demand for the company's products as well as the company's production capacity and speed. Management should consider the high costs of maintaining excessive inventory. Management could specify the ending inventory as a percentage of the next period's estimated sales. Other alternatives include maintaining a steady level of inventory, increasing inventory for expected periods of high demand, or using a just-in-time system. The inventory policy affects whether a company has constant production with variable inventory levels or variable production with constant inventory levels.

After management prepares the production budget, management can then prepare the direct materials purchases budget. Exhibit 9-15 illustrates a materials purchases budget. Management can also prepare the direct labour budget  Management bases the direct labour hours needed on the standard hours allowed. The wage rate includes fringe benefits. Exhibit 9-16 illustrates a direct labour budget. The engineering and human resources departments decide the necessary personnel for the factory, the sales force, and the office staff.

In addition, management can prepare the manufacturing overhead budget. Management must specify manufacturing overhead costs as fixed or variable before they can prepare the manufacturing overhead budget. Management must also separate mixed costs into their fixed and variable components. The manufacturing overhead budget usually shows total manufacturing overhead as well as separate totals for cash expenditures for manufacturing overhead and depreciation. The total cash items of manufacturing overhead are brought forward to the cash budget. Depreciation is a cost that does not require the outflow of cash.  Exhibit 9-17 illustrates a manufacturing overhead budget.

Management prepares the selling, general, and administrative (S&A) budget in a manner similar to the manufacturing overhead budget. Management must specify costs as fixed or variable. The total costs less depreciation flow through to the cash budget. The S&A budget, however, uses budgeted sales rather than production as the activity level. Exhibit 9-18 provides an example of an S&A budget.

The capital budget expresses management's plans for the purchase of plant and equipment. The capital budget is an important budget although it is not part of the master budget. The capital budget does affect the master budget because acquisitions of plant and equipment increase depreciation costs and require expenditures. These expenditures can be for the full purchase price or for repayment of loans including interest used to acquire plant and equipment. Exhibit 9-19 provides a brief example of a capital budget.

Management prepares the cash budget after preparing all the other budgets. The cash budget may be the most important budget that an organization prepares. No organization can survive without adequate cash. Cash budgets reveal when the organization will need short-term loans and when the cash will be available to repay those loans. Management also uses the cash budget to evaluate the performance of the accounts receivable and accounts payable departments by comparing actual to scheduled collections, payments, and discounts taken.

Management must translate the sales revenue from the sales budget into the pattern for cash collections.  Management must determine the pattern of cash collections from accounts receivable to prepare a schedule of cash collections that will flow through to the cash budget.  Also, the management calculates the budgeted balances for accounts receivable and allowance for uncollectible accounts for the pro forma balance sheet.  Exhibit 9-20 gives an example of a collection pattern for sales.  Exhibit 9-21 illustrates a schedule of cash collections.

Management must translate information from the purchases budget into the pattern for cash disbursements.  Also, management must determine the pattern for cash disbursements for accounts payable to prepare a schedule of cash disbursements.  The totals from this schedule also flow through to the cash budget.  Management also computes the budgeted balance for accounts payable for the pro forma balance sheet.  Exhibit 9-22 illustrates a schedule of cash disbursements for accounts payable.

Exhibit 9-23 illustrates a cash budget.  The beginning cash balance for the quarter as a whole is equal to the beginning cash balance for the first month of the quarter.  Also, the ending cash balance for the quarter as a whole must equal the ending cash balance for the last month in the quarter.

The last step in the budgeting process is the preparation of the pro forma financial statements.  Before management can prepare a pro forma income statement, however, management must prepare a pro forma cost of goods manufactured schedule.  Management uses the cost of goods manufactured in computing the cost of goods sold.  Exhibit 9-24 illustrates a pro forma cost of goods manufactured schedule.  Exhibit 9-25, Exhibit 9-26, and Exhibit 9-27, illustrate a pro forma income statement, a pro forma balance sheet, and a pro forma cash flow statement, respectively.

The cash flow statement shows the sources and uses of cash from three major activities:  (1) operating, (2) investing, and (3) financing.  Management finds such knowledge useful in deciding the company's ability to meet fixed cash outflow obligations, adapt to adverse business conditions, and assume new commitments.  The cash flow statement also helps managers in evaluating the quality of the company's earnings.  In addition, the pro forma cash flow statement allows management to assess whether the budgeted cash flows are consistent with the company's strategic goals and objectives.

The cash flow statement is a financial statement required for external reporting.  Management may prepare the operating section using either the direct method or the indirect method.  The direct method shows cash collections and cash disbursements from operating activities.  The indirect method begins with net income and makes adjustments to arrive at cash flow from operations.

Traditional budgeting often has limited usefulness as a control tool.  The reason is that some organizations use poor budgeting techniques such as basing the current year's appropriations on the expenditures in the prior year.  Thus, organizations fund activities without regard for priorities or alternative methods of achieving the organization's objectives.  Such an approach often results in the creeping commitment syndrome.

Government has used zero-based budgeting as a means to eliminate the creeping commitment syndrome.  Zero-based budgeting is a systematic approach to budgeting that considers the organization's priorities and alternatives for reaching the organization's objectives. Zero-based budgeting requires managers to reevaluate all activities at the beginning of the budgeting process to decide which activities the organization should continue, eliminate, or reduce.  Exhibit 9-28 shows some of the differences between traditional budgeting and zero-based budgeting.

Three steps involved in zero-based budgeting are (1) converting the organization's activities into decision packages, (2) ranking each decision package, and (3) allocating resources based on the organization's priorities. A decision package includes information about the activity such as objectives and benefits, consequences of not funding, necessary costs, and staffing requirements.

Zero-based budgeting, a process with both costs and benefits, is a demanding exercise that requires substantial time, effort, and commitment to be successful. An organization considering zero-based budgeting should weigh the costs and benefits of doing so.

Budgeting has been a standard and acceptable management practice for U.S. manufacturing and retail firms since it was introduced in the 1920s. In recent years, despite the general and long-term acceptance of budgeting, a movement has developed among many major firms to discontinue budgeting. The Beyond Budgeting Round Table (BBRT) was formed in 1998 to discuss best practices to replace traditional budgeting.

After reviewing the problems with traditional budgeting and examining what many of its member organizations have been doing to replace traditional budgeting, the BBRT recommended that traditional budgeting be replaced with an alternative that includes the use of an enterprise resource planning (ERP) system that allows all parts of the organization to be tied together via information. Operations should be managed in terms of activities rather than in terms of finances.

With the activity and information orientation, the organization should be measured against its strategy – not in financial terms, but in operational terms from multiple perspectives with a balanced scorecard. Using the balanced scorecard, performance should be benchmarked against peers internally and externally.

If balanced scorecard and benchmarking are used to measure operational or physical performance, budgeting is not needed as the ERP systems can be used frequently to forecast the expected financial results to the end of the next month, quarter, or year.

Estimating the demand for a company's products is pivotal to the budgeting process. Managers use all available information and various estimation techniques to forecast sales demand. Combining several estimation techniques serves as a check on the other methods and helps to reduce uncertainty. Methods of forecasting sales demand include the following: (1) asking salespeople for a subjective consensus, (2) extrapolating past trends, (3) using market research, and (4) using statistical and mathematical models.

Sensitivity analysis is one modeling technique that managers can use to assess risk in the budgeting process. Managers use sensitivity analysis to find the amount of change in one variable that must occur before they would make a different decision.

After management completes the preparation of the master budget including the pro forma financial statements, management can use the master budget for a variety of purposes. In addition to using the master budget for planning, the master budget enables management to make comparisons between actual results and the master budget. These differences are variances. Management uses these variances in control and in performance evaluation.

## SELF TEST

### TRUE/FALSE

1.  T  F  A master budget is a comprehensive set of all budgetary schedules and the pro forma financial statements of an organization.

2.  T  F  The intentional underestimation of revenues and/or overestimation of expenses is budget slack.

3.  T  F  The sales budget is the first budget that management prepares.

4.  T  F  The production level is the activity level used in preparing the selling, general, and administrative expenses budget.

5.  T  F  Management prepares the capital budget separately from the master budget.

6.  T  F  Imposed budgets are essential for multinational companies.

7.  T  F  The two acceptable formats for preparing the operating section of the cash flow statement are the direct method and the indirect method.

8.  T  F  A budget prepared from the bottom up is a participatory budget.

9.  T  F  An imposed budget is a budget that top management prepares with little or no input from operating personnel.

10. T  F  A continuous budget adds a new month as each current month expires.

11. T  F  The master budget is flexible rather than static.

12. T  F  The cash budget is an example of a financial budget.

13. T  F  The sales volume variance is the difference between the actual sales volume and the budgeted sales volume multiplied by the actual sales price.

14. T  F  If the sales price variance is positive, it is favourable (F).

15. T  F  One of the advantages of zero-based budgeting is that it requires little time and effort to implement.


### MULTIPLE CHOICE

1. Budgets derived from the bottom up are known as:

   A.  imposed budgets.
   B.  participatory budgets.
   C.  strategic budgets.
   D.  zero-based budgets.

2. Which of the following is an advantage of an imposed budget?

    A. enhances coordination among divisional plans and objectives
    B. causes a feeling of teamwork
    C. improves the morale of the workers
    D. encourages initiative in the lower-level managers

3. Which of the following is an advantage of a participatory budget?

    A. develops fiscal responsibility and budgetary skill among employees
    B. includes specific resource requirements
    C. is generally more realistic
    D. all of the above

4. A budget that adds one month as the current month expires is a:

    A. slack budget.
    B. continuous budget.
    C. capital budget.
    D. current budget.

5. Participatory budgets are more appropriate for:

    A. extremely small businesses.
    B. times of economic crisis.
    C. well-established organizations.
    D. start-up organizations.

6. Which budget does management prepare first?

    A. production budget
    B. cash budget
    C. pro forma income statement
    D. sales budget

7. Sensitivity analysis is a modeling technique that management can use for assessing:

    A. the change in the quantity demanded divided by the change in price.
    B. the direct method of preparing the operating section of the cash flow statement.
    C. risk in the budgeting process.
    D. the quality of a company's earnings.

8. The measure of activity used in preparing the selling, general, and administrative expenses budget is:

    A. sales.
    B. units produced.
    C. machine hours.
    D. direct labour hours.

9.  Which budget does management prepare separately from the master budget?

    A.  cash budget
    B.  capital budget
    C.  sales budget
    D.  selling, general, and administrative expenses budget

USE THE FOLLOWING INFORMATION TO ANSWER QUESTIONS 10 AND 11

Dunn Company prepared a production budget by month (January, February, and March) for the first quarter of the year and for the first quarter as a whole.

10.  The ending inventory for the first quarter as a whole equals:

    A.  the sum of the ending inventories for January, February, and March.
    B.  the ending inventory for March.
    C.  the beginning inventory for January.
    D.  the ending inventory for January.

11.  The beginning inventory for the first quarter as a whole equals:

    A.  the sum of the beginning inventories for January, February, and March.
    B.  the ending inventory for March.
    C.  the beginning inventory for January.
    D.  the ending inventory for January.

USE THE FOLLOWING INFORMATION TO ANSWER QUESTIONS 12 AND 13

Odom Company is preparing a cash budget by month for the fourth quarter of the year (October, November, and December) and for the fourth quarter as a whole.

12.  The beginning cash balance for the quarter as a whole equals:

    A.  the sum of the beginning cash balances for October, November, and December.
    B.  the ending cash balance for December.
    C.  the beginning cash balance for December.
    D.  the beginning cash balance for October.

13.  The ending cash balance for the quarter as a whole:

    A.  also goes on the pro forma balance sheet.
    B.  equals the beginning cash balance for December.
    C.  equals the beginning cash balance for October.
    D.  equals the sum of the ending cash balances for October, November, and December.

14.  The final step in the master budgeting process is the development of:

    A.  the cash budget.
    B.  the capital budget.
    C.  the selling, general, and administrative expenses budget.
    D.  budgeted or pro forma financial statements.

15.  The indirect method of preparing the cash flow statement begins the operating section with:

    A.  net sales.
    B.  net income.
    C.  total cash collections.
    D.  the ending cash balance.

16.  Robertson Company makes all of its sales on account.  Robertson collects its accounts as follows:  70 percent in the month of sale, 25 percent in the month following sale, and 4 percent in the second month following sale.  Uncollectible accounts are 1 percent of sales.  Robertson expects sales for the first three months of the year to be as follows:  January $450,000; February $475,000; and March $500,000.  How much cash should Robertson expect to collect in March?

    A.  $350,000
    B.  $486,750
    C.  $495,000
    D.  $500,000

17.  Camp Company expects its purchases for April to be $650,000 and its purchases for May to be $620,000.  Camp pays for 60 percent of its purchases in the month of purchase and receives a 2 percent discount.  Camp pays for the remaining 40 percent in the next month without any discount.  For purchases only, what are the expected cash payments in May?

    A.  $620,000
    B.  $624,560
    C.  $632,000
    D.  $636,960

18.  Franks Company has a policy of maintaining an ending inventory of finished goods equal to 10 percent of the current month's sales.  Franks met this requirement for October.  Sales for October were 24,000 units, and Franks expects sales for November to be 30,000 units.  How many units should Franks produce in November?

    A.  29,400
    B.  30,600
    C.  33,000
    D.  35,400

19.  Short Company plans to produce 3,200 units during August.  Each unit requires 4 kilograms of materials.  Short Company desires an ending raw materials inventory of 1,600 kilograms.  The raw materials inventory on August 1 contained 1,200 kilograms.  How many kilograms of materials should Short purchase in August?

    A.  12,400
    B.  12,800
    C.  13,200
    D.  14,400

20. Lane Company bases its manufacturing overhead budget on machine hours. Estimated machine hours for the quarter are 50,000. Lane estimates its variable manufacturing overhead costs at $7.00 per machine hour. Lane projects its fixed manufacturing overhead costs for the quarter to be $80,000 including $25,000 in depreciation. By how much will manufacturing overhead costs affect the cash budget for the quarter?

    A. $350,000
    B. $375,000
    C. $405,000
    D. $430,000

21. Kehr Company makes all of its sales on account. Kehr collects its accounts as follows: 20 percent in the month of sale, 70 percent in the month following sale, and 10 percent in the second month following sale. Uncollectible accounts are so low as to be disregarded. Kehr budgets sales for the first quarter of the year as follows: January $88,000; February $84,000; and March $100,000. The accounts receivable balance on January 1 was $55,000 for sales made in November and December of the previous year. What is Kehr's budgeted balance for accounts receivable at the end of March?

    A. $ 80,000
    B. $ 88,400
    C. $ 95,600
    D. $143,400

22. Pillow Company had net income of $298,000 for the year. Depreciation expense was $40,000; accounts receivable increased $24,000; accounts payable decreased $19,000; and inventory decreased $6,000. What was the cash flow from operations?

    A. $258,000
    B. $295,000
    C. $298,000
    D. $301,000

## USE THE FOLLOWING INFORMATION TO ANSWER QUESTIONS 23 AND 24

Terry Company makes all purchases of materials on account. Terry pays for 60 percent of each month's purchases in the month of purchase taking a 2 percent discount. Terry pays for the remaining 40 percent of each month's purchases in the month following purchase with no discount. Terry budgets purchases for the second quarter as follows: April $300,000; May $340,000; and June $350,000. The accounts payable balance for purchases was $125,000 on April 1 for purchases made in March.

23. What are Terry's expected cash payments for April?

    A. $176,400
    B. $180,000
    C. $301,400
    D. $305,000

24. What is Terry's budgeted accounts payable balance on June 30?

    A. $140,000
    B. $210,000
    C. $265,000
    D. $335,000

25. Thompson Company budgeted sales in units for the last quarter of the year as follows: October 60,000; November 70,000; and December 80,000. The finished goods inventory on hand October 1 is 20,000 units. Thompson desires an ending inventory on December 31 of 15,000 units. How many units should Thompson produce for the last quarter?

    A. 205,000
    B. 215,000
    C. 225,000
    D. 245,000

## USE THE FOLLOWING INFORMATION TO ANSWER QUESTIONS 26, 27, AND 28

Bolton Company's budgeted and actual results for the last year were as follows:

|  | Budgeted | Actual |
|---|---|---|
| Sales in units | 45,800 | 41,390 |
| Average sales price | $50 | $52 |

26. What is the sales price variance?

    A. $82,780 F
    B. $82,780 U
    C. $91,600 F
    D. $91,600 U

27. What is the sales volume variance?

    A. $220,500 F
    B. $220,500 U
    C. $229,320 F
    D. $229,320 U

28. What is the total revenue variance?

    A. $137,720 F
    B. $137,720 U
    C. $312,100 F
    D. $312,100 U

29.  Zero-based budgeting:

   A.  bases appropriations on the prior year's expenditures.
   B.  requires time, effort, and commitment to implement.
   C.  is applicable for manufacturing companies only.
   D.  is applicable for government agencies only.

30.  One of the major benefits of zero-based budgeting is that:

   A.  it focuses more on money than on goals and objectives.
   B.  it begins with the prior year's funding level.
   C.  little time is required to implement it.
   D.  managers focus on identifying unnecessary activities.

## ESSAY QUESTIONS AND PROBLEMS

1.  Define and explain operating budgets and financial budgets.

2.  Discuss the alternatives for establishing a desired ending inventory.  What should management consider before deciding how much inventory to keep on hand?

3.  What must management do to manufacturing overhead costs before estimating them?  What manufacturing overhead costs flow through to the cash budget?

4.  Explain how the capital budget relates to the master budget.

5.  Explain the basic differences between imposed budgets and participatory budgets.

6.  Define budget slack and explain its potential effects on the organization.

USE THE FOLLOWING INFORMATION FOR QUESTIONS 7 THROUGH 13

Gray Company makes only one product.  Its sales price is expected to be $80 per unit.

Actual sales:
November  6,000 units
December  6,500 units

Gray budgets its sales for the next six months as follows:
January    5,500 units
February   5,000 units
March      4,500 units
April      4,900 units
May        4,800 units
June       5,600 units

All sales are on account.  Gray collects its accounts as follows:
80 percent in the month of sale
15 percent in the month following sale
5 percent in the second month following sale
Uncollectible accounts are negligible and can be disregarded.

The beginning inventory on January 1 is 500 units.  Gray desires an ending finished goods inventory of 10 percent of the next month's budgeted sales.

Each unit of finished goods requires 3 kilograms of raw materials at a cost of $5.00 a kilogram.  Gray desires an ending inventory of raw materials equal to 20 percent of the following month's production needs.  Assume that Gray met this requirement at the end of December of the previous year.  Gray makes all purchases on account on terms net 30.  Gray pays its accounts payable as follows:  40 percent in the month of sale and 60 percent in the month following sale.  Purchases in December were $60,000.

7.  Prepare a sales budget by month for the first quarter and for the first quarter as a whole.

8.  Prepare a production budget by month for the first quarter and for the first quarter as a whole.

9.  Prepare a purchases budget by month for the first quarter and for the first quarter as a whole.

10. Prepare a schedule of cash collections from sales.

11. Prepare a schedule of cash disbursements for accounts payable.

12. Calculate the budgeted accounts receivable balance at March 31, 20xx.

13. Calculate the budgeted accounts payable balance at March 31, 20xx.

14. Hedrick Company's budgeted and actual sales results for the last year are as follows:

|  | Budgeted | Actual |
|---|---|---|
| Sales in units | 400,000 | 402,590 |
| Average sales price | $75 | $73 |

(A) Compute the sales price variance.

(B) Compute the sales volume variance.

(C) Compute the total revenue variance.

15. Define zero-based budgeting and explain how it differs from traditional budgeting.

## SELF TEST ANSWERS

### TRUE/FALSE

| | | | | | | | | | |
|---|---|---|---|---|---|---|---|---|---|
| 1. | T | 4. | F | 7. | T | 10. | T | 13. | F |
| 2. | T | 5. | T | 8. | T | 11. | F | 14. | T |
| 3. | T | 6. | F | 9. | T | 12. | T | 15. | F |

### MULTIPLE CHOICE

| | | | | | | | | | | | |
|---|---|---|---|---|---|---|---|---|---|---|---|
| 1. | B | 7. | C | 13. | A | 19. | C | 25. | A |
| 2. | A | 8. | A | 14. | D | 20. | C | 26. | A |
| 3. | D | 9. | B | 15. | B | 21. | B | 27. | B |
| 4. | B | 10. | B | 16. | B | 22. | D | 28. | B |
| 5. | C | 11. | C | 17. | B | 23. | C | 29. | B |
| 6. | D | 12. | D | 18. | B | 24. | A | 30. | D |

### ESSAY QUESTIONS AND PROBLEMS

1.  Management includes operating budgets and financial budgets in the master budget. Operating budgets contain information both in units and in dollars. Financial budgets contain information in dollars but not in units. The financial budgets include the cash budget and the pro forma financial statements. The capital budget is also a financial budget although management does not include it in the master budget. Management uses the information in dollars from the operating budgets to help prepare the financial budgets.

2.  Management could decide that the ending inventory should be a percentage of the next period's expected sales. Management could elect to keep a constant amount of inventory, change inventory levels based upon expected demand, or use the just-in-time approach of keeping a minimal amount of inventory. Before deciding how much inventory to keep on hand, management should consider the high carrying costs associated with inventory.

3.  Before management can estimate manufacturing overhead costs, management must specify the costs as fixed or variable, because some manufacturing overhead costs are fixed while other overhead costs vary with the number of units produced. Management must separate mixed costs into their fixed and variable components. The total manufacturing overhead costs less depreciation flow through to the cash budget as cash payments for manufacturing overhead. Depreciation is a cost that does not require the outflow of cash.

4.  The capital budget is not a part of the master budget. The capital budget, however, affects the master budget. Acquisitions of plant and equipment will affect the depreciation on the overhead budget and perhaps on the selling, general, and administrative expenses budget. Also, the capital budget will affect the cash budget because of the cash payments for plant and equipment or payments on loans used to acquire plant and equipment.

5.      Companies develop imposed budgets from the top down, and companies develop participatory budgets from the bottom up.  Participatory budgets involve joint decision making by top management and operating personnel.  Imposed budgets increase the chances that the organization will incorporate its strategic goals into the budget.  Imposed budgets are more appropriate for small organizations.  Imposed budgets may contribute to poor morale. Participatory budgets are more appropriate for large, well-established organizations.  Participation in the budgeting process fosters a spirit of teamwork and seems to cause a greater commitment to the budget.  Participatory budgets take more time to prepare than do imposed budgets.  They are generally more realistic than imposed budgets.  Budget slack may exist in participatory budgets, but budget slack usually does not exist in imposed budgets.

6.      Budget slack is the intentional underestimation of revenues and/or overestimation of expenses in preparing budgets.  Imposed budgets seldom contain budget slack.  Budget slack allows managers to reach their objectives with less effort than would otherwise be required.  Budget slack can result in operational problems because of the interaction of the various budgets.  If the company underestimates sales, problems can occur in other departments.

7.      Gray Company

Sales Budget
For the First Quarter Ending March 31, 20xx

|  | January | February | March | First Quarter |
|---|---|---|---|---|
| Sales in units | 5,500 | 5,000 | 4,500 | 15,000 |
| Price per unit | $80 | $80 | $80 | $80 |
| Sales in dollars | $440,000 | $400,000 | $360,000 | $1,200,000 |

8.      Gray Company

Production Budget
For the First Quarter Ending March 31, 20xx

|  | January | February | March | First Quarter |
|---|---|---|---|---|
| Sales in units | 5,500 | 5,000 | 4,500 | 15,000 |
| Add:  Desired ending inventory | 500 | 450 | 490[*] | 490 |
| Total needed | 6,000 | 5,450 | 4,990 | 15,490 |
| Less:  Beginning inventory | 500 | 500 | 450 | 500 |
| Units to be produced | 5,500 | 4,950 | 4,540 | 14,990 |

[*]April sales 4,900 x 10% = 490

9.    Gray Company

**Purchases Budget**
**For the First Quarter Ending March 31, 20xx**

| | January | February | March | First Quarter |
|---|---|---|---|---|
| Units to be produced | 5,500 | 4,950 | 4,540 | 14,990 |
| Add:  Ending inventory in whole units | 990 | 908 | 978** | 978 |
| Total units needed | 6,490 | 5,858 | 5,518 | 15,968 |
| Less:  Beginning inventory | 1,100* | 990 | 908 | 1,100 |
| Purchases in whole units | 5,390 | 4,868 | 4,610 | 14,868 |
| x kilograms per unit | 3 | 3 | 3 | 3 |
| Total kilograms to be purchased | 16,170 | 14,604 | 13,830 | 44,604 |
| x Price per kilogram | $ 5.00 | $ 5.00 | $ 5.00 | $ 5.00 |
| Total cost of materials | $80,850 | $73,020 | $69,150 | $223,020 |

*The beginning inventory for January is the same as the ending inventory for December.  The ending inventory for December met the 20 percent of the units to be produced for January: 5,500 x 20% = 1,100.

**Units to be produced in April = April sales 4,900 units + ending inventory (4,800 x 10%)  - beginning inventory 490 = 4,900 + 480 - 490  =  4,890.

Desired ending inventory for March = 4,890 x 20% = 978.

10.                                   Gray Company
**Schedule of Cash Collections**
**For the First Quarter Ending March 31, 20xx**

| | January | February | March | First Quarter |
|---|---|---|---|---|
| From: | | | | |
| November: | | | | |
| 6,000($80)( 5%) | $24,000 | | | $24,000 |
| December: | | | | |
| 6,500($80)(15%) | 78,000 | | | 78,000 |
| 6,500($80)( 5%) | | $26,000 | | 26,000 |
| January: | | | | |
| 5,500($80)(80%) | 352,000 | | | 352,000 |
| 5,500($80)(15%) | | 66,000 | | 66,000 |
| 5,500($80)(5%) | | | $22,000 | 22,000 |
| February: | | | | |
| 5,000($80)(80%) | | 320,000 | | 320,000 |
| 5,000($80)(15%) | | | 60,000 | 60,000 |
| March: | | | | |
| 4,500($80)(80%) | | | 288,000 | 288,000 |
| Totals | $454,000 | $412,000 | $370,000 | $1,236,000 |

11.

Gray Company
Schedule of Cash Disbursements for Accounts Payable
For the First Quarter Ending March 31, 20xx

|  | January | February | March | First Quarter |
|---|---|---|---|---|
| From: |  |  |  |  |
| December: |  |  |  |  |
| $60,000(60%) | $36,000 |  |  | $36,000 |
| January: |  |  |  |  |
| $80,850(40%) | 32,340 |  |  | 32,340 |
| $80,850(60%) |  | $48,510 |  | 48,510 |
| February: |  |  |  |  |
| $73,020(40%) |  | 29,208 |  | 29,208 |
| $73,020(60%) |  |  | $43,812 | 43,812 |
| March: |  |  |  |  |
| $69,150(40%) |  |  | 27,660 | 27,660 |
| Totals | $68,340 | $77,718 | $71,472 | $217,530 |

12.    Budgeted Accounts Receivable at March 31, 20xx:

From February Sales 5,000($80)( 5%)  =  $20,000
From March Sales    4,500($80)( 20%) =   72,000
Budgeted Accounts Receivable Balance   $92,000

13.  Budgeted Accounts Payable Balance at March 31, 20xx:

From March Purchases $69,150(60%) = $41,490

14.    (A) Sales price variance =
($73 - $75) x 402,590 = -$805,180 = $805,180 U

(B) Sales volume variance =
(402,590 - 400,000) x $75 = $194,250 = $194,250 F

(C) Total revenue variance =
(402,590 x $73) - (400,000 x $75) = - $610,930 = $610,930 U or
$194,250 + -$805,180 = $194,250 - $805,180 = -$610,930 = $610,930 U

15.    Zero-based budgeting is a system of budgeting that requires managers to justify planned expenditures in the current period without regard to the level of expenditures in the prior period.  Zero-based budgeting does not necessarily mean that managers must justify all activities from a zero base.  Rather, managers must reevaluate priorities annually within the context of organizational objectives to determine which ones to continue, eliminate, or fund at a lower level.  Zero-based budgeting is difficult to implement and does not provide measures of efficiency.  Traditional budgeting bases the current budget on the prior year's budget. Compared to zero-based budgeting, traditional budgeting focuses more on money and less on goals and objectives.  Also, traditional budgeting does not systematically consider alternatives to current operations. Traditional budgeting produces one level of appropriation for an activity.  Zero-based budgeting produces alternative levels of funding based on the availability of funds and objectives.

# CHAPTER 10
## CAPITAL ASSET SELECTION AND CAPITAL BUDGETING

## CHAPTER OVERVIEW

Companies invest in long-term assets to generate revenues or to reduce costs. These long-term assets are capital assets. Capital assets include plant, equipment, capital leases, and patents. Capital budgeting is the process of evaluating proposed investments in capital assets.

Management must make the best investments in capital assets within the constraints of limited resources. Making good capital budgeting decisions is critical to the long-term success of the company. This chapter describes four methods for evaluating proposed investments in capital assets. These methods are payback period, net present value, profitability index, and internal rate of return.

This chapter also discusses qualitative aspects that management should consider in capital budgeting decisions, especially for proposed investments in high-technology manufacturing equipment. The chapter also covers capital budgeting aspects of research and development costs and environmental costs.

Appendix 10A discusses the time value of money. Understanding the time value of money is vital to understanding the three discounted cash flow techniques for capital budgeting. Appendix 10B shows how to compute the accounting rate of return for a project. The accounting rate of return is another way to evaluate proposed investments. Appendix 10C discusses the impact of taxation on cash flows. For the best results, discounted cash flow methods should use after-tax cash flows.

## CHAPTER STUDY GUIDE

All companies must decide which investment opportunities to pursue from many potential projects. Making investment decisions is a most important responsibility of management. The investment in long-term assets often accompanies the execution of major strategies such as the development of new product lines or acquisitions of other companies. Companies also make such investments to improve product or service quality through acquisition of new technology. Companies make other capital investments to maintain or support existing operations. Capital asset acquisitions involve the investment of large sums of money for a long time.

Capital budgeting is the process of evaluating long-term investment proposals. A future activity or project usually includes the purchase, installation, and operation of a capital asset. Management must evaluate proposed capital assets to identify those that will best fulfill the company's goals and objectives.

Management must decide whether the project is worth the investment. This evaluation requires answers to the following four questions: (1) Is the activity worth the investment? (2) Which assets can the company use for the activity? (3) Of the suitable assets, which are the best investments? (4) Which of the best investments should the company select?

Management uses cost-benefit analysis to measure an activity's worth. Benefits can include qualitative benefits and financial benefits.

If management finds that the activity is worth the investment, management then must decide which assets the company can use for the activity. Cost information is necessary for this purpose and includes the initial cost of the asset and projected operating costs. Management must also estimate any revenues the asset will generate. Other factors that management should consider include the asset's useful life, salvage value, labour requirements, service availability, and revenues to be generated. Exhibit 10-1 shows these factors.

Next, management must decide which asset is the best for the activity.  Management must make two types of decisions--a screening decision and a preference decision.  A screening decision involves deciding whether the capital asset is acceptable based on predetermined criteria.  A preference decision involves ranking acceptable investments according to their ability to meet the company's objectives.  Management should attempt to fund the projects that, within budget limitations, will maximize shareholder wealth over the long run.  Exhibit 10-2 shows some criteria often used to rank capital investments.

Finally, management must decide in which assets to invest.  Because companies have limited resources, they may not be able to invest in all of the assets that are desirable.  Investments can be mutually exclusive, independent, or mutually inclusive.  Exhibit 10-3 shows the typical investment decision process.

Mutually exclusive investments accomplish the same task or function--if management selects one asset, it does not invest in the other assets under consideration.  When a company is considering the replacement of an existing asset with a new asset, the assets are mutually exclusive.  The company either keeps the existing asset or acquires the new asset and sells the old asset.

If investments are independent, investing in one asset has no specific effect on the decision to invest in the other possible investments.  Although limited resources may prevent the company from investing in all desirable investments, the investments themselves would not be mutually exclusive.

If investments are mutually inclusive, the selection of one investment means that the company must also select the other related investments.  On the other hand the rejection of the primary investment means that the company will reject the related investments also.

Management expects every investment to earn a return.  Using cash flows allows management to compare the return on a potential investment with the returns available on alternative investment opportunities.  Management must convert accounting income, which is on the accrual basis, to cash flows to use the cash flow methods.

Cash receipts include the revenues the investment generates and collects in cash.  Also included in cash inflows are the reductions in operating costs realized by the investment.  The salvage value of the asset and the working capital released at the end of its useful life are other cash inflows.

Cash disbursements include the acquisition cost of the asset and the investment in working capital caused by the asset's acquisition.  The operating costs of the asset are other cash outflows.

Any interest cost associated with financing the acquisition of the asset is not a cash outflow for this purpose.  The method used to finance the investment is not a factor in deciding whether to invest in it.  Capital budgeting decisions are investment decisions, but deciding how to finance an investment is a financing decision.  Management should not combine the cash flows associated with these two types of decisions.  Management must justify the decision to invest in a capital asset before deciding how to finance it.

For simplicity analysts assume that cash flows occur at the beginning of the period or at the end of the period.  Analysts also assume that acquisition costs occur at the beginning of the period.  In addition, analysts assume that revenues and expenses occur at the end of the period.  A timeline shows the timing of the cash inflows and cash outflows from an investment.  Cash flows that are a recovery of the original investment are a return of capital.  Cash flows in excess of the recovery of capital represent a return on capital.  Exhibit 10-4 illustrates the cash flows associated with a decision to purchase a fleet of trucks.

The payback period is the time that the investment takes for it to generate cash flows to recover the original investment. Managers often use the payback period as a measure of the risk of a project. The quicker the payback period, the less is the perceived risk of a project. The payback period has three shortcomings: (1) it ignores the time value of money; (2) it ignores the company's desired rate of return; and (3) it ignores cash flows after the payback period.

An annuity is a series of equal cash flows at equal intervals. If the cash flows are an annuity, the payback period is the investment divided by the annuity. If the cash flows are not equal per period, the payback period occurs at the time when the company has received enough cash flows to recover the original investment.

Money has a time value. Appendix 10A covers this topic in more depth. The process of converting cash flows to be received in the future to their present values is discounting. Discounting removes the interest element and allows management to state all cash flows in terms of their present values. Most capital budgeting techniques use discounted cash flows. Management does not discount current cash outlays because the present value of a current cash outlay is equal to itself.

Management must estimate the company's required rate of return on capital. This return is the discount rate and should be greater than or equal to the company's cost of capital. The cost of capital can be the weighted-average cost of the various sources of debt and equity that make up the company's capital structure.

Three discounted cash flow techniques are the net present value method, the profitability index, and the internal rate of return. The textbook discusses and illustrates these techniques.

The net present value method discounts the cash flows to present value using the desired rate of return. The cost of capital is generally the minimum desired rate of return. Companies may adjust the cost of capital up or down to give a discount rate that reflects differences in factors underlying the investment projects. The net present value of a project is the present value of the cash inflows less the present value of the cash outflows. Exhibit 10-5 illustrates the net present value method. Appendix B at the end of the textbook contains tables of present value factors. Table 1 contains the present value factors for a single amount. Table 2 contains present value factors for an ordinary annuity.

If the net present value is zero, the projected return on the project is equal to the discount rate. If the net present value is positive, the projected rate of return is greater than the discount rate. If the net present value is negative, the projected rate of return is less than the discount rate. The project is acceptable if the net present value is greater than or equal to zero.

Management must use the same project life span for all projects under consideration, because the company can use the cash flow released at the end of a project with a shorter life to invest in another project. The other project would generate additional cash inflows and outflows.

Also, management should not use the net present value method to compare independent projects with significantly different costs. Management can use a variation of the net present value method called the profitability index to compare projects with uneven investments. Management computes the profitability index by dividing the present value of the net future cash inflows by the net investment. The profitability index provides a measure of the company's efficiency of capital use. The higher the profitability index, the more efficient is the company's use of capital.

For the profitability index to provide better information than the net present value method, the projects must be mutually exclusive or the availability of investment funds must be limited.  The profitability index should be greater than or equal to 1.00 for a project to be acceptable.

The internal rate of return method calculates the rate of return earned on the project if the company can reinvest all cash flows at the internal rate of return.  The internal rate of return is the rate of return that, when it is used as the discount rate, causes the net present value to be zero.

If the cash flows an investment generates are equal per period for several periods, one can calculate the internal rate of return using the table for present value factors of an ordinary annuity.  The investment divided by the annuity equals a present value factor.  Then, one identifies the interest rate that matches the present value factor for that number of periods.  That interest rate is the internal rate of return.

If the cash flows are not equal, one can solve the internal rate of return using a trial-and-error approach or using a calculator or computer.  Exhibit 10-6 illustrates a trial-and-error approach for estimating the internal rate of return for a project.

Management compares the internal rate of return of a project with its discount rate or hurdle rate.  The hurdle rate is the lowest rate of return acceptable to management, which is usually greater than or equal to the cost of capital.  If the internal rate of return is greater than or equal to the hurdle rate, the investment is acceptable.  If the internal rate of return is less than the hurdle rate, management will reject the investment.

All capital budgeting techniques have two identical shortcomings:  (1) they do not take management's preferences about the timing of cash flows into account; and (2) they use a single measure of cash flow amounts rather than a range of values based on probabilities.  Exhibit 10-7 summarizes the assumptions and limitations of the five capital budgeting techniques including the accounting rate of return discussed in Appendix 10B.

Effective management of the capital budget helps managers to fulfill many important responsibilities.  One such responsibility is quality management.  Investing in capital investments is one means of managing prevention and appraisal costs.  Increased spending for prevention and appraisal costs is likely to lead to reductions in failure costs.  Management could prevent quality problems by purchasing sophisticated manufacturing technologies and training employees to use manufacturing techniques that reduce errors.  Management can apply statistical quality controls to assess operations and decide when production has exceeded acceptable error tolerances.

Management seldom considers quality issues in isolation in capital budgeting decisions.  Quality will be a secondary issue in some capital budgeting decisions.  An asset acquisition could be unacceptable if management only looked at labour savings.  If the new asset reduces defects, the savings in quality costs could increase the net present value of the project enough to make it acceptable.  Management should consider reductions in external failure costs and internal failure costs in making capital budgeting decisions.

Management should also think about training costs when making capital budgeting decisions.  Similar to investments in equipment, companies incur training costs to generate future benefits.  The benefits of training are likely to last for the duration of a person's employment.  Thus, the view that training provides benefits over multiple periods is proper.  Acquiring advanced technology and providing training to employees are basic tools of quality improvement.  Both technology and training result in an increase in prevention costs to be offset by lower failure costs in the future.

The capital budget is also important for managing research and development (R&D) costs. R&D activities are vital to create innovative products that will provide future revenues. Global competition increases the pressure to manage R&D activities effectively.

Because many companies have developed effective R&D programs, the life cycles of numerous products have decreased. Such reductions in life cycles occur when a competitor introduces a new product that an even newer product of another competitor soon makes obsolete. Competitors respond quickly to competitive threats from new products.

In this competitive market, the generation of future profits depends on good capital budgeting decisions. Research and development requires that a company invest cash and other resources to realize cash inflows from future sales. Using discounted cash flow techniques is important in analyzing research and development projects. Management should note that life cycles will probably become shorter. This trend will require that companies recoup their investments quickly if new products are to be profitable. The company's strategy is the major driver of R&D, but capital budget analysis is the major control tool.

Besides R&D, the purchase of high-technology assets related to quality initiatives, product life cycle management, and new product development has a major role in determining the success of companies today. Investments in high technology, however, require huge investments. Thus, managers must carefully evaluate the tangible and intangible benefits that these investments will provide. Management must consider the effects that these investments will have on the company. Investments in high technology can reduce labour costs, improve quality, increase the quantity produced, and shorten processing time. Such investments, however, can increase costs for maintenance, training, and utilities. Exhibit 10-9 lists several characteristics of high-technology capital projects.

Managers may need to modify the traditional capital budgeting analysis in evaluating proposed investments in automated equipment. Managers must be careful not to set the hurdle rate too high. Management should consider quantitative and qualitative benefits. Managers have often not considered the qualitative benefits such as reduced product development time, shortened delivery time, and improved competitive position. Management should remember that investments in high-tech equipment are interrelated and not freestanding. Management must also consider the opportunity cost of not investing in high-tech equipment. If competitors acquire such equipment, the company could be at a competitive disadvantage if it did not also invest in high-technology equipment.

Management should attempt to quantify all benefits and costs that they can with any reasonable degree of accuracy. Managers could use probabilities in assigning quantitative value to qualitative benefits. Alternatively, management could make subjective assessments of nonquantifiable items to ensure that they weight such items properly in the decision model.

The most popular investments of manufacturing companies in high technology are flexible manufacturing systems (FMSs). Flexible manufacturing systems use computer systems to make many high-quality, customized products at low cost. FMSs are costly, but they can pay for themselves through increased sales at higher prices and through lower costs.

Another area of growing concern to companies is the effect of its operations on the environment. The impact of operations on the environment can significantly affect future costs. Companies can control these effects in part by capital budgeting decisions.

Accountants are becoming more concerned with measuring business performance with respect to environmental issues and management of environmental costs. In the future, some investors will want to evaluate a company's environmental track record in addition to its financial record in making investment decisions.

Management of environmental costs requires that a company consider environmental issues in every aspect of operations. Environmental issues cross the entire value chain. A major issue is accounting for the future disposal costs of products made now and in the past. Reducing adverse effects of operations on the environment is a worthy goal, but some impact on the environment is unavoidable.

In managing environmental costs, accountants must analyze environmental aspects of investment decisions. Accountants can help managers by including quality and environmental benefits in the analysis. The analysis should include any cost savings from lower energy use. If the company must control pollution, the analysis should recognize the financial impact.

The management of environmental costs includes the following managerial issues discussed in this chapter: (1) managing quality, (2) managing research and development, and (3) managing technology acquisition. Many cases suggest that quality and environmental costs are highly related. For example, a reduction in scrap and waste from better quality helps to reduce the environmental costs of waste disposal.

Through research and development, companies identify new products and production processes and develop new materials. The design of the products affects the following: (1) the types and quantities of the materials the companies will produce, (2) the types and quantities of waste, scrap, and byproducts the companies will produce, (3) the amount of energy that the companies will consume in the production process, and (4) the potential for gathering and recycling products when they become obsolete.

Technology acquisition also has many effects on the environment. Technology affects the following: (1) energy consumption and conservation, (2) environmental emissions, (3) the types, quantities, and features of future obsolete equipment, (4) the rate of defective output produced, (5) the quantities of scrap, waste, and byproducts produced, and (6) the nature and extent of support activities required to keep the technology operating.

In a post-investment audit, management compares the actual results of an investment to expected results. The comparison should use the same techniques that management used to decide the acceptance of the project. Companies intend the post-investment audit to accomplish at least the following four objectives: (1) serve as a financial control tool, (2) furnish information for future capital budgeting decisions, (3) eliminate psychological and political barriers often associated with asset control and abandonment, and (4) influence those proposing capital budgeting projects.

Management must decide when to conduct the post-investment audit. Sometimes, start-up costs of the first year would not be good indicators of future costs. Companies should allow for any necessary learning or training in the first year. Once the project is stable, management can use actual costs and benefits to predict future costs and benefits more accurately. Management should compare the actual cash flows to expected cash flows using the same technique or techniques used to accept the project. Management should also take action to find the causes of any adverse differences and the means, if possible, of remedying them.

Conducting a post-investment audit is not easy for several reasons. The actual information could be in a form different from that of the original estimates. The project may yield important benefits that are difficult to quantify. In addition, the returns on a project can vary over time. Despite the difficulties, post-investment audits provide managers with information that can help them make better capital investment decisions.

ERP systems impact capital budgeting at three stages:  (1) the capital project preparation and approval stage, (2) the operational stage, and (3) the post-audit stage.  During the first stage, an ERP system will allow the revenue and cost items to be linked to actual activities.  ERP systems, in effect, allow capital projects to be modelled as mini independent businesses.  These models are used to analyze the projects.  For the second stage, the models can be accessed after the capital project is implemented to ascertain on an ongoing basis whether the assumptions were validated.  For the third stage, the models can be accessed to do a post-audit to determine the success of the project and to provide feedback on the capital budgeting process.

The main advantage of ERP systems is that they provide the opportunity to plan a capital project from component activities up to the impact on the financial statements.  To be successful, project goals must be precisely described and the project activities to be performed must be structured.  A project is structured hierarchically and functionally.  Hierarchically structured means that the involved divisions, departments, and units must be specified in order to collect costs and revenues.  Functionally structured means that processes and activities must be specified.

Hyperion Activity Based Management (HABM) is software from Hyperion Solution Corporation that can be used with various ERP systems to undertake various analyses including capital budgeting.  In addition to capital budgeting, HABM allows managers to evaluate proposed initiatives and new product ideas, and even complete business scedarios.

## APPENDIX 10A--TIME VALUE OF MONEY

Appendix 10A covers the time value of money.  Money to be received in the future is worth less than the same amount of money to be received today because one can invest money received today to earn interest.  Present value is what a future amount of money is worth today at a given rate of interest.  Future value is the amount that a sum of money would be worth at a specified time in the future if one invests it at a given rate of interest.  Future value and present value depend on three things:  (1) the amount of the cash flow, (2) the interest rate, and (3) the timing of the cash flow.

The discounted cash flow capital budgeting techniques generally assume compound interest.  Compound interest means that one adds the interest earned in prior periods to the investment so that the interest and principal earn interest.  In contrast, simple interest means that only the principal earns interest.

A series of equal cash flows per period is an annuity.  In an ordinary annuity, the cash flows occur at the end of the period.  Cash flows from an annuity due occur at the beginning of the period. Each cash flow is a rent. Appendix 10A illustrates the calculation of the present value of a single amount and the present value of an annuity.

## APPENDIX 10B--ACCOUNTING RATE OF RETURN

Appendix 10B covers the accounting rate of return, another capital budgeting technique.  The accounting rate of return measures the expected rate of earnings on the average capital investment over the investment's life.  The accounting rate of return method uses accrual accounting net income rather than cash flows. The accounting rate of return is the average annual income from the project divided by the average investment in the project.  The average investment is generally equal to one-half of the sum of the original investment, including working capital, and the sum of the salvage value and working capital released at the end of the project's useful life.  Management compares the accounting rate of return to some predetermined standard to decide the acceptability of the investment.

## APPENDIX 10C--THE EFFECT OF TAXATION ON CASH FLOWS

Income taxes are a significant part of capital budgeting decisions.  In evaluating potential investments, managers should use after-tax cash flows because it is only the amount of cash that remains after paying taxes that is available for reinvestment.

Depreciation is calculated annually under GAAP to represent the benefits accrued to a business for using fixed assets for that period.  For tax purposes, accounting depreciation is not a deductible expense.  In its place, the *Income Tax Act* permits the deduction of Capital Cost Allowance (CCA), which is effectively tax depreciation.  For tax purposes, similar assets are placed together in a particular class.  Each class is assigned a specific write-off rate.  For most classes, CCA is calculated using the declining balance method.  Exhibit 10-8 provides examples of various classes of assets and their CCA rate.

Although it is not a cash flow, CCA is a deductible expense for tax purposes.  As taxable income decreases, so do the taxes that must be paid.  Thus, CCA reduces the outflow of cash for income taxes.

The CCA rate stated in the *Income Tax Act* is the maximum rate that can be claimed in a year.  Profitable businesses generally find it advantageous to claim the maximum CCA deduction permitted.  By reducing the amount of taxable income, CCA becomes a tax shield for revenues.  The tax shield produces a tax benefit equal to the CCA amount multiplied by the tax rate.

Income tax laws regarding CCA are subject to periodic revision.  In analyzing capital investments, managers should be sure to use the most current CCA regulations to calculate cash flows from projects.  Changes may also occur in the tax rate structure.  A reduction in the tax rate lowers the tax benefit provided by the tax shield.

As previously mentioned, for tax purposes, similar assets are placed together in a particular class.  Each class is assigned a specific write-off rate.  In the year of acquisition, the half-year rule applies.  As a result, the amount of CCA that can be claimed in the year of purchase is one-half of the calculated amount.  When additions and disposals of assets are made in any year, only the net additions (additions less disposals) are subject to the half-year rule.

For tax purposes, similar assets are placed together in a particular class.  Pooling of assets allows for gains and losses on disposal of assets to be spread over the life of the pool.  If a positive balance exists and there are no more assets remaining in the pool, a terminal loss can be claimed for the balance.  If, at any time, there exists a negative balance in the pool, there will be a recapture of previously claimed CCA.
On disposal, the maximum deduction from the undepreciated capital cost (UCC) is the lower of cost or proceeds.  If an asset sells for more than its original cost, a capital gain occurs.

Exhibit 10-9 illustrates the effect of taxes on cash flows from an investment in an advanced computerized system to monitor pipeline flows.

**SELF TEST**

<u>TRUE/FALSE</u>

1.  T  F  The process of converting future cash flows to their present values is discounting.

2.  T  F  The payback method ignores cash flows after the payback period.

3.  T  F  A reduction in scrap and waste from better quality helps to reduce the environmental costs of waste disposal.

4.  T  F  A return of capital represents income.

5.  T  F  Investment projects that have no specific bearing on other investment projects are independent projects.

6.  T  F  Analysts assume that a project's revenues occur at the end of the period.

7.  T  F  The discount rate used to determine the present value of future cash flows should equal or exceed the company's tax rate.

8.  T  F  The internal rate of return is the rate that when used as the discount rate in the net present value formula causes the net present value to be zero.

9.  T  F  Increasing the discount rate causes the net present value of a project to increase.

10.  T  F  Projects with uneven investments can be compared by using a profitability index.

11.  T  F  For the profitability index to provide better information than the net present value method, the projects must be mutually exclusive or the availability of investment funds must be limited.

12.  T  F  All of the capital budgeting techniques use a single measure of cash flow amounts rather than ranges of cash flows based on probabilities.

13.  T  F  The payback period for a project with equal annual cash flows is the annual cash flow divided by the original investment.

## APPENDIX 10A--TIME VALUE OF MONEY

14.  T  F  If compounding occurs more than once a year, the analyst must multiply the annual interest rate by the number of compounding periods per year to get the interest rate per compounding period.

## APPENDIX 10B--ACCOUNTING RATE OF RETURN

15.  T  F  Analysts compute the accounting rate of return by dividing the average annual cash flow by the average investment.

MULTIPLE CHOICE

1.  Which of the following capital budgeting techniques does not use discounted cash flows?

    A.  net present value
    B.  internal rate of return
    C.  profitability index
    D.  payback period

2.  What is the major driver of research and development?

    A.  the company's strategy
    B.  the product life cycle
    C.  the net present value method
    D.  the internal rate of return method

3.  Investments in high technology can:

    A.  reduce labour costs.
    B.  improve quality.
    C.  increase the quantity produced.
    D.  all of the above.

4.  The payback period:

    A.  ignores cash flows after the payback period.
    B.  does not discount cash flows to their present values.
    C.  ignores the company's desired rate of return.
    D.  all of the above.

5.  When management must select related projects after choosing the primary project, the projects are:

    A.  independent.
    B.  mutually exclusive.
    C.  mutually inclusive.
    D.  always unprofitable.

6.  Investment projects that have no specific bearing on other investment projects are:

    A.  independent.
    B.  mutually exclusive.
    C.  mutually inclusive.
    D.  a tax shield.

7.  When the selection of one project causes management to reject all other projects under consideration, the projects are:

    A.  independent.
    B.  mutually exclusive.
    C.  mutually inclusive.
    D.  the profitability index.

8. The profitability index is the present value of net cash inflows:

    A. divided by the present value of the investment.
    B. less the present value of the investment.
    C. plus the present value of the investment.
    D. times the present value of the investment.

9. Deciding how to rank projects that meet the minimum acceptance criteria on their impact on the achievement of company objectives is a:

    A. preference decision.
    B. screening decision.
    C. financing decision.
    D. timeline decision.

10. Removing the portion of the future cash flows that represents interest and reducing those cash flows to present values is:

    A. compounding.
    B. discounting.
    C. removing.
    D. reducing.

11. Comparing actual project results to expected results is a:

    A. timeline.
    B. post-investment audit.
    C. present value index.
    D. screening decision.

12 The benefits of training are likely to last for:

    A. one year.
    B. two years.
    C. five years.
    D. the duration of a person's employment.

13. The discount rate used to compute the imputed interest portion of future cash flows should generally equal or exceed the company's:

    A. tax rate.
    B. contribution margin ratio.
    C. cost of capital.
    D. return on sales.

14. The internal rate of return is the discount rate at which the net present value of the cash flows equals:

    A. the cost of capital.
    B. the tax rate.
    C. zero.
    D. the contribution margin ratio.

15. What are the three discounted cash flow techniques of capital budgeting?

    A. payback period, internal rate of return, and net present value
    B. accounting rate of return, internal rate of return, and net present value
    C. accounting rate of return, internal rate of return, and profitability index
    D. internal rate of return, net present value, and profitability index

16. The most likely reason why companies have not invested in high-technology manufacturing equipment is that such an investment:

    A. requires a large outlay of funds.
    B. would cause too much unemployment.
    C. would hurt employee morale.
    D. has adverse tax effects.

17. What has management often ignored in making capital budgeting decisions?

    A. income taxes.
    B. labour savings.
    C. qualitative benefits.
    D. maintenance costs.

18. Once management knows the internal rate of return on a project, they compare it to the:

    A. tax rate.
    B. discount rate or hurdle rate.
    C. net present value of the project.
    D. tax shield.

19. Why is performing a post-investment audit not easy?

    A. Information may be in a form different from original estimates.
    B. Some benefits may be difficult to quantify.
    C. Project results can vary considerably over time.
    D. All of the above.

20. An investment costs $72,000.  The investment will provide after-tax cash flows of $22,000 at the end of each of the next five years.  The investment will have no salvage value at the end of five years.  The discount rate is 12 percent.  To the nearest dollar, what is the investment's net present value?

    A. $7,306
    B. $12,483
    C. $79,306
    D. $122,993

21. A project costs $58,000 and will provide net cash flows of $19,000 at the end of each of the next five years. The discount rate is 10 percent. The project will have no salvage value at the end of five years. What is the profitability index?

A. 0.242
B. 0.328
C. 1.242
D. 3.053

22. An investment costs $93,861.60 and will provide net after-tax cash flows of $28,000 a year at the end of each of the next five years. The investment will have no salvage value at the end of five years. What is the internal rate of return?

A. 15.00%
B. 20.00%
C. 29.83%
D. 59.66%

23. A machine costs $44,000 and has a useful life of 10 years. The machine will provide net cash inflows of $11,000 for each of the next 10 years. What is the payback period?

A. 0.10 years
B. 0.25 years
C. 4.00 years
D. 10.00 years

24. A machine costs $45,000 and will provide net cash inflows as follows:

Year 1  $20,000
Year 2  $19,000
Year 3  $12,000
Year 4  $ 9,000
Year 5  $ 6,000

What is the payback period?

A. 2.50 years
B. 3.00 years
C. 3.41 years
D. 3.50 years

## APPENDIX 10A--TIME VALUE OF MONEY

25. A series of equal cash flows per period in which each cash flow occurs at the beginning of the period is called a(n):

A. rent.
B. ordinary annuity.
C. annuity due.
D. up-front annuity.

26. A series of equal cash flows per period that occur at the end of each period is a(n):
    A. ordinary annuity.
    B. annuity due.
    C. hurdle annuity.
    D. payback annuity

27. Each equal cash flow of an annuity is a:

    A. payment.
    B. rent.
    C. principal payment.
    D. payment due.

## APPENDIX 10B--ACCOUNTING RATE OF RETURN

28. Which capital budgeting technique uses net income rather than cash flows?

    A. accounting rate of return
    B. payback period
    C. net present value
    D. internal rate of return

29. Anderson Company bought a machine for $50,000.  The machine will provide cash flows of $16,000 a year for each of the next five years.  At the end of the five years, the machine will have no salvage value. Anderson uses straight-line depreciation.  What is the accounting rate of return?

    A. 12 percent
    B. 24 percent
    C. 32 percent
    D. 64 percent

## APPENDIX 10C--THE EFFECT OF TAXATION ON CASH FLOWS

30. Melton Company has a tax rate of 40 percent, a contribution margin ratio of 30 percent, and a cost of capital of 15 percent.  Capital cost allowance on the tax return is $200,000.  What is the tax benefit from CCA?

    A. $ 24,000
    B. $ 60,000
    C. $ 80,000
    D. $110,000

ESSAY QUESTIONS AND PROBLEMS

1.  How does effective management of the capital budget help in quality management?

2.  Under what conditions will the profitability index provide better information than the net present value method?  If the company is making capital budgeting decisions based on profitability, what is an acceptable profitability index?

3.  Define mutually inclusive projects, mutually exclusive projects, and independent projects.

4.  What are the four decisions that management must make in capital budgeting decisions?

5.  What modifications should managers make in traditional capital budgeting analysis when considering investments in high-tech equipment?

6.  What is a post-investment audit?  Why is performing a post-investment audit not easy?

7.  How does a change in the discount rate affect the determination of net present value?  How does a change in the amounts of the estimated cash flows affect the determination of net present value?

8.  Why should management consider training costs when making capital budgeting decisions?

9. What do flexible manufacturing systems do? What must a company understand for flexible manufacturing systems to be useful? Why is investing in flexible manufacturing systems important?

10. What does management of environmental costs require?

USE THE FOLLOWING INFORMATION TO ANSWER PROBLEMS 11 THROUGH 15

Cost of investment: $200,000
Discount rate: 10 percent (cost of capital)
Tax rate: 40 percent
Useful life: 5 years
Capital cost allowance: $40,000
Salvage value: None
Incremental cash contribution margin per year: $72,770.52

11. Compute the following:

(A) the income tax per year, (B) the after-tax net income per year, and (C) the net after-tax cash flow per year.

12. Calculate the internal rate of return.  Is the investment acceptable?  Why?

13. Compute the net present value and the profitability index.  Is the investment acceptable?  Why?

14. Compute the payback period.

## APPENDIX 10B--ACCOUNTING RATE OF RETURN

15. Compute the accounting rate of return.

## SELF TEST ANSWERS

### TRUE/FALSE

| | | | | | | | | | |
|---|---|---|---|---|---|---|---|---|---|
| 1. | T | 4. | F | 7. | F | 10. | T | 13. | F |
| 2. | T | 5. | T | 8. | T | 11. | T | 14. | F |
| 3. | T | 6. | T | 9. | F | 12. | T | 15. | F |

### MULTIPLE CHOICE

| | | | | | | | | | | | |
|---|---|---|---|---|---|---|---|---|---|---|---|
| 1. | D | 7. | B | 13. | C | 19. | D | 25. | C |
| 2. | A | 8. | A | 14. | C | 20. | A | 26. | A |
| 3. | D | 9. | A | 15. | D | 21. | C | 27. | B |
| 4. | D | 10. | B | 16. | A | 22. | A | 28. | A |
| 5. | C | 11. | B | 17. | C | 23. | C | 29. | B |
| 6. | A | 12. | D | 18. | B | 24. | A | 30. | C |

### ESSAY QUESTIONS AND PROBLEMS

1.      Investing in capital equipment can help companies to reduce defects and quality costs. Increased spending for prevention and appraisal costs is likely to lead to reductions in failure costs. Management could prevent quality problems by purchasing sophisticated manufacturing technologies and training employees to use manufacturing techniques that reduce errors. Management can apply statistical quality controls to assess operations and decide when production has exceeded acceptable error tolerances. If the new asset reduces defects, the savings in quality costs could increase the net present value of the project enough to make it acceptable. Management should consider reductions in external failure costs and internal failure costs in making capital budgeting decisions.

2.      The profitability index will provide better information than the net present value method only when (1) the projects are mutually exclusive; or (2) availability of investment funds is limited. The profitability index should be 1.00 or greater for a project to be acceptable based on its profitability.

3.      Mutually inclusive projects are projects for which management must accept related projects once management chooses the primary project. Mutually exclusive projects are projects that perform the same basic function. The acceptance of one of these projects under consideration precludes the acceptance of all the other projects. Independent projects are projects that have no specific connection with one another.

4.      The four basic questions that management must answer in capital budgeting decisions are as follows: (1) Is the activity worth the investment?  (2) Which assets can the company use for the activity? (3) Which is the best asset for the activity?  (4) Should the company invest in the asset?

5.      Managers should modify the traditional capital budgeting analysis in evaluating investments in high-tech equipment by (1) being careful to not set the discount rate too high, (2) giving more weight to the qualitative benefits, (3) remembering that investments in high-tech equipment are interrelated and not freestanding, (4) considering the opportunity cost of not investing in high-tech equipment, and (5) attempting to quantify even the intangible benefits that the high-tech equipment will provide.

6.      A post-investment audit is a comparison of the actual results of an investment project to the expected results.  A post-investment audit is not easy to conduct because (1) the actual information may be in a form different from that used for estimates; (2) the project may yield benefits that are difficult to quantify; and (3) the returns on a project can vary over time.

7.      The net present value reacts inversely to a change in the discount rate or to a change in the estimated cash outflows.  Increasing the discount rate decreases the net present value.  Decreasing the discount rate increases the net present value.  An increase in the estimated cash outflows decreases the net present value, and a decrease in the estimated cash outflows increases the net present value. On the other hand, the net present value changes in the same direction as a change in the estimated cash inflows.  An increase in the estimated cash inflows increases the net present value, and a decrease in the estimated cash inflows decreases the net present value.   All of the previous statements assume that the analyst makes only one change in the estimates.  If the cash flows and discount rate change at the same time, the analyst must make a new calculation to compute the effect of the changes on net present value.

8.      Training costs are somewhat similar to investments in equipment. Companies incur training costs to generate future benefits.  The benefits of training are likely to last for the duration of a person's employment.  Thus, regarding training benefits as multi-period is proper.  Providing training to employees is a basic tool of quality improvement.  It results in an increase in prevention costs to be offset by lower failure costs in the future.

9.      Flexible manufacturing systems (FMSs) use computer systems to make many high-quality, customized products at low cost.  The keys to customization are small lot sizes, quick setup, and abundant information.  Such flexibility is useful only if a company understands its customers and market.  FMSs are costly, but they can pay for themselves through increased sales at higher prices and through lower costs.

10.     Management of environmental costs requires that a company consider environmental issues in every aspect of operations.  Environmental issues cross the entire value chain.  A major issue is accounting for the future disposal costs of products made now and in the past.

        In managing environmental costs, accountants must analyze environmental aspects of investment decisions.   The analysis should include any cost savings from lower energy use.  If the company must control pollution, the analysis should recognize the financial impact.   Many cases suggest that quality and environmental costs are highly related.  A reduction in scrap and waste helps to reduce the environmental costs of waste disposal.

11.     Incremental cash contribution margin before taxes        $72,770.52
        Less:  CCA                                              (40,000.00)
        Income before taxes                                     $32,770.52
        Income tax  ($32,770.52 x 40%)                          (13,108.21)
        After-tax net income                                    $19,662.31

        Incremental cash contribution margin                    $72,770.52
        Less: income tax                                        (13,108.21)
        Net after-tax cash flow                                 $59,662.31

12.     The investment divided by the annuity (net after-tax cash flow per year) equals the present value of an annuity factor.

$200,000 ÷ $59,662.31 = 3.3522

The present value of an ordinary annuity factor of 3.3522 for five periods corresponds to an interest rate of 15 percent.  Thus, the internal rate of return is 15 percent.  The project is acceptable because the internal rate of return is greater than the 10 percent cost of capital.

13.    PV of net cash inflows   $59,662.31 x 3.7908 =  $226,167.88
       PV of cost of investment                        (200,000.00)
       Net present value (NPV)                         $ 26,167.88


The project is acceptable due to its positive net present value.

Profitability index:  $226,167.88 ÷ $200,000.00  = 1.13

The project is acceptable because its profitability index is greater than 1.00.

14.    Payback period:  $200,000.00 ÷ $59,662.31 per year = 3.352 years

15.    Accounting rate of return:   $\frac{\$19,662.31}{(\$200,000 + \$0\,) \div 2}$ = 19.66%

# CHAPTER 11
# RESPONSIBILITY ACCOUNTING AND TRANSFER PRICING
# IN DECENTRALIZED OPERATIONS

## CHAPTER OVERVIEW

Many companies become so large that their corporate structures impede rather than aid in the achievement of their goals and objectives. In such cases, top management may decide to change those structures so that the company can employ its resources more effectively. Each company's structure changes in response to changes in its goals, technology, and employees. For many companies, the change is from centralization to decentralization.

Decentralization is the transferring of authority from top management to lower levels of management. The opposite of decentralization is centralization. In centralization top management retains most of the authority and responsibility for making decisions. The amount of decentralization in a company depends on many factors and can vary from little to a great deal. Both decentralization and centralization have advantages and disadvantages.

The degree of decentralization reveals a chain of command, authority and responsibility connections, and decision-making capabilities. Responsibility accounting is an accounting system that gives top management information about the performance of an operational unit in the organization. Responsibility accounting focuses on the managers who control the operational units (also known as responsibility centres) in the organization. The more decentralized an organization is, the more extensive is its responsibility accounting system.

Many decentralized companies exchange goods and services internally. The price charged for such an exchange is a transfer price. This chapter discusses how companies determine transfer prices for products and services both for domestic and international transfers.

## CHAPTER STUDY GUIDE

The degree of decentralization in a company is a continuum from totally centralized to totally decentralized. In a totally centralized company, one person makes all decisions and retains all authority for the company's activities. A completely decentralized company has almost no central authority, and each subunit acts as an independent unit. Most companies have structures that function between these extremes. A business segment that operates in a dynamic environment is likely to have a more decentralized structure so that it can respond to new problems quickly. Exhibit 11-1 lists factors that affect a company's degree of decentralization.

Managers in decentralized companies must be goal-oriented, assertive, decisive, and creative. They must be willing to accept the authority that top management gives them and have their performance evaluated by the results of their decisions. Some units of a company may be more decentralized than others. Also, top management may retain authority over some decisions rather than delegating them to subunit managers.

Exhibit 11-2 lists some of the advantages and disadvantages to decentralization. One advantage is that decentralization allows managers to develop their abilities and provides an excellent training ground for aspiring managers. Decentralization encourages healthy competition among a company's managers. Top management evaluates managers of the various units based on the results of their unit compared to the results of other units in the company. Managers in a decentralized company derive more satisfaction from their work and develop a feeling of importance to the company. Employees have more challenging work that provides them with greater opportunities for advancement.

Decentralization is often more effective in achieving the company's goals and objectives because the unit manager has more knowledge of the local operating environment. This proximity to actual operations results in (1) a reduction in time to make decisions, (2) a reduction of difficulties in attempting to communicate problems and instructions through a chain of command, and (3) faster perceptions of changes in the operating environment. Decentralization also allows the use of the management by exception principle. Top management can address results that are significant exceptions to plans rather than spending a great deal of time reviewing operations that are proceeding according to plans.

Although decentralization has many advantages, it also presents some disadvantages. The division of authority and responsibility among managers may result in lack of goal congruence. Goal congruence occurs when the personal and organizational goals of managers throughout a company are consistent and mutually supportive. Because of the competition inherent in a decentralized company, managers may make decisions that help their unit but hurt other units or the entire company. The result of such decisions is suboptimization.

A decentralized company requires that it use more effective methods in communicating plans, activities, and achievements. Top management delegates authority but still has responsibility for the results of the decisions made at lower levels of management. Thus, top management must be continually aware of the operations of the various units of the company. If decentralization gets out of control, top management must be willing to intervene and take appropriate action.

Decentralization may disturb some employees. They may feel that top management asks too much of them too soon. Top management may have difficulty in giving up control or may be unable to delegate effectively.

Decentralization can also be expensive because of the cost of training lower-level managers and the potential cost of poor decisions by those managers. Decentralization causes a duplication of activities and the cost of developing and maintaining a complex planning and reporting system. This reporting system is known as a responsibility accounting system.

A responsibility accounting system provides information about the performance of an organizational subunit and produces responsibility reports. These reports help top management in evaluating the performance of subordinate managers and their units. The responsibility reports should reflect only the costs, revenues, and assets under the control of a unit manager. A responsibility accounting system is the key in making decentralization work effectively.

One purpose of a responsibility accounting system is to get control at the point of cost incurrence rather than assigning costs to all remote products and processes. This treatment is in accordance with the concepts of standard costing and activity-based costing. Standard costing traces variances to the person or machine responsible for the variance. Activity-based costing traces as many costs as possible to the activities that cause the costs rather than using aggregated allocation methods. Managers in decentralized organizations implement control procedures to promote effectiveness, efficiency, and a reasonable utilization of plant and equipment.

A responsibility accounting system implies that lower-level managers accept the authority that top management gives them. Lower-level managers have control over the revenues and/or costs for which they are responsible. Exhibit 11-3 illustrates the five basic control functions. A responsibility accounting system uses budgets to communicate expectations and spending authority. Managers of the responsibility centers should participate in the budgeting process because top management will evaluate their performances using reports of comparisons of actual results to the master budget and to the flexible budget.

By the time top management receives these comparisons, the unit managers should have corrected the problems that resulted in significant variances. If the unit managers have not corrected such problems, the unit managers should offer explanations or top management may need to intervene under the management by exception principle.

The amount of detail in responsibility reports becomes less as subordinate managers prepare them for successively higher levels of management. Upper-level managers who want more specific information can review the responsibility reports prepared for their subordinates. Exhibit 11-4 illustrates a set of performance reports. Besides financial reports, many responsibility accounting systems now provide information on critical nonmonetary performance measures. Exhibit 11-5 lists several nonmonetary performance measures that management can include on responsibility reports.

The focus of the responsibility accounting system is on people. Responsibility reports not only provide a means for control, but they also can motivate managers to influence operations in ways that will result in positive performance. The subunit under a manager's control is called a responsibility centre. Responsibility accounting systems identify, measure, and report on the performance of the managers of the responsibility centres. The four types of responsibility centres are (1) cost centres, (2) revenue centres, (3) profit centres, and (4) investment centres, as illustrated in Exhibit 11-6.

The manager of a cost centre has control only over costs. Thus, the manager's evaluation depends on how well the manager controlled costs. In a standard costing environment, the manager's focus is often on minimizing unfavourable variances. Management should investigate all significant variances whether unfavourable or favourable, however, because unfavourable and favourable variances may be related.

Some responsibility centres may receive revenues that are not under the manager's control or are difficult to measure. For example, a government agency may receive taxes for which it does not have the power to assess and collect. Another example is discretionary cost centres in which measuring the outputs related to the costs incurred is difficult. In these cases, the revenues should not appear on the manager's responsibility accounting report.

In a revenue centre, the manager has responsibility only for the generation of revenues. Thus, top management would evaluate the manager of a revenue centre by the amount of revenue generated. Managers of revenue centres may also be involved in planning and control related to some of the centre's costs. For example, top management may hold the manager of a revenue centre responsible for travel costs of the centre's sales staff. A more appropriate term for such revenue centres is revenue and limited cost centres.

Managers of revenue centres need to consider three possible reasons why actual revenues differ from budgeted revenues: (1) sales price differences, (2) sales mix differences, and (3) volume differences. A company can calculate variances for each of these three reasons. Exhibit 11-7 illustrates these variance calculations.

In a profit centre, managers are responsible for generating revenues and controlling costs. Top management evaluates managers of profit centres on the net income of their centres. Profit centre managers should have the authority to acquire resources at the lowest prices and to sell products at the price that will generate the most revenue. Manufacturing companies, retail stores, and service firms all use profit centers. Exhibit 11-8 illustrates a comparison of a profit centre's actual results to those estimated in the master budget. Comparing actual results to a flexible budget, however, provides better information for assessing cost control. Exhibit 11-9 shows a comparison of a profit centre's actual results to a flexible budget.

Managers of cost centres, revenue centres, and profit centres have no control over the assets invested in their responsibility centres.  A manager of an investment centre has control over revenues, costs, and the assets invested in the unit.  A company evaluates managers of investment centres on their return on investment or their residual income.  Chapter 13 discusses these topics.

One primary goal of any business is to generate profits.  A company earns profits when it satisfies its critical success factors.  A not-for-profit organization may seek to provide services and break even.  If an organization consistently fails to satisfy its critical success factors, it will cease to exist.  The following five critical success factors are common to most organizations:  (1) quality, (2) customer service, (3) efficiency, (4) cost control, and (5) responsiveness to change.  If an organization manages these five factors properly, the organization should be financially successful.

All members of the organization should work toward the same basic objective to satisfy the critical success factors.  When individual managers work toward goals and objectives that are in their own interest rather than in the company's best interest, this divergence is suboptimization.  Top management must be aware of possible suboptimal behaviour and find ways to avoid it.  One way to reduce suboptimal behavior is to communicate corporate goals to all organizational units.  Exhibit 11-10 illustrates the steps that a company can take to limit suboptimal behaviour.

Responsibility centres of a company may sell products or services to another segment of the company.  The price charged is a transfer price. A company may base transfer prices on cost, the market price, or a price negotiated between the buying segment and the selling segment.  Transfer pricing is useful for managerial purposes, but for external reporting the company must eliminate profits on intracompany sales and show the cost at the producing segment's cost.

If both the buying and selling managers have the authority to negotiate the transfer price, the maximum transfer price is the lowest market price that the buying segment would pay an external company for the same product.  The minimum transfer price is the selling segment's incremental production costs plus the opportunity costs of the facilities used.  The difference between the maximum transfer price and the minimum transfer price times the number of units transferred is the savings that the entire company will realize by intracompany sales rather than buying externally.

One difficulty in basing transfer prices on cost is how to define cost.  A company could define cost as variable cost or absorption cost.  Another issue is whether to use actual cost or standard cost.  If the company uses actual costs, it may not correct inefficiencies in the selling division because these costs are simply transferred to the buying division.  On the other hand, if the company uses standard cost and actual costs are less than standard, the buying division would be paying more than actual cost.

Some companies use market-based transfer prices to avoid the problems in defining cost.  They believe that the market price is objective and is similar to the price that would be charged if the divisions were independent companies.  Several problems can arise when using market-based transfer prices.  The products may not match exactly products sold in the external market.  Market price may not be appropriate because of internal cost savings from reductions in bad debts, advertising, packaging, and delivery.  Determining the right market price when the market is depressed may be difficult, especially if sellers quote different prices to different buyers.

A bargaining process between the selling and buying unit managers determines the transfer price in a negotiated transfer price setting.  The authority to negotiate a transfer price implies that the division managers have the autonomy to buy or sell products on the external market if they cannot negotiate a mutually acceptable transfer price.  When the negotiation process breaks down, top management may allow each party to set a different transfer price.

In a dual pricing arrangement, a company uses a different transfer price for the buying segment and the selling segment. The selling division records the sale at the market or negotiated market price. The buying division records the transfer based on cost.

The decision of which transfer pricing system to use should reflect the circumstances of the organizational units and the company's goals and objectives. No one method of transfer pricing is right in all instances. Exhibit 11-12 provides the results of a transfer pricing survey of Canadian multinational corporations. This survey shows that transfer pricing is a major concern, especially for income tax reasons.

A carefully set transfer price will provide the following advantages: (1) a means of encouraging what is best for the company as a whole, (2) an appropriate basis for calculating and evaluating divisional performance, (3) the rational acquisition or use of goods and services between corporate divisions, (4) the flexibility to respond to changes in demand or market conditions, and (5) a means of motivating managers in decentralized operations.

Although transfer prices for products are rather common, transfer pricing for services is less common but is an effective technique for some types of service departments. Examples of services where a company could use transfer prices are computer services, secretarial services, legal services, and maintenance services. Exhibit 11-13 lists questions that management should answer before using transfer prices for services and gives suggestions about how to set the transfer price.

A department must select what capacity level to use in determining transfer prices for services. This decision is similar to that made in setting a predetermined overhead rate for manufacturing companies. Using expected capacity results in a higher transfer price than using practical capacity.

Transfer prices are useful when service departments provide well-defined, measurable benefits to other departments or provide services having a definite cause-and-effect relationship. Under these conditions, using transfer prices provides the company with certain advantages in both the revenue-producing and service departments. The first advantage is that transfer prices encourage more interaction between the user and service departments. Using transfer prices for services also causes managers to be more cost conscious. Finally, transfer prices can be useful in evaluating managerial performance. Exhibit 11-14 discusses these advantages.

Using transfer prices for services also has its disadvantages. First, the unit managers may disagree as to the appropriate transfer price. Second, implementing transfer prices in the accounting system requires additional time and money. Third, transfer prices may not work equally well for all types of service departments. Fourth, a transfer price may result in dysfunctional behaviour among the organizational units. For example, a segment may use certain services too much or too little. A company should weigh the advantages and disadvantages of using transfer prices for services before reaching a decision.

Setting transfer prices can be difficult for companies engaged in multinational operations due to differences in tax systems, import/export regulations, and foreign exchange controls. Exhibit 11-15 shows how the internal and external objectives of transfer pricing in multinational companies differ.

Multinational companies may use different transfer prices for the same product depending on which country transfers or receives the product. A company should not price transfers to a foreign subsidiary at a price that would transfer most of its costs to a subsidiary in the country with the highest tax rate unless that pricing method is reasonable and equitable to all subsidiaries. Usually, the company should price such transfers at an arm's length price.

Tax authorities in both the home and host countries are now carefully scrutinizing transfer prices by multinational companies. The Government of Canada and the Canada Customs and Revenue Agency (CCRA) are concerned that companies could avoid paying Canadian income taxes by using misleading or inaccurate transfer prices. The CCRA may be more likely to investigate Canadian subsidiaries that operate in low-tax countries or areas.

Transfers among countries are becoming easier because of various trade arrangements. These arrangements should help reduce the significance of transfer price manipulations through the harmonization of tax laws and reductions in import/export fees, tariffs, and capital movement restrictions.

## SELF TEST

TRUE/FALSE

1. T F Critical success factors are items so important that if an organization fails to satisfy them, the organization would cease to exist.

2. T F Goal congruence occurs when unit managers make decisions that are good for their units but detrimental to other units or the entire company.

3. T F Decentralization can be costly in terms of time and money.

4. T F A manager of a profit centre is responsible for return on assets.

5. T F In a revenue centre, managers are responsible for revenues and controlling all expenses.

6. T F Setting transfer prices for companies engaged in multinational operations can be difficult.

7. T F The division of authority and responsibility among managers in a decentralized organization may result in lack of goal congruence.

8. T F Management should ignore the favourable variances of a cost centre.

9. T F Decentralization is often less effective in achieving the company's goals and objectives because top management usually has better knowledge of local operating environments.

10. T F The amount of detail in responsibility reports increases as subordinate managers prepare them for successively higher levels of management.

11. T F Managers of profit centres are responsible for generating revenues and controlling costs.

12. T F One way to reduce suboptimization is to communicate corporate goals to all organizational units.

13. T F For external financial reports, companies must eliminate profits on intracompany sales.

14. T F When a service department determines a transfer price for its services, using expected capacity results in a lower transfer price than using practical capacity.

15. T F One purpose of a responsibility accounting system is to obtain control at the point of cost incurrence.

MULTIPLE CHOICE

1. The focus of responsibility accounting is on:

    A. manufacturing overhead costs.
    B. selling costs.
    C. people.
    D. throughput.

2. The manager of a revenue centre is responsible for:

    A. return on assets.
    B. cost containment.
    C. net income.
    D. revenue generation.

3. A company achieves its ultimate goal when it satisfies its:

    A. critical success factors.
    B. budgeted net income.
    C. target return on investment.
    D. desired throughput.

4. What exists when the personal and organizational goals of managers throughout a company are consistent and mutually supportive?

    A. suboptimization
    B. management by exception
    C. goal congruence
    D. critical success factors

5. Which of the following would most companies consider to be a critical success factor?

    A. an increase in income each year
    B. quality
    C. achieving a target return on investment
    D. an increase in sales every year

6. What is a possible disadvantage of decentralization?

    A. the cost of poor decisions by subordinate managers
    B. the cost of training subordinate managers
    C. expensive duplication of activities
    D. all of the above

7. An internal charge established for the exchange of products or services between units of the same company is a(n):

    A. differential cost.
    B. fair-return price.
    C. transfer price.
    D. elastic price.

8. Which is a traditional method for determining transfer prices?

    A. cost-based prices
    B. market-based prices
    C. negotiated prices
    D. all of the above

9. What is an advantage of using transfer prices for services?

    A. encourages more involvement between the user and the service department
    B. no additional organizational costs are involved
    C. no dysfunctional behaviour can occur
    D. all of the above

10. When the selling division has idle capacity, the maximum transfer price should be:

    A. no greater than the selling division's incremental production costs.
    B. no less than the price the selling division charges outside companies.
    C. no greater than the lowest market price at which the buying division can buy the product or service externally.
    D. no less than the lowest market price at which the buying division can buy the product or service externally.

11. The use of a different transfer price for the buying segment and the selling segment is:

    A. price fixing.
    B. a dual pricing arrangement.
    C. price discrimination.
    D. incremental transfer pricing.

12. When a company uses a different transfer price for the buying segment and the selling segment, the buying division records the transfer at:

    A. a cost-based amount.
    B. fair market value.
    C. a negotiated price.
    D. the price top management dictates.

13. The degree of a company's decentralization reflects:

    A. a chain of command.
    B. authority and responsibility relationships.
    C. decision-making capabilities.
    D. all of the above.

14. What is the key in making decentralization work effectively?

    A. transfer prices
    B. training for unit managers
    C. a responsibility accounting system
    D. top management intervention

15. A possible problem in instituting decentralization is that top management may:

    A. have difficulty in giving up control
    B. be unable to delegate effectively
    C. both of the above
    D. none of the above

16. In addition to financial reports, many responsibility accounting systems now provide information on:

    A. personnel policies.
    B. critical nonmonetary performance measures.
    C. recent CCRA rulings.
    D. recent laws passed by the Government of Canada.

17. When a company uses a different transfer price for the buying segment and the selling segment, the selling division records the transfer at:

    A. a cost-based amount.
    B. standard cost.
    C. a market or negotiated market price.
    D. the price dictated by top management.

18. Which of the following is an advantage of decentralization?

    A. it is usually very inexpensive
    B. it may result in lack of goal congruence
    C. it allows the use of management by exception
    D. it requires more effective communication abilities

19. A company should design its responsibility accounting system so that it captures actual information in conformity with:

    A. asset accounts.
    B. shareholders' equity accounts.
    C. budgetary accounts.
    D. subsidiary ledger accounts.

20. A company evaluates the manager of a cost centre on the basis of:

    A. net income.
    B. product margin.
    C. return on investment.
    D. cost control.

21. A company evaluates the manager of a profit centre on the basis of:

    A. cost control.
    B. return on investment.
    C. net income.
    D. revenues.

22. An accounting system that provides information to top management about the performance of organizational units is:

    A. internal auditing.
    B. responsibility accounting.
    C. organizational accounting.
    D. authority accounting.

23. Which of the following is not an external objective of transfer pricing in multinational companies?

    A. increased taxes and tariffs
    B. lower foreign exchange risk
    C. better competitive positions
    D. better relations with government

### USE THE FOLLOWING INFORMATION TO ANSWER QUESTION 24 THROUGH 26.

Consolidated Industries has two divisions – the Bates Division and the Sutton Division. Sutton makes a part that Bates is currently buying from an outside company for $41 per unit. Sutton's variable production costs for this part are $25 per unit, variable selling costs are $5 per unit, and fixed manufacturing overhead costs are $6 per unit. Sutton will avoid $3 in variable selling costs on any sales to Bates. Sutton normally charges $42 to outside companies for this part. Sutton has enough idle capacity to make the 5,000 units of this part that Bates needs.

24. What is the highest price that Bates would be willing to pay?

    A. $16
    B. $22
    C. $41
    D. $42

25. What is the lowest transfer price that the Sutton Division would accept?

    A. $27
    B. $30
    C. $33
    D. $39

26. What is the potential increase or decrease in before-tax profit to Consolidated Industries if the Bates Division buys 5,000 units of this part from Sutton rather than from an outside company?

    A. $5,000 decrease
    B. $10,000 increase
    C. $40,000 increase
    D. $70,000 increase

USE THE FOLLOWING INFORMATION TO ANSWER QUESTION 27 THROUGH 30.

The Hutchison Division of Miller Company is a revenue centre. The Hutchinson Division sells lawn mowers and weed trimmers. Hutchinson's sales budget for the period was as follows:

|  | Units | Unit Price | Revenues | Standard Mix for Budgeted Volume |
|---|---|---|---|---|
| Lawn mowers | 6,000 | $150 | $900,000 | 75% |
| Weed trimmers | 2,000 | 50 | 100,000 | 25% |
| Totals | 8,000 |  | $1,000,000 | 100% |

Hutchison's actual results for the period were as follows:

|  | Units | Unit Price | Revenues |
|---|---|---|---|
| Lawn mowers | 5,200 | $165 | $858,000 |
| Weed trimmers | 3,800 | 40 | 152,000 |
| Totals | 9,000 |  | $1,010,000 |

27. What was the price variance?

    A. $ 40,000 F
    B. $ 40,000 U
    C. $367,500 F
    D. $367,500 U

28. What was the mix variance?

    A. $337,500 F
    B. $337,500 U
    C. $367,500 F
    D. $367,500 U

29. What was the volume variance?

    A. $337,500 F
    B. $337,500 U
    C. $367,500 F
    D. $367,500 U

30. What was the total revenue variance?

    A. $ 10,000 F
    B. $ 10,000 U
    C. $ 40,000 F
    D. $367,500 F

## ESSAY QUESTIONS AND PROBLEMS

1. What factors affect the degree of decentralization in a company?

2. What are the advantages of decentralization?

3. What are the disadvantages of decentralization?

4. Name the four types of responsibility centres and the means by which a company should evaluate each one.

5.  What are critical success factors?  Name five critical success factors that are common to most organizations.

6.  What is suboptimization?  What can top management do to limit suboptimization?

7.  What difficulties would a company encounter in using cost-based transfer prices?

8.  What are the advantages and disadvantages of using transfer prices for services?

9.  Why is determining transfer prices for multinational companies difficult?

10.  Why do tax authorities such as the Canada Customs and Revenue Agency carefully scrutinize the transfer prices of multinational companies?

11.  What characteristics must managers have for decentralization to be effective?

12.  What are the advantages and disadvantages of using market-based transfer prices?

13.  What benefits will a carefully set transfer price provide a company?

14.  The Rivers Division of Horton Company is a revenue centre. The Rivers Division sells two versions of its product–the deluxe model and the regular model.  River's sales budget for the period was as follows:

|  | Units | Unit Price | Revenues | Standard Mix for Budgeted Volume |
|---|---|---|---|---|
| Deluxe model | 2,000 | $80 | $160,000 | 20% |
| Regular model | 8,000 | 70 | 560,000 | 80% |
| Total | 10,000 | | $720,000 | 100% |

Rivers' actual results for the period were as follows:

|  | Units | Unit Price | Revenues |
|---|---|---|---|
| Deluxe model | 3,000 | $85 | $255,000 |
| Regular model | 9,000 | 66 | 594,000 |
| Total | 12,000 | | $849,000 |

Calculate the following:

(A) the price variance

(B) the mix variance

(C) the volume variance

(D) the total revenue variance

15.  The Bolton Division of Amalgamated Industries, Inc. is currently buying 5,500 units per year of a component used in making its product from an outside company at a price of $98 per unit. The Sanders Division of Amalgamated Industries makes this component and usually sells it for $100 per unit. Sanders' per-unit costs to make and sell this component are as follows:

| | |
|---|---|
| Direct materials | $ 25.00 |
| Direct labour | 10.00 |
| Variable manufacturing overhead | 5.00 |
| Fixed manufacturing overhead | 12.00 |
| Variable selling and administrative costs | $ 63.00 |

The fixed manufacturing overhead costs are allocated and would not increase if Sanders makes the 5,500 units for Bolton.  The variable selling and administrative costs would be reduced by $3 per unit on any sale to the Bolton Division. The Sanders Division has ample idle capacity to meet the demand for the components needed by the Bolton Division. Sanders has no alternative use for the idle capacity.

Calculate the following:

(A) the maximum transfer price that the Bolton Division would pay.

(B) the minimum transfer price that the Sanders Division would accept.

(C) the increase in before-tax profit to Amalgamated Industries if the Bolton Division buys the 5,500 units from the Sanders Division rather than from an outside company.

(D) Now assume that the Sanders Division has no idle capacity. Rather, the Sanders Division sells all of the products that it can make on the external market for $100 per unit. All other facts remain the same. What is the minimum transfer price that the Sanders Division would accept?

## SELF TEST ANSWERS

### TRUE/FALSE

| | | | | | | | | | |
|---|---|---|---|---|---|---|---|---|---|
| 1. | T | 4. | F | 7. | T | 10. | F | 13. | T |
| 2. | F | 5. | F | 8. | F | 11. | T | 14. | F |
| 3. | T | 6. | T | 9. | F | 12. | T | 15. | T |

### MULTIPLE CHOICE

| | | | | | | | | | |
|---|---|---|---|---|---|---|---|---|---|
| 1. | C | 7. | C | 13. | D | 19. | C | 25. | A |
| 2. | D | 8. | D | 14. | C | 20. | D | 26. | D |
| 3. | A | 9. | A | 15. | C | 21. | C | 27. | A |
| 4. | C | 10. | C | 16. | B | 22. | B | 28. | A |
| 5. | B | 11. | B | 17. | C | 23. | A | 29. | D |
| 6. | D | 12. | A | 18. | C | 24. | C | 30. | A |

### ESSAY QUESTIONS AND PROBLEMS

1.      The factors that affect the degree of decentralization in a company include the (1) company's age, (2) company's size, (3) stage of product development, (4) growth rate, (5) expected impact of poor decisions on profits, (6) confidence of top management in lower-level managers, (7) historical degree of control, (8) use of technology, and (9) rate of change in the company's market.

2.      The advantages of decentralization include the following: (1) managers can develop their abilities; (2) an excellent training ground exists for aspiring managers; (3) healthy competition is encouraged among managers; (4) managers derive more satisfaction from their work and develop a feeling of importance to the company; (5) top management can use the management by exception principle; and (6) the company's goals and objectives can be achieved more effectively. The last reason results in (1) less time to make decisions, (2) a reduction of difficulties in attempting to communicate problems through a chain of command, and (3) faster perceptions of changes in the operating environment.

3.      Decentralization has the following disadvantages: (1) possible lack of goal congruence, (2) suboptimization, (3) need for more effective communication of plans, activities, and performance measures, (4) the requirement of top management's continual awareness of the operations of the various units of the company, (5) the cost of training lower-level managers, (6) the potential cost of poor decisions by lower-level managers, (7) costly duplication of activities, (8) unwillingness of top management to give up control, (9) top management's inability to delegate effectively, and (10) the cost of developing and maintaining a complex planning and reporting system.

4.      The four types of responsibility centres are: (1) cost centres, (2) revenue centres, (3) profit centres, and (4) investment centres. In a cost centre, the manager is evaluated on the basis of how well the manager controlled costs. In a revenue centre, the manager would be judged by the revenue that was generated. In a profit centre, managers are evaluated on the net income of their centres. Managers of investment centres are evaluated on their return on investment or their residual income.

5.  Critical success factors are those factors that a company must satisfy to maintain its existence. The following five critical success factors are common to most organizations: (1) quality, (2) customer service, (3) efficiency, (4) controlling costs, and (5) responsiveness to change.

6.      Suboptimization occurs when individual managers pursue goals and objectives that are in their own and/or their segment's best interest instead of in the company's best interest. Top management must first be aware of suboptimization. One way for top management to limit suboptimization is to communicate corporate goals to all organizational units. Other ways top management can limit suboptimization include (1) requiring appropriate transfer prices between units, (2) gathering appropriate information, (3) making measurements in the appropriate time frame, (4) considering the operating environment, (5) defining measurements properly and taking a long-range perspective on actions, (6) having a commitment to the quality of performance, (7) using a responsibility accounting system, (8) using multiple performance measures including nonfinancial measures, (9) setting up an appropriate reward structure, and (10) ensuring goal congruence between units.

7.      Companies using cost-based transfer prices must decide how to define cost. Companies could define cost as variable cost or absorption cost. Variable cost could be defined as variable production cost or as total variable cost. Another difficulty is whether the company should use actual cost or standard cost. If the company uses actual cost, the selling division may not correct inefficiencies in production because the buying division will cover its cost. On the other hand, if the company uses standard cost and actual cost is less than standard, the buying division will be paying more than actual cost. Using cost-based transfer prices does not provide the selling division with the same amount of income that it could earn by selling the products externally.

8.      Advantages of using transfer prices for services are as follows: (1) more involvement occurs between user departments and service departments; (2) managers become more cost conscious; and (3) the resulting information is useful for performance evaluation. The disadvantages include the following: (1) user and provider departments may disagree on the transfer price; (2) additional organizational costs and employee time are required to implement the transfer prices within the accounting system; (3) transfer prices do not work equally well for all service departments; and (4) dysfunctional behaviour may occur.

9.      Differences in tax systems, customs duties, freight and insurance costs, import/export regulations, and foreign exchange controls make determining transfer prices for a multinational company difficult. Also, the internal and external objectives of transfer pricing in multinational companies differ.

10.    The Canada Customs and Revenue Agency and tax authorities in other countries carefully scrutinize transfer prices for multinational companies because the transfer prices determine which country taxes the income from the transfer. Companies could reduce their tax liability by using misleading or inaccurate transfer prices. Companies do so by charging higher transfer prices to subsidiaries in countries with high tax rates. Thus, the income in the high-tax countries will be less, and the income in low-tax countries will be greater. The Canada Customs and Revenue Agency and tax authorities in other countries want transfer prices to reflect market prices so that income will be taxed appropriately.

11.    For decentralization to be effective, managers must be goal oriented, assertive, decisive, and creative. Subordinate managers must be willing to accept the authority that top management gives them. They must be willing to have top management evaluate their performances by the results of their decisions.

12.    An advantage of using market-based transfer prices is that the company avoids the problem in defining cost. Market-based transfer prices are objective and are similar to the prices that would be charged if the segments were independent companies. A disadvantage of using market-based transfer prices is that the products may not be exactly the same as products sold in external markets. Another problem with market-based transfer prices is that deciding on the appropriate market price is difficult if the market is depressed, especially if different sellers are quoting different prices to different buyers.

13.    A carefully set transfer price will provide a company with the following benefits: (1) a means of encouraging what is best for the company as a whole, (2) an appropriate basis for calculating and evaluating divisional performance, (3) the rational acquisition or use of goods and services between corporate divisions, (4) the flexibility to respond to changes in demand or market conditions, and (5) a means of motivating managers in decentralized operations.

14.    Let AV = Actual Volume; AM = Actual Mix; AP = Actual Price; SP = Standard Price; SM = Standard Mix; and BV = Budgeted Volume.

(A)    (AV x AM x AP) – (AV x AM x SP)
    [(3,000 x $85) + (9,000 x $66)] – [(3,000 x $80) + (9,000 x $70)]
    = ($255,000 + $594,000) – ($240,000 + $630,000)
    = $849,000 - $870,000
    = -$21,000 = $21,000 U

(B)    (AV x AM x SP) – (AV x SM x SP)
    [(3,000 x $80) + (9,000 x $70)] – [(3,000 x 20% x $80) + (9,000 x 80% x $70)]
    = ($240,000 + $630,000) – ($48,000 + $504,000)
    = $870,000 - $552,000
    = $318,000 = $318,000 F

(C)    (AV x SM x SP) – (BV x SM x SP)
    [(3,000 x 20% x $80) + (9,000 x 80% x $70)] – [(2,000 x $80) + (8,000 x $70)]
    = ($48,000 + $504,000) – ($160,000 + $560,000)
    = $552,000 - $720,000
    = -$168,000 = $168,000 U

(D)    (AV x AM x AP) – (BV x SM x SP)
    [(3,000 x $85) + (9,000 x $66)] – [(2,000 x $80) + (8,000 x $70)]
    = ($255,000 + $594,000) – ($160,000 + $560,000)
    = $849,000 - $720,000
    = $129,000 = $129,000 F
    Reconciliation: $21,000 U + $318,000 F + $168,000 U = $129,000 F

15.     (A) The maximum transfer price that the Bolton Division would pay is $98 per unit. Bolton will not pay Sanders any more for the component than the price charged by the outside company.

|  |  |  |
|---|---|---|
| (B) | Direct materials | $25 |
| | Direct labour | 10 |
| | Variable manufacturing overhead | 5 |
| | Variable selling and administrative costs ($11 - $3) | 8 |
| | Minimum transfer price | $48 |

The fixed manufacturing overhead costs are not relevant because they would not increase if Sanders produces 5,500 more units for Bolton.

|  |  |  |
|---|---|---|
| (C) | Maximum transfer price | $98 |
| | Less: Minimum transfer price | 48 |
| | Per-unit increase in profit | $50 |

$50 per unit x 5,500 units = $275,000 increase in before-tax profit to Amalgamated Industries, Inc.

|  |  |  |
|---|---|---|
| (D) | Direct materials | $25 |
| | Direct labour | 10 |
| | Variable manufacturing overhead | 5 |
| | Variable selling and administrative costs ($11 - $3) | 8 |
| | Total variable costs on sale to the Bolton Division | $48 |
| | Lost contribution margin ($100 - $51) | 49 |
| | Minimum transfer price | $97 |

The lost contribution margin represents the opportunity cost of selling to the Bolton Division rather than to the external market. The variable costs on a sale to the external market are $51 because there are no variable cost savings on a sale to the external market. Another way to compute the minimum transfer price when there is no idle capacity is to subtract the variable cost savings for an internal transfer from the price that the selling division receives on the external market. Therefore, the minimum transfer price in this case is computed as follows: $100 - $3 = $97

# CHAPTER 12
# COST MANAGEMENT AND PERFORMANCE MEASUREMENT SYSTEMS

## CHAPTER OVERVIEW

Managerial accountants provide information for managers' planning, controlling, performance-evaluation and decision-making needs.  Cost management and performance measurement systems are parts of an organization's overall control system.

This chapter discusses how enterprise resource planning (ERP) systems integrate cost management and performance measurement systems.  This chapter also explains how Wal-Mart's ERP system has contributed to the company's success.

Three factors that should be considered in designing cost management and performance measurement systems are the organizational form, structure, and culture; organizational mission and critical success factors; and the competitive environment.  Cost management and performance measurement systems must be designed using elements from three groups of management control tools:  motivational, informational, and reporting elements.

Gap analysis is the key to identifying differences, or gaps, between the ideal cost management and performance measurement systems and the existing systems.

## CHAPTER STUDY GUIDE

A cost management system (CMS) is a group of standard methods devised for controlling a company's activities that cause costs compared with its goals and objectives.  The goal of a CMS is not necessarily to reduce total costs.  The CMS should help a company to realize the maximum benefits from the costs incurred.  A cost management system should help managers to do the following:  (1) identify the cost of resources consumed in doing vital activities of the organization, (2) measure the efficiency and effectiveness of the activities completed, (3) identify and assess new activities that can improve the future performance of the organization, and (4) achieve the three previous objectives in an environment of changing technology.  The information provided by the CMS should integrate and help all the functional areas of the company.  Exhibit 12-1 illustrates a functionally integrated cost management system.

By integrating all functional areas, a cost management system attempts to meet five main goals:  (1) compute reasonably accurate product or service costs, (2) evaluate product or service profitability over the whole life of the product or service, (3) increase understanding of internal processes and activities, (4) control costs, and (5) aid in the pursuit of the company's strategies.

Primarily, a cost management system should enable the company to compute reasonably accurate product or service costs.  Thus, the company must design the system to accumulate information in a way that allows the company to trace costs to products and services.  The system does not have to be the most accurate because the company must balance increased accuracy with the cost of obtaining additional accuracy.  The system will generate approximate though inaccurate costs.  Information technology, such as bar coding and the Internet, has made the tracing of costs easier.

The product or service costs provided by the cost management system are the inputs to managerial processes.  Managers use these costs to plan, prepare financial statements, evaluate individual product or service and period profitability, set prices, and establish a basis for performance measurements.  If the costs the cost management system accumulates and assigns are not reasonably accurate, the information generated by the CMS will not be suitable for control and decision making.

Companies may calculate product or service profitability periodically for use in preparing external financial statements. The financial accounting system, however, does not reflect life-cycle information. The cost management system should provide information about the life-cycle performance of a product or service. Managers need such life-cycle information to relate costs incurred in one stage of the life cycle to revenues and costs in other stages. Also, companies using target costing must establish allowable cost based on life-cycle rather than period-by-period relationships among price, cost, and profit margin.

Finally, a company must obtain information necessary to determine present and future costs regarding its organizational strategies. The information the CMS generates enables managers to do strategic analyses on issues such as the following: (1) determining core competencies, (2) managing resources from a cost-benefit viewpoint, (3) assessing the positive and negative financial and nonfinancial factors of investment and operational plans, and (4) engaging in employee empowerment by using new management techniques.

A company must base its cost management system partially on accounting information. Most companies still generate all of their accounting information from one accounting system and set of accounts. Historically, the primary purpose of the accounting system was to generate financial statements. Management adapted the information to meet internal needs.

An activity-based costing (ABC) system is an alternative approach used to accumulate accurate cost information on products and customers. As noted in Chapter 6, ABC is an accounting information system that identifies the various activities performed in an organization and collects costs on the basis of the underlying nature and extent of the activities.

The four steps in developing an ABC system are as follows: (1) compile the list of activities; (2) determine how much the organization is spending on each of its activities; (3) identify the organization's products, services, and customers; and (4) select activity cost drivers that link activity costs to the organization's products, services, and customers.

An ABC system must first identify the activities being performed by the indirect or overhead costs. Standard activity dictionaries have been developed that provide a template for determining the appropriate activity classification for nearly all overhead activities. Activity dictionaries can vary, containing from as few as 10 activities to hundreds of activities and more, with more activities being related to size and complexity of the organization and the desire for detailed costs.

The second step involves attaching the respective indirect costs to the respective activity in the activity dictionary. The third step is to identify the activities' products, services, and customers. In the fourth step, activity cost drivers are used to link the activity costs in step 2 with the products, services, and customers in step 3.

Three generic types of activity drivers form a framework for determining appropriate drivers: (1) transaction drivers count how often an activity is performed; (2) duration drivers measure the amount of time required for the activity; and (3) intensity drivers charge directly for the time required for the activity. To be an effective driver, the change in the driver level must be highly correlated with the costs of the activities.

A performance measurement system provides economic feedback to managers and operators about process efficiency and effectiveness; it should help managers and operators to understand business processes and organizational activities. Only by understanding how an activity is accomplished in terms of nonfinancial performance measures, and the reasons for performance variation, can managers make cost-benefit improvements in products and services.

Cost management systems are not sufficient.  The cost data are important and necessary; however, managers must also gather data on the efficiency and effectiveness of the performance of activities.  Activities can be controlled only when the activity is known and its performance compared to standards.  The performance measurement system should generate information that will assist managers in the measurement and evaluation of human and equipment performance and the assessment of future decision alternatives.

To maintain a competitive position in an industry, a company must generate performance information necessary to define and implement its strategies.  A performance measurement system for reporting on activity accomplishments complements a cost management system, which reports on the cost of activities.

Four stages have been identified for evolution of cost and performance measurement systems:  (I) inadequate for financial reporting, (II) financial reporting-driven, (III) customized, managerially relevant, standalone, and (IV) integrated cost management, financial reporting, and performance measurement.

Stage I systems are not able to record costs accurately and do not have the means to accurately allocate overhead costs to products and services.  These systems exist in both new and mature organizations.

Stage II systems are adequate for valuing inventory for financial reporting purposes and for preparing periodic financial reports.  However, these systems produce highly distorted product costs due to use of traditional allocation systems instead of ABC.  Stage II systems do not provide adequate information to managers for planning, decision making, and control.

When companies operate at Stage III, they have a financial reporting system, one or more activity-based costing systems, and performance measurement systems of various types.  However, these systems are freestanding rather than integrated.

Rather than separate systems for financial reporting, cost management, and performance measurement, Stage IV organizations have ABC and performance measurement systems that are integrated.  The transition to Stage IV systems is generally facilitated by the installation of enterprise resource planning (ERP) systems.

An enterprise resource planning system is a fully integrated, full-service suite of software with a common database that can be used to plan and control resources across an entire organization.  An ERP is able to integrate financial reporting, cost management, and performance measurement along with all other systems in an organization.

ERP systems consist of relatively rigid sets of software for processing transactions and information.  In implementing an ERP system, there is minimal customization of the software to meet the organization's requirements; rather, it is economically more viable to adjust the organization to the software.  This is called business process redesign.  There are three basic approaches for ERP business process redesign:  (1) change all processes to achieve the ideal set of business processes, (2) accept the ERP design, and (3) redesign with the ERP system in mind.

The re-engineering of business processes in connection with ERP involves the elimination of technical and organizational bottlenecks, the improvement in quality of information, the replacement of out-of-date processes and activities, the integration of processes, and the reduction in standalone systems and interfaces.

To be effective, an ERP system will contain an extensive chart of accounts or codes for accurate recording and tracking of activities and costs.  An important characteristic of an ERP system is the coding of activities that allows activity costs to be used to construct ABC for products and services as well as for periodic reporting.  The same activity-based costs of an ERP system can be used for financial reporting to external parties.

An ERP system permits daily access to information on activity costs and activity drivers.  Frequent feedback on costs and cost drivers facilitates learning, which makes for improved performance and decision making.  The ERP system maintains a record of resource use; therefore, performance can be measured in physical terms and compared to standards, which allows for the computation of variances.  Performance measurement deals with demand, the success in meeting that demand, delays, defects, backlogs, outputs, defects, etc.

Performance measurement and ABC are complementary.  ABC determines the cost of activities in dollar terms.  When activity costs exceed expectations, the changes that need to be made involve resource utilization and performance measurement.

The textbook provides a description of Wal-Mart's enterprise resource planning system and discusses how the ERP system has contributed to the company's outstanding success.

A company needs cost management and performance measurement systems to compute product or service costs, to manage its business, to meet customer expectations, and to satisfy external reporting requirements.  In designing or improving cost management and performance measurement systems, managers and accountants must consider the unique characteristics of the company.

Effective cost management and performance measurement systems successfully implement a company's strategies and, as a result, achieve their company's goals and objectives.  Each company needs a cost management system designed for its unique needs.

The legal form and organizational structure of the company affect its cost management needs.  How top management organizes business segments will have an impact on the design of the cost management system.  Senior management must decide what to do internally and what to outsource.  The extent of decentralization is especially important because it decides who will be accountable for cost management and performance measurement.  An information system must provide relevant information to managers who make decisions with cost and performance implications.

A company's culture also affects the design of cost management and performance measurement systems.

Awareness of a company's mission is a primary consideration in the design of a cost management and performance measurement system.  The mission provides a long-term goal that the company wants to achieve.

Critical success factors are aspects of operations that are vital to a company's survival.  Examples include timeliness, quality, customer service, efficiency, cost control, and responsiveness to change.  Once managers agree on the company's critical success factors, they can design the cost management and performance measurement system to gather information to measure those factors and generate output about those factors in forms useful to management.

As noted in Chapter 1, two generic strategies are differentiation and cost leadership.  For a company adopting a differentiation strategy, critical success factors would focus on how the products or services are achieving differentiation.  For a company adopting a cost leadership strategy, the critical success factors would need to identify that the company was in fact the low-cost producer in its markets.

Cost management and performance measurement systems are composed of three main elements: motivational, informational, and reporting.  Exhibit 12-2 gives details about these elements.  Managers design cost management and performance measurement systems by choosing elements from each of the three main categories.  The elements selected must be consistent with the strategies and missions of the business subunits.  The individual control elements should help in carrying out the company's strategies for the company as a whole and for the individual subunits.

Management should select cost and performance measures that are consistent with the company's goals and objectives and that will motivate managers toward specified achievements.  These performance measures may be quantitative or qualitative, financial or nonfinancial, and short-term or long-term.

The cost management and performance measurement system should encourage managers to act in the best interest of the company and the subunits.  Management should link the criteria used for cost management and performance measurement with the company's incentive system.  This performance-reward link ensures that managers will receive rewards based on the quality of their decisions and their contributions to achieving the company's mission.

The company can use different types of rewards for short-term performance and long-term performance.  Cash compensation is an obvious choice for rewarding short-term performance.  Companies use stock options to encourage and reward long-term performance.  Companies can use a combination of short-term and long-term rewards for top management.  The rewards should be consistent with the company's mission.

Managers will evaluate decision alternatives considering the measurement and reward criteria.  The cost management and performance measurement systems must have performance benchmarks and provide measurement information to the proper individuals for evaluation purposes.  Companies often judge current performance compared with past or expected performance.

The cost management and performance measurement systems should support management's functions of planning, controlling, performance evaluation, and decision making.  For the planning function, the cost management and performance measurement systems should provide a good foundation for budgeting.  Budgets specify expected achievement and provide benchmarks with which to compare actual performance.  Besides providing the required financial information for the budgeting process, the cost management and performance measurement systems should identify the factors that cause the company to incur costs.  The knowledge of such cost drivers allows management to compare alternative scenarios.  Also, the system can highlight activities in the budgeting process that provide no tangible benefits so that management can mark them for reduction or elimination.  Thus, management can reduce the time for budget preparation.

As maintaining competitive advantage becomes more difficult, companies must emphasize management of the product life cycle.  Companies may use the Japanese tool of target costing to evaluate their competitive positions.  Information about managing costs must focus on decisions made in the early stages of the product life cycle.

Product life cycles are becoming shorter as companies become more skillful at making products similar to their competitors' products. Accordingly, companies must use the cash from older products to support new product development. Companies must adapt quickly to changing market conditions. Flexibility will be an important attribute and will cause managers to change the emphasis of control systems as shown in Exhibit 12-3.

The cost management and performance measurement systems must link resource consumption and cost with alternative product and process designs. Also, managers will need to consider the effects on the company's cost structure, long-run competitive benefits, and cash flow in evaluating research and development investment decisions.

The reporting elements of cost management and performance measurement systems point to methods of providing information to persons with evaluation responsibilities. The cost management and performance measurement systems must support the calculation of inventories and cost of goods sold for the external financial statements. The reporting elements must also address the internal needs of the responsibility accounting system. For each subunit, the responsibility accounting system tracks appropriate costs and revenues. Managers compare actual performance with expected performance to learn which managers and subunits exceeded, met, or failed to meet expectations. Management can tie this information to the reward system.

The trend toward more decentralization and outsourcing has elevated the importance of a useful reporting system. Top managers depend on the reporting system to keep the subunits on course to achieve their missions and to help in achieving the company's goals and objectives.

Managers must understand that the company incurs different costs and activities for different purposes. The company incurs some costs and activities to realize an immediate benefit. Other costs and activities will yield benefits only in the long run.

By connecting cost to activities and activities to strategies, managers gain an understanding of the benefits of cost incurrence. Thus, managers should sort activities by their strategic roles to promote effective cost management and performance measurement. This notion suggests that dividing the company into subunits will facilitate effective management.

Most companies already have cost management and performance measurement systems. Therefore, most design issues relate to changes for existing systems. After the company and its subunits decide their needs and the structure of the cost management and performance measurement systems, the company should evaluate its current information systems. The company should compare the information needed to the information currently available using a gap analysis. Any difference represents a gap that the system needs to fill. Exhibit 12-4 describes how companies can use gap analysis to make design changes in their cost management and performance measurement systems.

Eliminating all gaps in the system is often impossible in the short run. The company should specify the methods of reducing or eliminating the gaps including all technical requirements and changes to feeder systems. These methods should be stated in terms of costs and benefits. Cost management and performance measurement systems require continuous improvement to reflect ongoing organizational and environmental changes.

If the company has limited resources, top management may need to decide which gaps to fill and in which order. As system modifications occur, management should assess the effectiveness of the improvements and consider the need for other improvements. A company's cost management and performance measurement information needs change over time. Thus, management should engage in continuous improvement efforts to ensure that the cost management and performance measurement systems will continue to provide relevant information to their users.

## SELF TEST

### TRUE/FALSE

1. T F  The primary purpose of a cost management system is to minimize the costs incurred by an organization.

2. T F  Most companies use different accounting systems for different purposes.

3. T F  A performance measurement system provides economic feedback to managers and operators about process efficiency and effectiveness.

4. T F  A Stage I System exists in a new organization only.

5. T F  Rather than separate systems for financial reporting, cost management, and performance measurement, Stage IV organizations have ABC and performance measurement systems that are integrated.

6. T F  Implementing an enterprise resource planning (ERP) system is straightforward and simple.

7. T F  Business process redesign is pursued both before and after ERP implementation.

8. T F  Organizational form refers to the nature of the legal entity created for a business enterprise.

9. T F  An entity's culture plays an important role in designing cost management and performance measurement systems.

10. T F  For a company pursuing a cost leadership strategy, the critical success factors would need to identify that the company was in effect the low-cost producer in its markets.

11. T F  Companies use stock options to encourage and reward long-term performance.

12. T F  Rewards for top management should consist of long-term incentives only.

13. T F  Product life cycles are generally becoming longer.

14. T F  The movement toward decentralization and outsourcing has decreased the importance of an effective reporting system.

15. T F  Gap analysis is useful in making changes to existing cost management and performance measurement systems.

MULTIPLE CHOICE

1.  A cost management system should help managers to:

    A.  identify the costs of resources consumed in performing significant activities of the organization.
    B.  determine the efficiency and effectiveness of the activities performed.
    C.  identify and evaluate new activities that can improve the future performance of the organization.
    D.  accomplish all of the above objectives in an environment characterized by changing technology.

2.  A functionally integrated cost management system integrates cost accounting with:

    A.  financial accounting.
    B.  quality control.
    C.  research and development.
    D.  all of the above.

3.  A cost management system can be viewed as having _____ primary goals.

    A.  three
    B.  four
    C.  five
    D.  six

4.  Primarily, a cost management system should help the company to:

    A.  reduce or eliminate costs.
    B.  compute product costs with precision.
    C.  compute reasonably accurate product costs.
    D.  measure the performance of employees.

5.  The first step in developing an ABC system is to:

    A.  determine how much the organization is spending on each of its activities.
    B.  identity the organization's products, services, and customers.
    C.  develop the activity dictionary or list of activities.
    D.  select activity cost drivers that link activity costs to the organization's products, services, and
customers.

6.  A set of activities for a purchasing function would include all of the following except:

    A.  develop specifications and obtain a list of potential vendors.
    B.  send specifications to prospective vendors and request quotes from them.
    C.  review submitted quotes against specifications and award order.
    D.  receive merchandise and transfer to raw materials storeroom.

7.  Which of the following is not a generic type of activity driver?

    A.  transaction
    B.  operation
    C.  duration
    D.  intensity

8.  A(n) _____ provides economic feedback to managers and operators about process efficiency and effectiveness.

    A.  cost management system
    B.  performance measurement system
    C.  enterprise resource planning system
    D.  activity-based costing system

9.  Stage I systems:

    A.  are inadequate for financial reporting.
    B.  are not able to record costs accurately.
    C.  do not have the means to accurately allocate overhead costs to products and services.
    D.  all of the above

10.  A problem with Stage II systems is:

    A.  the inability to provide useful feedback to improve business processes.
    B.  the inability to meet financial reporting requirements.
    C.  the inability to collect costs accurately by responsibility centres.
    D.  the inability to prepare complete financial statements that require minimal postclosing adjustments.

11.  Stage III organizations have all of the following systems except for:

    A.  a financial reporting system.
    B.  one or more activity-based costing systems.
    C.  performance measurement systems.
    D.  an enterprise resource planning system.

12.  Rather than separate systems for financial reporting, cost management, and performance measurement, Stage IV organizations have _____ and _____ systems that are integrated.

    A.  ABC, performance measurement
    B.  ABC, cost management
    C.  cost management, performance measurement
    D.  ABC, ERP

13.  Which of the following is an organization that provides ERP systems?

    A.  PAS
    B.  PeopleSoft
    C.  Great Prairies
    D.  Prophesy

14. A(n)_____system has a common database or data warehouse that integrates all systems for all parts of the organization.

    A. job order costing
    B. process costing
    C. activity-based costing
    D. enterprise resource planning

15. _____is when an organization changes its business processes.

    A. Business process redesign.
    B. Process re-engineering.
    C. Simultaneous engineering.
    D. Concurrent engineering.

16. The re-engineering of business processes in conjunction with ERP would involve all of the following except for:

    A. the improvement in quality of information.
    B. the replacement of out-of-date processes and activities.
    C. the creation of technical and organizational bottlenecks.
    D. the integration of processes.

17. Global electronic commerce associations are recommending that retailers use_____bar codes that accompany the UPC beginning January 1, 2005.

    A. 12-digit
    B. 13-digit
    C. 14-digit
    D. 15-digit

18. Wal-Mart's success is a result of:

    A. outsourcing.
    B. the use of information technology.
    C. the improvement of productivity measurement and utilization rates at check-out.
    D. all of the above.

19. An entity's legal nature reflects its:

    A. organizational form.
    B. organizational structure.
    C. organizational culture.
    D. organizational size.

20. Aspects of operations that are vital to a company's survival are:

    A. core competencies.
    B. performance measures.
    C. distribution costs.
    D. critical success factors.

21. Which of the following would be considered a critical success factor by most organizations?

    A. timeliness
    B. quality
    C. customer service
    D. all of the above

22. What are the three primary elements of cost management and performance measurement systems?

    A. planning, control, and decision making
    B. budgeting, control, and performance evaluation
    C. motivational, informational, and reporting
    D. planning, control, and motivational

23. Which of the following is not a motivational element of cost management and performance measurement systems?

    A. preparation of financial statements
    B. performance measurements
    C. reward structure
    D. support of organizational mission and competitive strategy

24. Which of the following is not an informational element of cost management and performance measurement systems?

    A. support of budgeting process
    B. provision of details for responsibility accounting system
    C. differentiation of value-added and non-value-added activities
    D. assessment of core competencies and support of decision making

25. Which of the following is a reporting element of cost management and performance measurement systems?

    A. emphasis on product life cycle
    B. support of target costing
    C. provision of details for responsibility accounting system
    D. focus on cost control

26. Cost and performance measurements may be:

    A. quantitative or nonquantitative.
    B. financial or nonfinancial.
    C. short-term or long-term.
    D. all of the above.

27.  What specifies expected achievements and provides benchmarks against which to measure actual performance?

     A.  external financial statements
     B.  budgets
     C.  product life cycle
     D.  critical success factors

28.  Most cost reduction efforts occur in:

     A.  the late stages of the product life cycle.
     B.  the middle stages of the product life cycle.
     C.  the early stages of the product life cycle.
     D.  equal amounts in each stage of the product life cycle.

29.  Which of the following is not a nonfinancial performance measure?

     A.  customer satisfaction measures
     B.  capacity utilization
     C.  budgetary figures
     D.  research and development activities

30.  Any difference between the information the current cost management and performance measurement systems provide and the information management needs is a:

     A.  violation of generally accepted accounting principles.
     B.  gap that the system needs to fill.
     C.  variance from standard.
     D.  core competency.


## ESSAY QUESTIONS AND PROBLEMS

1.  How should a cost management system help managers?

2.  What are the five main goals of a cost management system?

3.  Why do managers need information about the life-cycle performance of a product?

4.  How does a cost management system help managers to define and carry out strategies?

5.  What four steps have been identified in developing an ABC system?

6.  What are the four stages of cost management and performance measurement systems?

7.  Describe the three systems that are in place when an organization is operating at Stage III.

8.  What are the three basic approaches for ERP business process redesign?

9.  What were the four improvements in Wal-Mart's organization of functions and tasks that were noted by the McKinsey Global Institute (MGI)?

10.  Why is selecting the organizational form one of the most important decisions made by business owners?

11.  Define critical success factors and explain how they affect the design of cost management and performance measurement systems.

12.  What three groups of elements affect the design of cost management and performance measurement systems?

13.  What factors should management consider in establishing performance measures?

14.  How do cost management and performance measurement systems support the responsibility accounting system?

15. What steps should a company take in modifying its cost management and performance measurement systems?

## SELF TEST ANSWERS

### TRUE/FALSE

| | | | | | | | | | |
|---|---|---|---|---|---|---|---|---|---|
| 1. | F | 4. | F | 7. | T | 10. | T | 13. | F |
| 2. | F | 5. | T | 8. | T | 11. | T | 14. | F |
| 3. | T | 6. | F | 9. | T | 12. | F | 15. | T |

### MULTIPLE CHOICE

| | | | | | | | | | |
|---|---|---|---|---|---|---|---|---|---|
| 1. | D | 7. | B | 13. | B | 19. | A | 25. | C |
| 2. | D | 8. | B | 14. | D | 20. | D | 26. | D |
| 3. | C | 9. | D | 15. | A | 21. | D | 27. | B |
| 4. | C | 10. | A | 16. | C | 22. | C | 28. | C |
| 5. | C | 11. | D | 17. | C | 23. | A | 29. | C |
| 6. | D | 12. | A | 18. | D | 24. | B | 30. | B |

## ESSAY QUESTIONS AND PROBLEMS

1.    A cost management system should help managers to do the following: (1) identify the cost of resources consumed in doing vital activities of the organization, (2) measure the efficiency and effectiveness of the activities completed, (3) identify and assess new activities that can improve the future performance of the organization, and (4) achieve the three previous objectives in an environment of changing technology. The information provided by the cost management system should integrate and help all of the functional areas of the company.

2.    The five main goals of a cost management system are as follows: (1) compute reasonably accurate product or service costs, (2) evaluate product or service profitability over the whole life of the product or service, (3) increase understanding of internal processes and activities, (4) control costs, and (5) aid in the pursuit of the company's strategies.

3.    Managers need life-cycle performance information to relate costs incurred in one stage of the life cycle to revenues and costs in other stages. Also, companies using target costing must establish allowable cost based on life-cycle rather than period-by-period relationships among price, cost, and profit margin.

4.      A cost management system helps managers to define and carry out strategies by providing the information necessary to perform strategic analysis on issues such as the following: (1) determining core competencies, (2) managing resources from a cost-benefit viewpoint, (3) assessing the positive and negative financial and nonfinancial factors of investment and operational plans, and (4) engaging in employee empowerment by using new management techniques.

5.      Four steps have been identified in developing an ABC system: (1) develop the activity dictionary or list of activities, (2) determine how much the organization is spending on each of its activities, (3) identify the organization's products, services, and customers, and (4) select activity cost drivers that link activity costs to the organization's products, services, and customers.

6.      The four stages of cost management and performance measurement systems are: (I) inadequate for financial reporting, (II) financial reporting-driven, (III) customized, managerially relevant, standalone, and (IV) integrated cost management, financial reporting, and performance measurement.

7.      The three systems that are in place when an organization is operating at Stage III are: (1) a traditional but well-functioning financial reporting system capable of basic accounting and transaction-capturing functions, such as preparing monthly and quarterly financial statements for external stakeholders; (2) one or more activity-based costing systems that use data from the financial reporting and other systems to measure the costs of organizational units, customers, products, services, processes, and activities; and (3) performance measurement systems of various types that provide front-line workers and their superiors with timely, accurate information – financial and nonfinancial – on the efficiency and effectiveness of activities and processes.

8.      There are three basic approaches for ERP business process redesign.  First, change all processes to achieve the ideal set of business processes.  With these changes, there may be difficulties with implementing an ERP system as the new processes may be inconsistent with the ERP system requirements.  Second, accept the ERP design.  This allows for fast implementation – and the saving of time, human energy, and money – because issues regarding process redesign are avoided.  Generally, with this approach the disadvantage is the lack of flexibility; business processes that use the ERP vendor's design might not be sufficiently appropriate for the organization.  Third, redesign with the ERP system in mind.  This approach is often called "ERP design by default."  The advantage of this approach is that for most processes the plain ERP system is adequate.  For those few cases where customized software is crucial, the extra cost needs to be incurred.

9.      The four improvements in Wal-Mart's organization of functions and tasks that were noted by MGI are: (1) the more extensive use of cross-docking and better flow of goods/palleting to maximize in-store labour efficiency, which was enabled by "sScan" or other electronic supply chain management tools; (2) the use of forecasting tools to better align staffing levels with demand; (3) the redefining of store responsibilities and cross-training employees through the pooling of labour across aisles and organization of tasks such as price changes on a functional rather than departmental level; and (4) the improvement of productivity measurement and utilization rates at check-out.

10.      Selecting the organizational form is one of the most important decisions made by business owners because that choice affects the cost of raising capital, of operating the business (including taxation issues), and, possibly, of litigating.

11.      Critical success factors are aspects of operations that are vital to a company's survival.  Examples include timeliness, quality, customer service, efficiency, cost control, and responsiveness to change.  Once managers agree on the company's critical success factors, they can design the cost management and performance measurement systems to gather information to measure those factors and generate output about those factors in forms useful to management.

12.      Cost management and performance measurement systems comprise a set of three primary elements: motivational, informational, and reporting.  The motivational elements consist of performance measurements, reward structure, and support of organizational mission and competitive strategy.  The informational elements consist of support of budgeting process, emphasis on product life cycle, differentiation of value-added and non-value-added activities, support of target costing, focus on cost control, and assessment of core competencies and support of decision making.  The reporting elements consist of preparation of financial statements and provision of details for responsibility accounting system.

13.      Management should consider the company's goals and objectives and establish performance measures that are consistent with them.  Also, managers should choose performance measures that will motivate managers toward specified achievements.  These performance measures may be quantitative or qualitative, financial or nonfinancial, and short-term or long-term.  The company can use different types of rewards for short-term performance and long-term performance.

         The performance measurement system should encourage managers to act in the best interest of the company and the subunits.  Management should link performance measures with the company's incentive system.  This performance-reward link ensures that managers will receive rewards based on the quality of their decisions and their contributions to achieving the company's mission.

14.      The reporting elements of cost management and performance measurement systems point to methods of providing information to persons with evaluation responsibilities.  The reporting elements of cost management and performance measurement systems address the internal needs of the responsibility accounting system.  For each subunit, the responsibility accounting system tracks appropriate costs and revenues.  Managers compare actual performance with expected performance to learn which managers and subunits exceeded, met, or failed to meet expectations.  Management can tie this information to the reward system.

         The trend toward more decentralization and outsourcing has elevated the importance of a useful reporting system.  Top managers depend on the reporting system to keep the subunits on course to achieve their missions and to help in achieving the company's goals and objectives.  Managers must understand that the company incurs different costs for different purposes.  The company incurs some costs to realize an immediate benefit.  Other costs will yield benefits only in the long run.

15.      After the company and its subunits decide their needs and the structure of the cost management and performance measurement systems, the company should evaluate its current information systems. The company should compare the information needed to the information currently available using a gap analysis. Any difference represents a gap that the system needs to fill.

         Eliminating all gaps in the system is often impossible in the short run.  The company should specify the methods of reducing or eliminating the gaps including all technical requirements and changes to feeder systems.  These methods should be stated in terms of costs and benefits.

         If the company has limited resources, top management may need to decide which gaps to fill and in which order.  As system modifications occur, management should assess the effectiveness of the improvements and consider the need for other improvements.  A company's cost management and performance measurement information needs change over time.  Thus, management should engage in continuous improvement efforts to ensure that the cost management and performance measurement systems will continue to provide relevant information to their users.

# CHAPTER 13
## MEASURING AND REWARDING PERFORMANCE

## CHAPTER OVERVIEW

Companies traditionally have measured performance using one-dimensional financial indicators. Financial measures alone, however, do not necessarily show how well a business unit is performing in a customer-driven, global marketplace. Many companies are now supplementing traditional financial measures with a variety of qualitative and nonmonetary quantitative measures. Success is now multidimensional and balances short-term and long-term considerations.

This chapter discusses conventional financial performance measures and innovative performance measures. Financial performance measures include cash flow, return on investment, and residual income. World-class, customer-driven companies often need more innovative performance measures to compete effectively. The chapter also includes a discussion of the employee rewards a company can use to balance short-term and long-term interests.

## CHAPTER STUDY GUIDE

Management evaluates subordinates' performances using various measures. The measures may be monetary or nonmonetary, quantitative or qualitative, or a combination of measures. Four general rules are appropriate for performance measurement: (1) performance measures should assess progress toward organizational goals and objectives; (2) the persons being evaluated should have some input in developing the performance measures and be aware of them; (3) persons whom management evaluates should have the necessary skills, equipment, information, and authority to be successful under the measurement system; and (4) management should provide feedback about performance in a timely and useful manner.

Management should consider the mission of the subunit in selecting performance measures. The use of profit measures for new divisions is not appropriate. Performance measures for new divisions are likely to include objectives for sales growth, market share, research and development success, and rate of new product introductions. Profit and cash flow performance measures are more appropriate for mature divisions.

Because companies have a variety of goals and objectives, a single performance measure is unlikely to assess a company's progress toward all its goals effectively. Even several similar measures are likely to be inadequate. A basic goal of any organization is to be financially solvent. Cash flow is a performance measure for solvency. A business often satisfies its solvency goal by generating a satisfactory profit compared with the assets invested. Companies usually use some measure of net income to assess financial performance.

Financial measures supply necessary indications of performance, but they do not consider some new issues essential for survival in the global economy. Accordingly, many companies have set goals of customer satisfaction, zero defects, minimal lead time to market, and environmental and social responsibility. Companies can develop nonfinancial performance measures that show progress, or lack of it, toward achievement of long-run critical success factors of world-class companies.

Exhibit 13-1 illustrates a balanced scorecard that links all aspects of performance to a company's strategies.  The balanced scorecard is defined as a performance measurement conceptualization that translates an organization's strategy into clear objectives, measures, targets, and initiatives organized by the four perspectives:  financial, customer, business processes, and human resources.  The balanced scorecard gives a comprehensive set of financial and nonfinancial performance measures that reflect both internal and external perspectives.

A balanced scorecard should have 15 to 25 measures that support a company's strategy and are linked together in the form of cause-and-effect hypothesis statements.

A company must set its performance targets at levels that will encourage its employees to do their best.  Employees must be familiar with the performance measures and targets management uses to evaluate them.  A company should also allow its employees to participate in designing performance measures, which will result in a type of social contract between the employees and their evaluators.

Performance measures should also encourage harmonious operations among a company's units.  All employees striving to achieve the same goals for the company is necessary to prevent suboptimization.

Management should place employees in jobs for which they are well suited, and   provide employees with the necessary equipment, information, authority, training, and support to perform their jobs in a manner consistent with the measurement process.  Without the necessary tools, management cannot expect employees to accomplish their tasks.

Management should monitor employee performance and provide feedback on a continuous basis.  Positive feedback reinforces favourable behaviors.  Negative feedback highlights areas that need correction or improvement.

The type of responsibility centre over which a manager has control impacts the financial measures used to evaluate managerial performance.  A manager of a cost or revenue centre is responsible for only one monetary item; therefore, performance measurements are limited to those relevant to that single monetary measure.  Profit and investment centre managers are responsible for their centres' revenues and expenses; therefore, a greater number of financial measures can be used to evaluate performance.

For a company to succeed, it must be profitable in the long run and always maintain liquidity.   For external reporting purposes, companies must prepare a cash flow statement.  This statement shows the cash inflows and outflows for three categories:  (1) operating, (2) investing, and (3) financing. Thus, another performance measure is cash flow.  However, like segment margin and net income, cash flows are subject to manipulation and emphasize the short run.

Top management often evaluates managers of investment centers using return on investment (ROI) and residual income.  Return on investment is income divided by assets invested.  However, management must define both terms specifically.  Exhibit 13-2 lists questions and answers regarding return on investment definitions.  Exhibit 13-3 illustrates ROI calculations.

Companies often express ROI using the Du Pont model.  According to this formula, ROI equals profit margin times asset turnover.  Profit margin is income divided by sales, and asset turnover is sales divided by assets invested.  Exhibit 13-4 illustrates the use of the Du Pont formula.

Management must compare the ROI to a benchmark used as a performance measure. Typically, the base of comparison could be expected return on investment, prior return on investment, or the ROI of similar companies or divisions. Managers can increase their ROI by increasing sales, decreasing expenses, or decreasing the investment in assets. However, decisions that affect one element of the ROI formula will probably affect the other elements. Thus, managers should make such decisions only after considering their dynamic effects. The elasticity of demand with respect to price is an important consideration regarding decisions about prices. Using ROI as a performance measure discourages managers from investing in new assets whose projected rate of return is less than the current return on investment. This reluctance sometimes is present even if the projected rate of return is greater than the target rate of return.

Management can also use residual income to evaluate the performance of investment center managers. Residual income (RI) is income less the product of a target rate of return times the assets invested. Unlike ROI, RI is a dollar number rather than a percentage. Thus, managers have an incentive to invest in new assets if the projected return on investment is greater than the target rate of return. Exhibit 13-5 illustrates the calculation of RI. Residual income has an inherent bias in favor of large divisions. Thus, managers should use it with care when comparing the performances of divisions of different size.

Return on investment and residual income have three primary disadvantages as shown in Exhibit 13-6: (1) three problems with income--managers can manipulate income, income depends on accounting methods, and income is based on accrual accounting not cash flows; (2) three problems with assets invested--asset investment is difficult to measure, assets invested may reflect the decisions of previous managers, and if the company does not adjust assets and income for inflation, investment centers with older assets will have greater returns on investment; and (3) the use of return on investment and residual income can motivate suboptimal behaviour by managers.

In today's business environment, assets with little or no book value are nevertheless important in competing successfully. For example, a patent with little book value may have a large market value and be vital to a company's success. Traditional accounting methods ignore intangible assets such as a reputation for high quality or customer loyalty.

Also, ROI and RI are short-term performance measures that are better for evaluating mature divisions than they are for high-growth divisions. For divisions with growth opportunities, ROI and RI punish managers who invest in assets in the current period that do not generate returns until future periods.

A new and popular performance measure is economic value added (EVA). This measure attempts to align the interests of shareholders and managers. EVA is conceptually similar to RI. The major difference is that EVA applies the target rate of return to the capital invested in the division or company as opposed to the book value or market value of assets used for RI. Capital invested is the sum of the market value of total equity and total interest-bearing debt. The target rate is the weighted-average cost of capital. Also, EVA uses after-tax profits as the measure of income. Thus, EVA is after-tax profits less the product of capital invested and the weighted-average cost of capital.

The more the divergence between the book value of capital and its market value, the greater is the difference between EVA and RI. The market value of a company may be significantly higher than its book value. Exhibit 13-7 illustrates RI and EVA calculations. Although EVA is a popular short-term performance measure, it cannot measure all dimensions of performance. EVA can discourage investments in long-term projects because such investments increase invested capital immediately but do not provide increased after-tax profits until some time in the future. Companies should supplement EVA with longer-term financial and nonfinancial performance measures.

Traditionally, companies have used only financial measures in performance evaluations.  Financial measures, however, reflect the results of past decisions.  Success requires that companies pay careful attention to the steps that they must take to compete effectively in the global marketplace.  Companies must focus on performing activities such as setup, customer service, product development, manufacturing, marketing, and delivery.  Performance measures should track the causes and occurrences of these activities.

A good performance measurement system uses several measures of performance.  Managers may evaluate subordinates using quantitative and qualitative measures.  Qualitative measures are often subjective.  Managers are usually more comfortable with quantitative measures because they are more objective.  Quantitative performance measures also are more effective in motivating employees because such measures provide a well-defined target.  Quantitative measures can be either financial or nonfinancial.

Nonfinancial measures include manufacturing cycle time, productivity, setup time, defect rate, on-time deliveries, number of unplanned production interruptions, and customer returns.  Nonfinancial measures that track factors necessary for world-class status are especially important.  Nonfinancial performance measures have two advantages over financial performance measures:  (1) they directly measure a corporation's performance in the activities that create shareholder wealth; and (2) they may better predict the direction of future cash flows.  Exhibit 13-8 depicts several financial and nonfinancial performance measures needed at various organizational levels for various purposes.

Before selecting nonfinancial performance measures, a company should identify its critical success factors.  For each critical success factor, management should choose a few attributes of each relevant nonfinancial performance measure for continuous improvement.  These attributes should include short-run and long-run measures to guide organizational activities properly.

After management selects performance measures, management should establish acceptable performance levels against which to compare actual results.  Management can develop these benchmarks internally or select them from external sources.

For each performance measure, an employee must agree (1) to accept specific responsibility for performance and (2) to be evaluated.  Management should install a system for monitoring and reporting comparative performance levels at regular intervals as shown in Exhibit 13-9.  A company determines performance measures for lower-level managers more often than for upper-level managers.

A general model for measuring the relative success of an activity involves dividing the number of successes by total activity volume.  For example, market share is the number of units sold by a specific company divided by the total units sold by the industry.

Throughput is becoming a more popular performance measure.   Synchronous management is a term that refers to all endeavors that help a company achieve its goals.  The goal of synchronous management is to increase throughput, reduce inventory, and reduce operating expenses simultaneously.  Throughput is the number of good units produced and sold within a particular time period.  The calculation of throughput involves three elements:  (1) manufacturing cycle efficiency, (2) process productivity, and (3) process quality yield.  The product of these three elements is the number of good units per hour of processing time.

Manufacturing cycle efficiency is the value-added processing time divided by the total processing time.  Process productivity is the total units started, completed, and sold divided by the value-added processing time.  Process quality yield is a measure of quality computed by dividing the number of good units by the total number of units.  A company can increase throughput by decreasing non-value-added activities, increasing total production and sales, decreasing the per-unit processing time, or increasing process quality yield.

A world-class company striving for growth and profitability should systematically measure quality and assess the cost of quality.  Such measures should focus on and be related to actions that add value to products and services in the mind customers.  Exhibit 13-10 gives several indicators of quality for each of the four quality cost categories, their cost drivers, and whether they are value-added or non-value-added.

Prevention is the only category of quality cost that is value-added.  Appraisal costs add no customer value because they cannot be added to products.  Internal failure costs and external failure costs add no value as they simply increase total costs for the company and for its customers.  These failure costs stem from poor quality.

A company can reduce the costs of appraisal, internal failure, and external failure by investing in prevention.  Many prevention activities involve one-time costs that improve quality now and in the future.  Employees may suggest some prevention measures that are fairly inexpensive.  Employee suggestion programs can be very effective in finding opportunities for continuous improvement.

Using nonfinancial performance measures can help a company to focus on activities that cause costs.  By controlling those activities, the company can control costs and improve processes more effectively.

Activity-based costing aims to reduce non-value-added activities to increase throughput.  Traditional performance measures in accounting are replete with factors that contribute to non-value-added activities.  For example, material and labour standards often include factors for waste and idle time.  Companies base predetermined manufacturing overhead rates on estimates of expected capacity usage, not full capacity usage.  Companies produce inventory to meet budget expectations, not to meet sales demand.  A company's accounting procedures often include detailed explanations of how to account for spoiled or defective units.  Exhibit 13-11 provides some traditional performance measures and some potential suboptimal results they may create.

To move toward world-class status, companies must eliminate non-value-added activities from performance measures and substitute value-added activities.  Activity-based costing focuses on value-added activities and emphasizes external performance measures.  Customers see good performance as performance that meets or exceeds their expectations for quality, cost, and delivery.  Nonfinancial performance measures can be more effective because they monitor the desired characteristics instead of monitoring internal financial goals.

When a company is aware that these external criteria determine its performance, it should start to implement ideas such as just-in-time inventory and total quality management.  These ideas have as their common themes making the company, its products, and its processes better and reducing costs to give better value to customers.

Companies with multinational operations face more complex issues than do companies that operate in one country only.  Thus, multinational companies should consider additional factors concerning performance measurement and evaluation.  Differences in cultures and economies are as important as differences in accounting and reporting practices.  The investment base required to create a particular type of organizational unit may differ significantly among countries.

In multinational settings, the use of income as the primary performance measure is inappropriate. The reasons include differences in tariffs and tax rates among countries, exchange rate fluctuations, and possible restrictions on the transfer of goods or currency out of a country. Also, government protection of local companies, government aid in some countries, and different wage rates may affect the income of multinational units. In addition, if the multinational units adopt the local country's accounting standards, differences in international accounting standards can make income comparisons difficult.

The International Accounting Standards Committee (IASC) is working for harmonization of international accounting standards. Many of its standards, however, result from compromise positions, allow for alternatives, and rely on voluntary compliance. Also, as discussed in Chapter 11, transfer prices between multinational units affect income and income taxes in multinational units.

Qualitative performance measures and nonfinancial quantitative measures may be more appropriate for multinational units. Using performance measures that limit suboptimization is essential for managing multinational responsibility centers properly. No single system is suitable for all companies or perhaps for all responsibility centers within the same company. Performance measurement involves people, and the performance measurement system should reflect the differences in people. People are usually concerned about how the performance measurement system will affect their compensation and rewards.

A company should compensate its employees in a way that motivates them to act in ways that cause them to achieve the company's goals efficiently and effectively. A rational compensation plan is a cohesive package of organizational goals, performance measurements, and employee rewards. Exhibit 13-12 presents a plan-performance-reward model that illustrates the relationships among these three elements.

In this model, the board of directors and top management determine the strategic goals for the company. From these strategic goals, management identifies the company's critical success factors and defines its operational targets. The board of directors and top management must also determine a compensation strategy for the company. This strategy serves as a foundation for the compensation plan by specifying the role compensation should play in the company. Management should communicate the compensation strategy to everyone in the company. Companies are reducing or eliminating automatic cost-of-living adjustments and annual pay raises. Compensation plans should promote greater levels of employee performance and loyalty while reducing costs and increasing profits.

To prevent suboptimization, management should highly correlate the company's incentive compensation plans with the company's operational objectives. This tight correlation should help to motivate employees to focus on productivity improvement. As shown in Exhibit 13-13, the entire package of decisions concerning performance measurements is a performance management system. Traditionally, performance measures have concentrated on short-run profits without giving enough attention to long-run performance. Pay-for-performance criteria should influence employees to take a long-run view.

To encourage a long-run perspective, many companies compensate their top executives largely in the form of stock or stock options. This can work well if the executives are committed to the organization for the long term.

Many companies have changed from evaluating employees based on their inputs to evaluating them based on their outputs. This change, however, has created new problems in the pay-for-performance relationship. The company should evaluate its managers and other employees only on the basis of controllable factors. Many performance measures tend to evaluate results that are a function of both controllable and uncontrollable factors.

Learning the contributions of the controllable and uncontrollable factors to performance is often difficult.  As a result, the employee bears the risk that a performance measure may stem from an uncontrollable cause.  Management should seek ways to reduce this risk.

At the basic worker level, performance measures should be specific and focus on cost and quality control.  At higher levels of responsibility, the critical success factors under a manager's control become more important.  Performance measures for upper management should be less specific and look more toward the long run.

Uncontrollable factors partially affect output.  Therefore, some would argue that companies should base their compensation on subjectively determined intangible measures instead of on the more objective performance measures.  These subjective measures might include leadership skills, flexibility, attitude, ability to work well with others, professional pride, and enthusiasm.  Management may combine such subjective measures with the more objective performance measures.  The subjective measures are important for long-range considerations while the objective measures emphasize short-run performance.

Conventionally, companies have based their compensation systems on current financial incentives.  Middle managers receive salaries with the opportunity for raises usually based on financial performance measures such as segment margin, return on investment, or residual income.  Lower-level workers receive wages based on the number of hours worked with possible bonuses based on some quantitative measure.  Companies usually reserve significant incentive pay for top management and perhaps the salesforce.  Thus, the traditional compensation system provides little incentive for employees other than top managers to improve a company's performance.

Individuals at different employment levels generally view monetary rewards differently.  At lower employment levels, more incentives should be monetary and short-term with some nonmonetary incentives that encourage long-term performance.  At higher employment levels, more incentives should be nonmonetary and long-term with some monetary incentives that encourage short-term performance.

Companies must also consider incentives for both groups and individuals since a great deal of work in automated factories emphasizes group rather than individual performance.  Group incentives are important, but some individual incentives are necessary to encourage all members of the group to perform rather than free-riding on the efforts of others in the group.

Employees also need nonmonetary rewards such as recognition, appreciation, and praise.  Allowing subordinates to participate in decisions helps to make employment more enjoyable.  Job security is another strong incentive.

A company must also be careful that its compensation strategy does not suppress creativity, innovation, risk taking, and proactive conduct of job responsibilities.  If the company withholds monetary rewards for risk-taking activities that result in failure, the company will discourage its employees from taking risky actions in the future.  Management should communicate that failure is merely a step on the road toward continuous improvement.

With international operations increasing, companies must develop compensation plans that treat expatriate employees fairly and equitably.  Expatriates are parent company and third-country nationals assigned to a foreign subsidiary, or foreign nationals assigned to the parent company.  A compensation package that employees think is fair and equitable in one country may not be considered fair and equitable in another country.

Expatriates' compensation packages must reflect labour market factors, cost-of-living considerations, currency fluctuations, and tax consequences. Companies may pay expatriates in the currency where the company has relocated them, in the currency of their home country, or a combination of both. A company should pay the fringe benefit portion related to retirement in the currency of the home country.

Connecting the compensation system to performance management is vital because what a company measures and rewards is what managers and other employees strive to achieve. Companies must focus their reward structures to motivate employees to succeed at all activities that will create shareholder wealth and personal value.

## SELF TEST

### TRUE/FALSE

1.  T  F  Throughput is a performance indicator that refers to the number of good units that a company manufactures and sells during a time period.

2.  T  F  Appraisal costs are value-added costs.

3.  T  F  Internal failure and external failure costs are non-value-added.

4.  T  F  Traditional performance measures in accounting are filled with factors that contribute to non-value-added activities.

5.  T  F  Activity-based costing is concerned with reducing non-value-added activities and increasing throughput.

6.  T  F  A company should evaluate its managers using quantitative measures only.

7.  T  F  Retirement contributions for expatriates should be paid in the currency of the country in which they are relocated.

8.  T  F  Managers are usually more comfortable with qualitative measures of performance.

9.  T  F  The first step in motivating employees to focus on productivity improvement is to correlate an organization's pay-for-performance plan with strategic goals.

10.  T  F  Return on investment is equal to assets invested divided by income generated.

11.  T  F  Residual income is the income of an investment centre less an amount charged for funds committed to that centre.

12.  T  F  Traditionally, performance measures have focused on long-run performance without giving adequate attention to short-term profits.

13.  T  F  The use of return on investment and residual income as performance measures may motivate managers to make suboptimal decisions.

14. T F  The use of income as the primary performance measure is extremely inappropriate for multinational segments.

15. T F  Economic value added defines income as after-tax profits.


MULTIPLE CHOICE

1.  Performance measurements should:

    A. reflect organizational goals and objectives.
    B. be specific and understandable.
    C. promote harmonious relations among units.
    D. all of the above.

2. Management attempts to increase productivity will enjoy limited success without:

    A. employee support.
    B. synchronous management.
    C. an activity-based cost system.
    D. enough cost centers.

3. How does economic value added (EVA) define capital invested?

    A. the book value of equity
    B. the book value of equity and interest-bearing debt
    C. the market value of equity
    D. the market value of equity and interest-bearing debt

4.  Top management has traditionally focused on what type of performance measures?

    A. quantitative financial
    B. quantitative operational
    C. qualitative financial
    D. qualitative operational

5. What is the preferred definition of income in determining an investment centre's return on investment?

    A. operating income
    B. operating income less interest
    C. net income after taxes
    D. segment margin

6. One difficulty in using return on investment as a performance measure is that it:

    A. measures performance only over the long run.
    B. is a dollar amount rather than a percentage.
    C. can result in suboptimal decisions.
    D. measures cash flows rather than income.

7. Income comparisons among multinational units may be invalid because of:

    A. differences in tax rates and tariffs.
    B. currency fluctuations.
    C. possible restrictions on the transfer of goods or currency.
    D. all of the above.

8. Profit margin equals:

    A. income ÷ sales.
    B. income ÷ average assets.
    C. average assets ÷ income.
    D. sales ÷ income.

9. A problem with using income to measure performance is that the individual components used to derive income are:

    A. often variable with volume.
    B. not subject to precise measurement.
    C. subject to manipulation.
    D. not reported on a timely basis.

10. What links all aspects of performance to a company's strategies?

    A. return on investment
    B. residual income
    C. economic value added
    D. balanced scorecard

11. The total number of good units produced divided by the total time available during the period is:

    A. process productivity.
    B. throughput.
    C. process quality yield.
    D. manufacturing cycle efficiency.

12. Return on investment equals:

    A. profit margin x asset turnover.
    B. income ÷ average assets.
    C. both of the above.
    D. none of the above.

13. The strategic objective of _____ is to increase throughput while simultaneously reducing inventory and operating expenses.

    A. management by exception
    B. synchronous management
    C. responsibility accounting
    D. decentralization

14. At the basic worker level, performance measures should usually focus on:

    A. enthusiasm.
    B. leadership skills.
    C. cost and quality control.
    D. residual income.

15. When employees become shareholders in their employing company, they tend to adopt the perspective of:

    A. short-run profits.
    B. long-run wealth maximization.
    C. throughput.
    D. expatriates.

16. For higher-level managerial employees, incentives should primarily be:

    A. monetary and short-term.
    B. nonmonetary and short-term.
    C. monetary and long-term.
    D. nonmonetary and long-term.

17. Management should monitor employee performance and provide feedback:

    A. once a year.
    B. once every six months.
    C. once every three months.
    D. on a continuous, ongoing basis.

18. Which of the four cost of quality categories is value-added?

    A. prevention
    B. appraisal
    C. internal failure
    D. external failure

19. Bradshaw Company made 500 billings during the year. Of these 500 billings, 490 were accurate. What was the billing error rate?

    A. 1.02%
    B. 2.00%
    C. 2.04%
    D. 98.00%

20. Kinder Company made 6,000 deliveries during the year of which 5,520 were on time. What was Kinder Company's delivery success rate?

    A. 8.000%
    B. 8.696%
    C. 92.000%
    D. 108.696%

21.  Hurt Company had a profit margin of 9 percent, sales of $900,000, and a return on investment of 27 percent.  What were the average assets?

A.  $ 100,000
B.  $ 243,000
C.  $ 300,000
D.  $2,700,000

22.  Jacobs Company had sales of $500,000, an asset turnover of 2, and a return on investment of 18 percent.  What was Jacobs Company's income?

A.  $ 45,000
B.  $ 90,000
C.  $180,000
D.  $250,000

USE THE FOLLOWING INFORMATION TO ANSWER QUESTIONS 23 THROUGH 26.

Harris Company presents you with the following information for the year:

Total units processed      10,000
Good units                        9,610
Value-added processing time 24,300 hours
Total time                       81,000 hours

23.  What was the manufacturing cycle efficiency?

A.  30.00%
B.  41.15%
C.  96.10%
D.  333.33%

24.  What was the process productivity?

A.  0.3955 units per value-added hour
B.  0.4115 units per value-added hour
C.  2.4300 units per value-added hour
D.  2.5286 units per value-added hour

25.  What was the process quality yield?

A.  11.86%
B.  30.00%
C.  39.55%
D.  96.10%

26. What was the throughput?

    A.  0.1186 units per hour
    B.  0.1235 units per hour
    C.  0.3955 units per hour
    D.  8.4287 units per hour

USE THE FOLLOWING INFORMATION TO ANSWER QUESTIONS 27 THROUGH 30.

Diggs Division had the following results for the year:

| | |
|---|---|
| Net sales | $300,000 |
| Income | $ 36,000 |
| Average assets | $150,000 |
| Target rate of return on average assets | 9% |

27. What was the profit margin?

    A.  2%
    B.  9%
    C.  12%
    D.  24%

28. What was the asset turnover?

    A.  2.00
    B.  8.33
    C.  12.00
    D.  24.00

29. What was the return on investment?

    A.  2%
    B.  3%
    C.  12%
    D.  24%

30. What was the residual income?

    A.  $ 9,000
    B.  $13,500
    C.  $22,500
    D.  $27,000

ESSAY QUESTIONS AND PROBLEMS

1. Why are financial measures inadequate to address new issues necessary for survival in the global economy?

2. How can a manager improve return on investment?

3. What two advantages do nonfinancial performance measures have over financial performance measures?

4. How should management select the nonfinancial performance measures the company or business unit uses?

5.  How can the use of activity-based costing help a company move toward world-class status?

6.  What are the three primary limitations of using return on investment and residual income as performance measures?

7.  What are the four general rules for performance measurement?

8.  Why is using income as the primary performance measure of a multinational segment inappropriate?

9.  Why must companies give special consideration to the compensation plans of expatriate employees?

10.  What is a balanced scorecard and what purpose does it serve?

11.  What is economic value added (EVA) and how does it differ from residual income?

12.  McFadden Company made a total of 500 deliveries during the month of which 478 were on time. Compute the following:
(A) delivery success rate

(B) delivery failure rate

13.  The Northern Division of Brock Company had the following results for the year:

| | |
|---|---|
| Sales | $2,500,000 |
| Income | $ 175,000 |
| Average assets | $1,250,000 |
| Target return on average assets | 11% |

Compute the following:

(A) profit margin

(B) asset turnover

(C) return on investment

(D) residual income

14.  Jarboe Company worked a total of 28,000 hours to produce 4,000 total units.  Of the 28,000 hours worked, 8,400 hours were value-added processing time.  Of the 4,000 units produced, 3,948 were good units.  Compute the following:

(A) manufacturing cycle efficiency

(B) process productivity

(C) process quality yield

(D) throughput

15. Collins Company provides you with the following information for their most recent year of operations:

| | |
|---|---:|
| Income before taxes | $ 500,000 |
| Income tax expense | 180,000 |
| Book value of invested capital | 900,000 |
| Market value of invested capital | 2,000,000 |
| Weighted-average cost of capita | 12% |

Calculate the economic value added (EVA).

## SELF TEST ANSWERS

### TRUE/FALSE

| | | | | | | | | | |
|---|---|---|---|---|---|---|---|---|---|
| 1. | T | 4. | T | 7. | F | 10. | F | 13. | T |
| 2. | F | 5. | T | 8. | F | 11. | T | 14. | T |
| 3. | T | 6. | F | 9. | T | 12. | F | 15. | T |

### MULTIPLE CHOICE

| | | | | | | | | | |
|---|---|---|---|---|---|---|---|---|---|
| 1. D | 7. | D | 13. | B | 19. | B | 25. | D |
| 2. A | 8. | A | 14. | C | 20. | C | 26. | A |
| 3. D | 9. | C | 15. | B | 21. | C | 27. | C |
| 4. A | 10. | D | 16. | D | 22. | A | 28. | A |
| 5. D | 11. | B | 17. | D | 23. | A | 29. | D |
| 6. C | 12. | C | 18. | A | 24. | B | 30. | C |

### ESSAY QUESTIONS AND PROBLEMS

1.      To succeed in the global economy many companies have set goals of customer satisfaction, zero defects, minimal lead time to market, and environmental social responsibility.  Companies cannot measure these goals with periodic income.  Companies that make inferior goods, deliver products late, abuse the environment, or fail to satisfy customers will lose market share and eventually cease to exist.  Companies can develop nonfinancial performance measures to track progress, or lack thereof, toward achievement of long-run critical success factors of world-class companies.

2.    A manager can improve return on investment in three ways: (1) increasing sales, (2) decreasing expenses, and (3) decreasing invested assets. However, a manager must consider the dynamic effects of any of these actions. Increasing sales increases return on investment because an increase in sales causes an increase in income (as long as the products are sold for more than their cost). If a manager attempts to increase sales by raising the sales price, this price increase leads to a decrease in the quantity demanded and will cause a decrease instead of an increase in return on investment if demand is elastic with respect to price. A decrease in expenses leads to an increase in return on investment because a decrease in expenses leads to an increase in income if all other things are held constant. However, if a manager reduced advertising expense, sales may decrease, which could lead to a decrease in return on investment. A reduction in the asset base will increase return on investment because the denominator is smaller. However, if a manager reduced needed inventory, sales might decrease causing a decrease in return on investment. Because of these dynamic factors, a manager must carefully consider any strategy designed to increase return on investment.

3.    Nonfinancial performance measures directly measure an organization's performance in the activities that create shareholder wealth, such as providing quality products and services. Second, nonfinancial performance measures may be able to predict the direction of future cash flows better.

4.    First, management should identify the company's critical success factors. For each factor chosen, management should select a few attributes of each relevant nonfinancial performance measure for continuous improvement. These attributes should include short-term and long-term measures to guide the company's activities properly. Usually, management should use a mixture of quantitative and qualitative nonfinancial performance measures. Management should specify acceptable performance levels against which to compare results.

5.    Activity-based costing is concerned with reducing non-value-added activities to increase throughput. For companies to move toward world-class status, they must remove non-value-added activities from performance evaluation measurements and substitute value-added activities. Activity-based costing focuses on the activities that add value from the customer's viewpoint. Thus, activity-based costing emphasizes external performance measures. Customers see good performance as products or services that meet or exceed their expectations as to quality, cost, and delivery. The company can use nonfinancial performance measures to monitor these characteristics necessary to achieve world-class status. Companies also implement concepts such as just-in-time inventory and total quality management. These concepts help to reduce costs and increase value to customers.

6.    Return on investment and residual income have three primary disadvantages: (1) three problems with income--managers can manipulate income, income depends on accounting methods, and income is based on accrual accounting not cash flows; (2) three problems with assets invested--asset investment is difficult to measure, assets invested may reflect the decisions of previous managers, and if assets and income are not adjusted for inflation,
investment centers with older assets will have greater returns on investment; and (3) the use of return on investment and residual income can motivate suboptimal behaviour by managers.

7.    Performance measures should assess progress toward organizational goals and objectives. The persons whom management evaluates should have input into developing the performance measures and be aware of them. The persons whom management evaluates should have the necessary skills and tools to be successful under the measurement system. Management should provide feedback relative to performance in a timely and useful manner.

8.    In multinational settings, the use of income as the primary performance measure is inappropriate because of differences in tariffs and tax rates among countries, exchange rate fluctuations, and possible restrictions on the transfer of goods or currency out of a country.

9.    Companies must give special consideration to the compensation plans of expatriate employees because what employees consider fair and equitable in one country may not be what is considered fair and reasonable in another country.  Expatriates' compensation plans must reflect labour market factors, cost-of-living considerations, currency fluctuations, and tax consequences.  Companies must also decide whether to pay expatriates in the currency of the country where the company has relocated them or in their home currency.  The company should pay the fringe benefit part of the package for retirement needs in the currency of the home country.

10.    A balanced scorecard is a set of financial and nonfinancial performance measures.  It links all aspects of performance to a company's strategies.  The balanced scorecard gives a comprehensive view of performance measures that reflect both the internal and external perspectives.  The complexity of managing a company today requires that managers be able to see performance in several areas simultaneously.  A balanced scorecard enables managers to do so.

11.    Economic value added (EVA) is a measure of profit produced above the cost of capital.  EVA is after-tax profits less the product of capital invested and the weighted-average cost of capital.  Capital includes the market value of equity and interest-bearing debt.  Residual income and EVA are similar.  The major difference between EVA and residual income is that EVA uses the total market value of capital invested rather than the market value or book value of book assets.

12.    (A) delivery success rate = $\dfrac{\text{number of on-time deliveries}}{\text{total deliveries made}} = \dfrac{478}{500} = 95.6\%$

(B) delivery failure rate = $\dfrac{\text{number of late deliveries}}{\text{total deliveries made}} = \dfrac{500 - 478}{500} = \dfrac{22}{500} = 4.4\%$

13.    (A) profit margin = $\dfrac{\text{income}}{\text{sales}} = \dfrac{\$\ 175{,}000}{\$2{,}500{,}000} = 7.00\%$

(B) asset turnover = $\dfrac{\text{sales}}{\text{average assets}} = \dfrac{\$2{,}500{,}000}{\$1{,}250{,}000} = 2.00$

(C) return on investment = $\dfrac{\text{income}}{\text{average assets}} = \dfrac{\$\ 175{,}000}{\$1{,}250{,}000} = 14.00\%$

ALSO

return on investment = profit margin x asset turnover

= 7.00% x 2.00 = 14.00%

(D)
| | |
|---|---:|
| Income | $175,000 |
| Less:  Target income ($1,250,000 x 11%) | (137,500) |
| Residual income | $ 37,500 |

14.  (A) manufacturing cycle efficiency = $\dfrac{\text{value-added processing time}}{\text{total time}}$

$$= \frac{8,400 \text{ hours}}{28,000 \text{ hours}} = 30\%$$

(B) process productivity = $\dfrac{\text{total units}}{\text{value-added processing time}}$

$$= \frac{4,000 \text{ units}}{8,400 \text{ hours}} = 0.476 \text{ units per value-added hour}$$

(C) process quality yield = $\dfrac{\text{good units}}{\text{total units}} = \dfrac{3,948 \text{ units}}{4,000 \text{ units}} = 98.7\%$

(D)

Throughput = manufacturing cycle efficiency x process productivity x process quality yield

$= \dfrac{\text{value-added processing time}}{\text{total time}}$ x $\dfrac{\text{total units}}{\text{value-added processing time}}$ x $\dfrac{\text{good units}}{\text{total units}} = \dfrac{\text{good units}}{\text{total time}}$

$\dfrac{8,400 \text{ hours}}{28,000 \text{ hours}}$ x $\dfrac{4,000 \text{ units}}{8,400 \text{ hours}}$ x $\dfrac{3,948 \text{ units}}{4,000 \text{ units}} = \dfrac{3,948 \text{ units}}{28,000 \text{ hours}} = 0.141$ units per hour

15.  Economic value added (EVA) = ($500,000 - $180,000) - ($2,000,000 x 12%)
                  = $320,000 - $240,000 = $80,000